BIOGRAPHY AND THE SOCIOLOGICAL IMAGINATION: CONTEXTS AND CONTINGENCIES

Contemporary Societies Series

Jeffrey C. Alexander, Series Editor

Andrew Abbott   *Methods of Discovery: Heuristics for the Social Sciences*

Arne Kalleberg   *The Mismatched Worker*

Judith Lorber   *Breaking the Bowls: Gender Theory and Feminist Change*

Douglas Massey   *Strangers in a Strange Land: Humans in an Urbanizing World*

Saskia Sassen   *A Sociology of Globalization*

Michael Schudson   *The Sociology of News*

Steven Seidman   *The Social Construction of Sexuality*

Bryan Turner   *The New Medical Sociology: Social Forms of Health and Illness*

Michael J. Shanahan and Ross Macmillan   *Biography and the Sociological Imagination: Contexts and Contingencies*

Forthcoming

Craig Calhoun   *The Public Sphere*

David Snow and Sarah Soule   *A Primer on Social Movements*

BIOGRAPHY AND THE SOCIOLOGICAL IMAGINATION: CONTEXTS AND CONTINGENCIES

Michael J. Shanahan
Ross Macmillan

CONTEMPORARY SOCIETIES
Jeffrey C. Alexander
SERIES EDITOR

 W. W. NORTON & COMPANY ◎ NEW YORK LONDON

W. W. Norton & Company has been independent since its founding in 1923, when William Warder Norton and Mary D. Herter Norton first published lectures delivered at the People's Institute, the adult education division of New York City's Cooper Union. The Nortons soon expanded their program beyond the Institute, publishing books by celebrated academics from America and abroad. By mid-century, the two major pillars of Norton's publishing program—trade books and college texts—were firmly established. In the 1950s, the Norton family transferred control of the company to its employees, and today—with a staff of four hundred and a comparable number of trade, college, and professional titles published each year—W. W. Norton & Company stands as the largest and oldest publishing house owned wholly by its employees.

Copyright © 2008 by W. W. Norton & Company, Inc.

Composition by PennSet, Inc.
Manufacturing by Quebecor World—Fairfield Division.
Production manager: Jane Searle.
Series design by Beth Tondreau Design.

Library of Congress Cataloging-in-Publication Data
Shanahan, Michael J.
    Biography and the sociological imagination : contexts and
contingencies / Michael J. Shanahan and Ross Macmillan.— 1st ed.
        p.   cm. — (Contemporary societies)
    Includes bibliographical references and index.
    ISBN 978-0-393-97608-3 (pbk.)
    1. Sociology—Biographical methods.   I. Macmillan, Ross.   II. Title.
HM527.S53 2008
301.072'3—dc22

                                                    2007013481

W. W. Norton & Company, Inc., 500 Fifth Avenue, New York, NY 10110-0017
www.wwnorton.com

W. W. Norton & Company Ltd., Castle House,
75/76 Wells Street, London W1T 3QT

1   2   3   4   5   6   7   8   9   0

To
Jeylan T. Mortimer,
treasured mentor, colleague, and friend

CONTENTS

INTRODUCTION   ix

CHAPTER ONE   What Is the Life Course?   3

CHAPTER TWO   The Life Course as a Paradigm   44

CHAPTER THREE   Macro Views of the Life Course   105

CHAPTER FOUR   Micro Views of the Life Course   181

CHAPTER FIVE   From Macro to Micro   235

CHAPTER SIX   Return to *The Sociological*
                   Imagination   278

NOTES   297

INDEX   311

INTRODUCTION

LET US BEGIN WITH a passage from Salman Rushdie's magnificent work of fiction, *Midnight's Children*. The main character, Saleem Sinai, is beginning the story of his life:

> And there are so many stories to tell, too many, such an excess
> of intertwined lives events miracles places rumours, so dense a
> commingling of the improbable and the mundane! I have been
> a swallower of lives; and to know me, just the one of me, you'll
> have to swallow a lot as well.[1]

Not surprisingly, a major theme running through *Midnight's Children* is the intricate and unique configurations of each person's life: how each person's biography reflects experiences with family, friends, acquaintances, complete strangers, communities, states, nations, and history. The result is that each life is a world unto itself.

Notice the lack of commas in "intertwined lives events miracles places rumours." The things that make up life run together, too interconnected to even begin to be teased apart. People's biographies are a jumbling multitude in time and space, all of the parts running together and colliding with each other. And notice the curious use of "swallow," which of course means to consume fully, to make something a part of oneself: "To know me, just the one of me, you'll have to swallow a lot as

well." The character Saleem Sinai (indeed, Mr. Rushdie himself) is saying that to understand one person's life, a whole
world must be experienced completely by the reader. And
when this happens, the reader is changed forever.

ORIGINS

This passage from *Midnight's Children* serves as a suitable starting point for our book, which is about how to study people's
lives as they reflect connections to other people, society, and
history. While we are devoted fans of Mr. Rushdie and of all
fiction writers who seek to capture this complexity, our approach differs from his and theirs in one important respect: our
inspiration and challenge is how to study people's biographies
as they reflect society and history *from a scientific point of view*.
No doubt, each life is a jumbled world of people and places
moving through time. But can we make sense of each life, each
world, by using the basic strategies of science?

The answer is an enthusiastic "yes" and the story of this
"yes" begins with another book, published in 1959, written by
C. Wright Mills (1916–62), and entitled *The Sociological Imagination*.[2] This book is, in fact, a classic cited approvingly to this
day in virtually every "Introduction to Sociology" class in the
United States. Its popularity is somewhat strange, though, because much of it is concerned with what most undergraduates
would view as an esoteric topic: a critique of American sociology after World War II, including a famous chapter attacking
the grand theory of Talcott Parsons.

Parsons was a prominent sociologist of the time who had
proposed a seemingly complete theory of social life, sometimes
called simple functionalism, in a series of complicated books.

In his critique, Mills's argued that Parsons's work was highly abstract, ideologically slanted, and difficult, if not impossible, to comprehend. A short excerpt from Parsons draws sympathy for Mills's position, at least with respect to comprehension: "An element of a shared symbolic system which serves as a criterion or standard for selection among alternatives of orientation which are intrinsically open in a situation may be called a value" (as quoted in Mills[3]). If one considers that Parsons wrote hundreds and hundreds of pages of such prose, one begins to sympathize with the desire to lampoon him. Clearly, sociology need not be a jargon-fueled exercise. We have tried to make this book as accessible as possible and have defined all scientific concepts in plain English.

One part of Mills's critique makes a particularly constructive point. He advocates that the study of human behavior should begin with humans, their behavior, and their settings, and not with highly abstract concepts that are imposed on people and their situations. The behavioral scientist, then, should start with the individual and ask what features of society produce such a person. According to Mills, the seemingly "personal" problems of one's biography are better understood as repercussions of broad social tensions, and he proposes the "sociological imagination" to empower people to think about how their lives reflect historical and social forces:

> The sociological imagination enables its possessor to understand the larger historical scene in terms of its meaning for the inner life and external career of a variety of individuals. Within that welter [of daily experience], the framework of modern society is sought, and within that framework the psychologies of

a variety of men and women are formulated. . . . [I]t is by means of the sociological imagination that men now hope to grasp what is going on in the world, and to understand what is happening in themselves as minute points of the intersections of biography and history with society.[4]

The eloquence and truth of such passages undoubtedly explains the enduring popularity and motivational power of *The Sociological Imagination*. Mills was on the right track in asserting that connections among person, place, and time should be studied in their particulars.

Such an insight, however, needs further elaboration. *How* can we study such connections? Mills's essay was a call to study society and biography, but it was silent on how such a task might be accomplished. Since Mills's celebrated call, much has been learned about how lives are socially organized, and indeed his formulation can be refined in two major ways. First, what he seemingly did not appreciate is that people age and that *the meaning of social change for people's lives depends on their age*. The fall of Communism throughout Eastern Europe, for example, meant very different things for young people and adults. Younger people were less committed to and "entrenched in" the Communist social order—its norms, social roles, and routines—and hence were capable of re-inventing themselves to fit into a new society. Adults, in contrast, could not so readily re-make themselves and often took the role of spectator as new opportunities arose. Mills asked how changing societies affect behavior, but the more precise question concerns how to make sense of connections between history, which refers to the many facets of societies as they change, and biography, which describes a lifelong pattern of experiences and behaviors.

Second, although there are substantial connections between society and biography, there is also substantial diversity in how lives are patterned in any given time and place. Put differently, in any given society, *social forces create patterns in biographies but a multitude of contexts and consequent contingencies nevertheless render each life distinct.* The result is that we can apprehend in each person's life both the common experience of the community and his or her unique constellation of social experiences. Biographies are obviously unique to each person, but they share many significant features within groups of people and so should be considered both individually and collectively.

This book builds on the constructive enterprise of C. Wright Mills by developing an imaginative framework with which people can think about how their lives reflect the imprint of society, how this imprint reflects the intersection of social changes and personal development, and how these processes are complicated by each person's unique location in society. Such an appreciation for the social foundations of the biography finds its basis in a subfield called "life course sociology."

GUIDEPOSTS

As an area of study, the life course is fundamentally an *imaginative framework* that encourages us to think about social change, aging, and how the two are interrelated. In so doing, life course sociology confronts several major intellectual challenges which, even if answered imperfectly, offer major insights into how lives are organized. These challenges may be viewed as "guideposts" because they direct our imaginations in highly significant ways.

First, *the central role of society and social change.* A focus on social change may seem to indicate an interest in obscure matters. Yet social change is everywhere. Readers who, like the authors, were born at the end of the Baby Boom, in the early 1960s, have already witnessed the massive social changes of the 1960s, substantial economic recessions (1981–83, 1990–94), sexual liberation and the AIDS crisis, the rise of religious fundamentalism, the rapid entry of women into the workplace, the emergence of a black middle class, significant gains in access to higher education for women and racial/ethnic minorities, a fundamental reorganization of the economy, the Vietnam War, the farm crisis, the first Gulf War, the tragedy of September 11, and American involvement in Afghanistan and then Iraq. And there are larger trends as well, including the move toward globalization, with its many diverse and often subtle manifestations. Beyond America's shores, famines, civil and multinational wars, genocide, political and economic re-organizations, the collapse of nations, and the catastrophic spread of diseases are, regrettably, not uncommon. Indeed, untold millions of people alive today have experienced such changes and their lives have been transformed because of them. To these large-scale historical changes we may add a set of household-level social changes that have affected millions of Americans: family breakup, geographic moves, serious illness or death in the family, dramatic loss of income, retirement, and so on.

All of these events and trends are *social* changes because they may affect society's institutions and organizations, as well as people's connections to society, to organizations, and to each other. They create new circumstances that call for new ways of thinking and behaving, and so represent excellent opportunities to study how society can shape our lives. Changes, large and small, near and far, suddenly and gradually occurring, are a constant of human experience. To study human development and aging without acknowledging social change is to indulge in a constrained and artificial view, one that neglects the essence of experience, which is adaptation to one's setting.

Second, *temporality in people's lives.* Many people are resolutely focused on the "here and now" of their society's current state (as opposed to the historical past) and also to their present personal situation (as opposed to their personal past and possible futures). History is commonly viewed as distinct from the present and, in any event, complicated and largely inaccessible. How could it be relevant to the patterns of our lives? For many people, one's past experiences are part of history, often vaguely recalled and hardly important to the present. And the future is even more opaque—an uncertain, uncharted terrain filled with promissory notes, the dreams of our ambitions, and the fears of our failures.

In actuality, the present is a fleeting instance when compared to what has been and what will be. All of our social ties—to society, to our community and neighborhood, and to institutions and organizations, as well as our interpersonal relationships—have a past and a future that are highly consequential for understanding the present. Consider common social positions such as "married," "junior in college," "accounts manager," and "grandparent." By themselves, these statuses tell us very little about a person. But knowing the personal experiences that have led to them and knowing where they might lead in the future makes them particularly consequential for study. Thus, a life is not only "what is" but also, if not more so, "what was" and "what will be."

Third, *macro and micro phenomena and their linkages.* "Macro" means large-scale with respect to time, place, and/or number of people (i.e., collectivities or aggregations). For example, are there distinct types of societies and, if so, how do they change over long periods of time? How are religions established and under what circumstances do they flourish or dissolve? What are the connections between the educational and family systems in different European countries today? These questions direct our attention to processes involving many people, many years, and great distances. "Micro" describes things that are small-scale with respect to time, place, and/or number of people. For example, how does one person shame another person (to promote conformity)? How do people emerge as leaders in small groups? What strategies do people use in order to cope with failures in their lives? These questions direct our attention to processes involving comparatively fewer people and shorter time frames and distances.

The macro/micro distinction actually defines two opposite ends of a continuum. Consider hybrid questions, drawing on the preceding examples: How has the nature of "shaming" changed through the nineteenth and twentieth centuries in the United States and Japan? How did people emerge as leaders of their communities in pre-, proto-, and postmodern England and Germany? How have people viewed "failure" in their lives in the West since the time of the Enlightenment? These questions all contain within them both macro and micro elements and so fall somewhere along the continuum between them. Because scholars often develop either micro or macro expertise, connecting the disparate pieces (e.g., the nature of shaming through history in two very different societies) is an exceedingly challenging enterprise for any one person.

How does the macro–micro continuum apply to the study of society and biography? A macro view asks how biographical organization changes over long periods of time and across large geographic units (such as nation-states), and why these changes have occurred. For example, how and why has the nature of "childhood" changed throughout the twentieth century in the West? At what age have women given birth to their first child throughout the seventeenth, eighteenth, nineteenth, and twentieth centuries in North America and what explains changes in the timing of first births across these centuries and geographic regions? A micro view asks how people organize their lives, with an emphasis on how they interpret their past experiences, make sense of the present, and formulate and pursue plans for the future. For example, on what bases do people develop ideas about when they would like to have a first child? How do adults' memories of adolescence compare with their actual experiences during adolescence? Why do some people make highly unrealistic educational plans?

Bridging the macro and micro can be quite difficult. Again, consider a hybrid question drawing on the preceding examples: Did young people's educational plans become increasingly unrealistic through the twentieth century and, if so, why? To answer this question, we must develop measures of "unrealistic educational plans" and observe how the values associated with these measures change over a hundred-year period with attention to regional, gender, and racial/ethnic differences, which reflects a macro focus. But the "why" part of the question can only be answered by attempting to link the observed historical changes with social psychological processes by which people think about themselves in the educational system, which reflects a micro focus. The ultimate goal is to link the two strands and, if possible, develop generalizations about how societal changes affect the practicality of young people's decisions about their educational careers.

Fourth, *the study of real people in the real world.* The study of links between society and biography is very challenging from a methodological perspective. A comparison between the so-called "hard" and "soft" sciences is instructive. Imagine how complicated chemistry (a "hard" science) would be if the nature of atoms and molecules changed every year. People and societies are in a constant state of change. Imagine how far physics (another "hard" science) would get if scientists could not perform experiments in carefully controlled settings. Very rarely can sociologists perform experiments and studies in carefully controlled settings. (Nor do they necessarily want to.) Imagine if biologists ("hard" science again) had to ask microorganisms about their behaviors and the microorganisms failed to tell the truth. Imagine if an atom or molecule being studied "thought" about how it wanted to act in front of a physicist. Sociologists often must ask people about their experiences and people sometimes omit or misrepresent key details. And despite all of these complexities, the social sciences receive a tiny fraction of the research funds that the "hard sciences" have at their disposal. At every stage of the scientific process, the study of society and human behavior is very difficult, at least as difficult as the so-called "hard sciences." This book is not about research methods but, as you will see in the chapters that follow, a wide range of research strategies are used to study people in social context. These four guideposts—societal change, temporality in people's lives, links between the societal and personal, and the study of real people in the real world—are ongoing sources of intellectual inspiration, struggle, and insight that distinguish life course sociology. Yet we also need to acknowledge some deep, ideological obstacles that may stand in the way of progress.

OBSTACLES

For most people, sociological thinking is a cultivated skill, not a natural tendency. As societies modernize, people become increasingly individualistic and, correspondingly, they are increasingly inclined to view behavior through the lenses of psychology and economics. Psychology emphasizes processes occurring "within" people: their cognitive patterns, their perceptual and motor abilities, their emotional states and motivations, and so on. Thus, modern people (including, in all likelihood, most readers of this book) have a strong tendency to think about things from a psychological perspective that largely highlights internal processes. At the same time, such internal processes are seen to produce a "calculating animal" that responds to circumstances and events using the economic logic of cost and benefit. Thus, the rational actor (i.e., calculating person) is a common image of people in society.

With such logic in play, we are often, if not typically, concerned with the *self*: our self-concept (including such things as self-esteem, self-efficacy, and self-authenticity), and the possibilities of self-help, self-actualization, self-awareness, and self-improvement. Indeed, a recent search of "self-help" books on the popular Amazon.com website yielded no fewer than 135,250 sources. Not surprisingly, we are likewise concerned about the state of our self. This includes our feelings, personality, intelligence, and so on. Many of today's media icons are purveyors of self-help (e.g., Oprah, Dr. Phil), and our stores and libraries are filled with books that claim to empower us so that we might fix what is wrong with ourselves. And yet the self-help movement is but a part of much bigger phenomenon. Research suggests that as societies become increasingly modern, the organizations and resources devoted to psychology proliferate.[5] America is a modern society and Americans are, not surprisingly, a very psychology-oriented people.

Given such inclinations, we are apt to think about our lives in terms of personal attributes: intelligence, personality, motivation, physical attractiveness, emotions, and the like. "As we all know," these factors explain achievements in school, occupational successes and failures, family life, and so on. We do not hesitate to describe our lives as a story of "what I did" in keeping with the literal meaning of "autobiography," the biography of one's self. Indeed, research shows that personal factors can be important in determining how people age and that people are likely to think about their biographies in very personal terms.

And yet, the importance of such factors notwithstanding, the focus of this book is *emphatically different:* to discover how our changing social experiences affect the way we age. Because society is in a constant state of change as people grow older, the sociological study of lives rightly calls on the one hand for the study of history, social change, and changes in our circumstances and on the other hand how we develop from birth to death. This shift to sociological thinking is the shift from the inner workings of the person to the social setting that encompasses and constitutes the person. For most readers, this sociological view will be a new and exciting way of looking at oneself and other people.

There is another ideological obstacle to the sociological study of the biography. Many students distrust sociology because it appears to threaten two cherished and interrelated beliefs: self-determination and personal responsibility. How, they reason, can social forces powerfully shape people's lives and yet people remain free to "be themselves"? In turn, if people are the products of their environments, how can they be accountable for bad deeds and praiseworthy for good ones? These questions are clearly serious ones given that most Western social institutions—legal, economic, religious, educational, and occupational—rest on the foundation that people are free and responsible for their actions. The sinner has earned punishment, the high achiever has earned the best grades and income, and so on.

Nevertheless, even an enthusiastic proponent of human freedom and responsibility will not doubt that social circumstances have *something* to do with one's life. Were this not the case, society would care little about how its institutions are organized. For example, if social circumstances do not affect people, then why the "continuing crisis" over the conditions of our schools? Why care about the organization of our health care system or laws and regulations governing work and family life? We care about such matters because we know that, to a significant degree, how social settings are organized can greatly affect people's lives. Indeed, the captains of industry know this to be true: there are many ways to organize the workers in a company, and some lead to higher productivity than others.

Whether people are free and accountable is a philosophical issue that cannot be resolved by science, but social arrangements clearly affect people's life chances, their families, productivity, and health and well-being. The issue then becomes: to what extent and in what ways does society shape people's lives, and how can we study these processes?

A MAP

Our purpose in writing this book is to see beyond the conventional, to encourage readers to overcome the common roadblocks that we have identified, and to appreciate the complex, richly social nature of how people are born into this world, grow up, work and love, and, if all goes well, live long and rewarding lives. Of course, most lives are not so neatly packaged, which adds yet more interest and urgency to the study of biography.

Because life course sociology is an imaginative framework, this book is less about "what we know" about the life course and more about "how to think" about changing societies and aging by drawing on life course ideas. We hope that it establishes how very far we have come since the days of Mills's essay, far beyond urging the study of society and lives and now deeply engaging the difficulties of this enterprise, aided by many useful ideas and concepts and analytic strategies. This book is fundamentally about those ideas, concepts, and analytic strategies. Beginning students will find some (but certainly not all) of the classics of life course research discussed and evaluated; more advanced students will find a synthetic, critical view that organizes these classics. We augment these discussions, both thick and thin, with pertinent research that highlights the theoretical issues under consideration. We recommend that interested readers consult cited works and we also suggest further readings at the end of each chapter.

It is our hope that, in addition to introducing life course studies, this book also spurs the imagination to consider alternative ways of organizing society and the implications of these alternatives for the biography. The American family is under intense pressures owing to strains between work careers and family responsibilities; the transition from school to work is not a smooth process for many young adults; growing up poor is filled with experiences that drain the human spirit and discourage people; many retired people face great hardship after decades of earnest work. Life course sociology promotes an appreciation for the connections between societies and lives, and so can help address such challenges.

Chapter 1 begins with a brief consideration of how sociology fits into the behavioral sciences, how sociology has typically looked at biography, and how life course sociology emerged to address weaknesses in traditional sociological views. Chapter 2 further explores the meaning of the life course by considering key principles and concepts that have been used to study lives in context. Chapter 3 explores some basic ideas and analytic strategies for the macro study of biography. (Given the state of scholarship, we are necessarily—and regrettably—constrained to the case of Western societies and indeed largely to the American experience.) Chapter 4 explores the micro perspective and considers how the lives of people are built through the complex interplay of agency and subjectivity. A key issue here is how temporality—the past, the present, and the future—shapes the micro dimensions of the life course. Chapter 5 then turns to a synthesis of the major ideas presented in the previous chapters by asking how the macro and micro perspectives can, together, inform the study of biography. This chapter illuminates both the concepts and ideas that have proven useful in studying how social changes affect the way people age and the specific processes at work. It also directs us towards new, emerging areas of inquiry, including those of behavioral genetics, the embeddedness of agency within historical context, and the implications of globalization.

In each of these chapters, we discuss several case studies to illustrate the life course imagination at work. Finally, in Chapter 6 we return to the unfinished task of C. Wright Mills, drawing upon the preceding chapters to formulate an imaginative framework with which people can think about the intersection between their biographies and society. In their totality, these chapters are meant to highlight the richness and complexity surrounding the study of social change and the biography.

We wish to acknowledge very helpful criticism from Professor Glen H. Elder Jr. and his exceptional Life Course Working Group at the University of North Carolina at Chapel Hill, the members of which include at this writing Daniel Adkins, Janel Benson, Tyson Brown, Matthew Dupre, Kathryn Henderson, Matthew Lloyd, Naomi Spence, Miles Taylor, Stephen Vaisey, Victor Wang, and David Warner. We thank Professors Elizabeth Fussell and Karl Ulrich Mayer for their contributions to Tables 3.1 and 3.3, respectively, and Frank J. Sulloway for useful comments on our case study of Charles Darwin. We also thank our helpful, friendly, and professional colleagues at W. W. Norton & Company, Karl Bakeman, Rebecca Arata, and Mike Fleming. The first author wishes to thank his wife, Lilly Shanahan, for her patience, support, and advice.

Finally, this book is dedicated to Professor Jeylan T. Mortimer, who, as Director of the Life Course Center at the University of Minnesota, an extraordinarily productive scholar, and a seemingly inexhaustible mentor, has inspired and educated us and many other students of the life course. The many talents that make her an outstanding scholar are matched by her generosity and grace.

FURTHER READING

The following references are to select overviews that build on the basic understanding of life course studies provided by *Biography and the Sociological Imagination.*

Elder, G. H., Jr., and Michael J. Shanahan. "The Life Course and Human Development." In *Handbook of Child Psychology*, vol. 1, edited by R.M. Lerner, 665–715. New York: John Wiley & Sons, 2006.

Overview of life course concepts and research with an emphasis on its intersections with the study of human development, particularly child and developmental psychology. This chapter is also useful in distinguishing life course sociology from life-span psychology, two subfields that are sometimes (erroneously) conflated.

Heinz, Walter R., and Victor W. Marshall, eds. *Social Dynamics of the Life Course: Transitions, Institutions, and Interrelations.* New York: Aldine de Gruyter, 2003.

Stimulating collection of essays reflecting interest in macro-micro links, cross-national comparative analyses, and connections between the adult workplace and other facets of the life course.

O'Rand, Angela M., and Margaret L. Krecker. "Concepts of the Life Cycle: Their History, Meanings, and Uses in the Social Sciences." *Annual Review of Sociology* 16 (1990): 241–262.

Very useful essay on the life cycle, which is often associated with the life course but is nevertheless distinct.

Mayer, Karl Ulrich. "The Sociology of the Life Course and Lifespan Psychology: Diverging or Converging Pathways." In *Understanding Human Development: Dialogues with Lifespan Psychology,* edited by Ursula M. Staudinger and Ulman Lindenberger, 463–481. Boston: Kluwer, 2003.

    Perceptive essay on the differences between life course sociology and its counterpart in psychology, life-span research. Considers possibilities of integrating these two approaches. See also, Dannefer (1984), listed in Chapter 2 Further Readings.

Mortimer, J. T., and Michael J. Shanahan, eds. *Handbook of the Life Course.* New York: Plenum-Kluwer, 2005.

    Many useful essays that collectively offer a state-of-the-art survey of life course research: concepts, methods, research findings, emerging directions. For an engaging reaction to this collection of essays, see Mayer, Karl Ulrich. Book review. *Social Forces* 84. 4 (2006): 2363–2365.

Settersten, Richard A., Jr., ed. *Invitation to the Life Course: Toward New Understandings of Later Life.* Amityville, NY: Baywood Publishing Company, 2003.

    Collection of essays that explores connections between life course studies and gerontology.

BIOGRAPHY AND THE SOCIOLOGICAL IMAGINATION: CONTEXTS AND CONTINGENCIES

Chapter One

WHAT IS THE LIFE COURSE?

*No social study that does not come back to the problems of biography, of
history, and of their intersection within a society has completed its intellectual journey.*

—C. Wright Mills

EVERY LIFE IS DIFFERENT and every life is the same.

On the one hand, each person is a unique combination of
experiences and attributes: some people are born into wealth
and privilege, while others are born into poverty and a lack of
meaningful opportunity. Some people are born into the "domi-
nant culture," with its racial, ethnic, religious, and sexual dimensions; others are born as "outsiders," minorities in their
societies who often face discrimination and prejudice. Some
people are born in sound physical and mental health, while
others are born with physical and mental challenges. It is a truism reaffirmed by the birth of every child: no two lives are the
same and each one of us is unique among the billions of people
who have ever lived and who will ever live.

And yet it is also a truism that the human condition brings
with it a set of seemingly universal experiences. We may or
may not understand the intricacies of Shakespeare's Elizabethan
prose, but all of us feel the corrosive envy of Othello, the buoy-
ant passion of Romeo, and the plaguing indecision of Hamlet.

Beyond these commonplace emotions, lives are similar in how they are "structured": people begin life as infants and proceed through a series of phases including childhood, adolescence, adulthood, and old age. Shakespeare himself acknowledged the phases of life, referring to old age, for example, as the "sixth age" in which the once vivacious young man "shifts into the lean and slipper'd pantaloon, with spectacles on nose and pouch on side, his youthful hose, well-sav'd, a world too wide for his shrunk shrank."[1] The audience can relate to this representation because they are familiar with the images: for centuries, old age was associated with physical decrepitude and disengagement from society. In fact, every phase of life has its unique images, opportunities, and limitations, all of which shape who we are, creating commonalities in our experiences and life patterns. And so, although it may appear contradictory at first glance, we can accurately observe that every life is different and every life is the same.

In today's society, we are entertained by Shakespeare's theatrical treatment of what it means to be human and to grow old, but we are also left asking a distinctly modern question: from the perspective of science, sociology in particular, how are biographies both different and the same and how does sociology make sense of this dualism?

To answer the question, we must briefly sketch a definition of "science" and explain how sociology fits into the "behavioral sciences." Early sociological approaches that attempted to link society with human lives are then considered. As interesting as these approaches still are, they failed to consider the full complexity of the biography. Building on and extending these approaches, life course sociology emerged in the 1970s as an analytic tool for the study of changing societies and the aging person.

THE BEHAVIORAL SCIENCES AND SOCIOLOGY

The Nature of Science

Science is part of a distinct worldview called empiricism, which assumes that we learn new things through observations made by our five senses. Moreover, observations must be systematic, which means that they are made according to a set of agreed-upon rules. These rules govern measurement (i.e., the task of assigning numbers to observations, or categorizing them in some other meaningful way), sampling (i.e., the task of determining who will be studied and how often to make observations), and research design (i.e., how to make comparisons among the observations in order to learn new things). Science is the practice of empiricism, fundamentally concerned with the mechanics of making systematic observations and interpreting them to yield an accurate understanding of the world. In other words, empiricism is a philosophical position that underscores the value of observations, and science is the "nuts and bolts" of how to make those observations. The result is empirical research, studies based on systematic observations.

Is there just one way to conduct empirical research? No. Any strategy that makes systematic observations is empirical. Perhaps the strategy involves survey data collected from a representative sample of Americans, interviews with adults who have spent time in prison, experiments exploring interpersonal conflict in the laboratory, analysis of newspaper articles appearing in the last two centuries, observation of people in a retirement home, and so on. Surveys, interviews, experiments, archival analyses, participant observations—all of these methods generate observations. As long as the investigator exerts her or his best effort to make these observations scientifically systematic, "an act of social science is being committed," to paraphrase the poet W. H. Auden.[2]

When many people think of science, they think of a Madame Curie or an Albert Einstein—a seemingly solitary figure who, by virtue of a giant intellect and hard work, arrives at insights or makes observations that prove helpful to the rest of humanity. This is a misleading view. Because science insists on the use of systematic observations, anyone can repeat (or "replicate") what has been purportedly observed. Furthermore, because everyone knows exactly how the observations were made, the community of scientists can evaluate their meaning and importance. (Indeed, Einstein did not make observations, focusing as he did on interpreting the observations of other scientists and suggesting observations that should be made.) The story of science is thus not the story of a great person but rather of communities of people who make observations, debate their meaning, and form a consensus about what is true. And this is a process that unfolds in history as each generation of scientists receives a consensus, adds to it, and sometimes challenges it.

But if science consisted only of making observations, it would not get very far because the world presents a seemingly infinite set of observations that could be made. Indeed, many of the early scientists devoted their lives to creating catalogs of observations. But they quickly realized that such catalogs needed to be organized: what observations should science make and, once made, how can they be organized in cohesive and meaningful ways? These are the functions of scientific theory: to direct the scientist's attention to specific observations and also to organize observations into coherent accounts of reality.

A scientific theory refers to a set of logically interrelated statements that include concepts (or words with specialized meanings). In turn, these statements lead to a hypothesis, or prediction, which identifies observations that are most useful. Oftentimes, the observations lead the scientist back to the theory: something new has been learned, and so the theory must be updated, perhaps expanded, perhaps modified, or perhaps rejected completely. The cycle then repeats, with the updated theory suggesting new observations, which will, in turn, have further implications for the theory.

Scientists can also use paradigms, which are sets of concepts that stimulate their imaginations. Unlike theories, paradigms are not comprised of statements that are interrelated according to the rules of logic. Rather, paradigms are ideas, concepts, models, and analytic strategies that loosely fit together and often lead scientists to generate new hypotheses. "Science" thus refers to communal efforts to study and understand phenomena via the continual interplay between systematic observations and theories or paradigms.

But what is "behavior?" The common definition refers to any action or reaction that a person has to external or internal stimuli. Behavior thus refers to a very broad range of phenomena. This includes things such as interacting with other people, studying, talking, or walking. But it also includes modes of thinking, feeling, and evaluating. In fact, "behavior" is used by some behavioral scientists to refer to *any* attribute of the person (including, for example, personality, motivation, motor and sensory skills, as well as the workings of hormones and genes, and physical and mental health) or to any attribute of two or more people (including, for example, cooperation, the use of power, and parenting practices). Throughout this book, "behavior" is used in this latter, broad sense.

Behavioral Science and Sociology

Given the complexity of behavior, different scientific communities have formed based on different presuppositions about its nature. A presupposition, or premise, refers to a "suppose that . . ." statement. A presupposition is not a fact, but rather a starting point for thinking about complicated things. The behavioral sciences are made up of different disciplines, and these disciplines are distinguished first and foremost by their different presuppositions about the origins and nature of behavior. For example: *Suppose that* behavior is fundamentally about the workings of mind, including cognition, emotion, motivation, and the mechanics that govern our sensory perceptions. This is a presupposition that animates the discipline of psychology. Or, instead: *Suppose that* human lives reflect the rational use of resources to maximize one's life chances and enjoyment. This is a presupposition that inspires economics. Such presuppositions fundamentally shape what questions (or types of questions) are asked, how findings are interpreted, and ultimately how explanations are organized.

What is the sociological presupposition to the study of biography? *Suppose that* the biography is fundamentally shaped by our relationships with other people and by the social structures that contextualize these relationships. The word "structure" appears in this sociological presupposition and this word is very abstract and important. A phenomenon is *structured* when it has organized elements that tend to repeat through time and space. Traditionally, science has been especially good at understanding things that have a structure. For example, viewed from an airplane at a high altitude, the landscape often takes on interesting features that repeat across the land (e.g., mountain ranges, coastlines, or patterns of color that characterize the soil and rocks) and that remain stable for long periods of time. A geologist might be interested in using science to explain how these geologic structures came about. Similarly, every human body is comprised of the same organs, which in turn are comprised of the same types of cells. A physiologist might be interested in studying these biological structures.

Sociologists are interested in social structures, which refer to organized patterns of behavior or experience that persist in space and time and which are created by two or more people. Notice that social structures do not refer to individual people, but rather to relationships and interactions among people or groups of people. Social structures can be thought of in terms of levels of aggregation, that is, levels of analysis roughly matching the number of people who are organized. There are many different levels of aggregation, including dyads (groups of two people), small groups, large groups, families, neighborhoods, communities, formal organizations (e.g., churches or schools), institutions (e.g., the American educational system), and large political units like states, provinces, and nations.

What are examples of social structures? Think about dyads, groups of two people, for a moment. The early sociologist Georg Simmel observed that relationships between two people are highly structured.[3] For example, they may be in love, and the expression of this love, as a set of ongoing interactions, is fairly predictable. The same may be said for hostility, competition, power, cooperation, or hatred. All of these concepts refer to qualities of relationships between two people, and these qualities tend to repeat across dyads (i.e., competition between Ben and Sheila will share basic properties with competition between Leah and Joseph). At a "higher level" of aggregation, formal organizations (e.g., companies or universities) may have similar relationships. For example, Companies X and Y may be locked in competition to secure a growing market share for their product (or, for that matter, Companies X and Y may decide to cooperate).

Another type of social structure involves status, or one's place within a group. Think, for example, of one's position in an organizational chart, which is made up of statuses, not specific people. At a modern-day American university, for example, the board of regents often has the highest status position in the university, followed by the president, chancellors, vice-chancellors, deans, and so on. The concept of status is critically important because every status brings with it certain opportunities and limitations and every status has a role, which is a set of expected behaviors. Thus, social expectations strongly dictate how the chancellor will appear (including his or her dress, speech, posture, and mannerisms) and behave. Similarly, people expect the head of Police and Parking to appear and behave in certain ways that differentiate him or her from the chancellor. Status may refer to a person's place in the family ("the older sister"), in the school ("she's a senior now"), in the workplace ("she's the sales manager"), and indeed in the society ("he's from an upper-middle-class suburban black family"). Sociologists consider race/ethnicity, gender, and social class to be principal indicators of status within a society.

Social structure is also comprised of codes, schemas, scripts, rules, and regulations, written and unwritten, explicitly stated and implicitly understood, that govern our behavior. These rules may be highly abstract (e.g., the Golden Rule to "do unto others as you would have them do unto you") or highly specific (e.g., the tax regulations governing charitable deductions). Some codes and rules refer to the expectations that we maintain about each of the phases of life: how a small child should behave versus what is required from an adolescent; when people should have left their parents' home and established their own household; what are the strengths and limitations of a young adult versus those of a "senior citizen." All of these types of expectations are internalized, more or less, which means that we gradually come to understand them and make them a part of the way we think. In turn, these internalized schemas, cohesive sets of rules, regulations, and expectations all combine to regulate our behavior.

Our purpose is not to be exhaustive but already it is clear that social structure refers to a complex, multifaceted set of phenomena that define a person's situation. These forces create the opportunities and constraints that fundamentally shape our lives. Each one of us is born into a "social location" reflecting the sum total of our social statuses. This social location profoundly shapes who we are and the range of possibilities that define who we are likely to become. No two social locations are identical, which creates inequalities of opportunity and differential exposure to risks. For example, compare and contrast the life chances of two persons: one is born in an impoverished rural area, the other in a wealthy, gated community. Who is more likely to do well in school, to secure a well-paying, interesting job, to have a satisfying family life, and to live into old age in relatively good health? And who is more likely to encounter difficulties with peer groups, to drop out of high school, to have a poor-paying job, and to die a comparatively early death? Although these two scenarios represent extremes, they illustrate a point that applies to each one of us: lives are powerfully shaped by the social circumstances into which we are born and which continue to shape us throughout our lives. Such circumstances ultimately produce unique, yet structured, biographies.

Sociology's interest in social structures also explains its interest in social change. By definition, social change refers to changes in social structures. Social change can reflect changes in culture, norms and values, changes in institutions and how they function, or very large-scale changes in the organization of populations. By observing these changes and behavioral patterns, we can learn much about how society and biography are linked. Understanding the links between such behavioral changes and social change is a challenge, but one that brings with it tremendous rewards.

Specifically, the challenge is how we can study social structure and biography scientifically. That is, how can we theorize about people's lives as they are shaped by social forces and then test these theories by making systematic observations? How can we empirically study how and why people are both the same and different, given that not everyone is affected by society and by social change in the same way? The answer to this question is the story of how life course sociology emerged from early sociology efforts that linked society and person.

SOCIOLOGY AND BIOGRAPHY

At first glance, the core sociological presupposition may seem obvious. Of course our relationships with other people and our place in society shape our lives! And yet, adherence to this idea can lead to new ways of viewing things and to an uncommon perspective on biography. Most people see their lives and the lives of others as resulting from personal efforts, talents, shortcomings, personality, intelligence, and the like. In contrast, the sociological view directs us to look at a person's life story as a social creation, reflecting a complex web of social forces peculiar to a historical time and place. Consider, for example, the life of Wolfgang Amadeus Mozart, perhaps the most admired composer in the history of Western music. A recent search of his biographies conveys the themes that most people think of when they think about Mozart. Here are some representative observations:

- Mozart was one of the greatest prodigies in the history of music.
- Mozart had a love-hate relationship with his overbearing father and never developed a normal adult balance in conducting his affairs.
- Mozart grew up to be undisciplined, unwordly, and gullible.
- Mozart's arrogance and impulsive behavior undermined him at every turn.
- Despite his emphatic success, Mozart went through a period of great trial and depression during his adult life.
- Mozart worked feverishly on his requiem (a religious ceremony for the dead), refusing both rest and food so that he might finish it before he died.

The lasting impression created by most biographies is that through hard work and great genius, Mozart wrote a large body of music that millions of people have come to enjoy. These themes, however, focus exclusively on Mozart's character traits and other psychological features: he is said to have been born with immense talent that made his great musical achievements "natural"; as an adult, he was psychosocially "immature"; he was successful, but had bouts of depression; he was hardworking, particularly at the very end of his life. In thinking about Mozart (or anyone else for that matter), most people are unwittingly drawn to the psychological presupposition that biography reflects the talents, motivations, and emotional state of the person.

By itself, such a view cannot account for the full richness of a life story, including Mozart's biography. Many musical prodigies have been born, many people have a love-hate relationship with their father, many adults are arrogant and impulsive, and many people are hardworking. Indeed, countless people have undoubtedly been born with all of these qualities. Nevertheless, one can (and should) view Mozart's life from the sociological presupposition that directs our attention to social structures. What would such a view look like?

In *Mozart: Portrait of a Genius,* the sociologist Norbert Elias notes that Mozart's life, particularly the peculiar pattern of enormous success on the one hand and poverty and depression on the other, can only be understood by locating Mozart in the society of his time and place.[4] According to Elias, Mozart lived during a transitional period in history, marking the boundary between a time when musicians were viewed as mere servants to nobility and a time when musicians could be "freelance" artists commanding the respect of the middle and upper classes through their accomplishments. In the late eighteenth century, musicians were heavily dependent on the church and aristocracy, who dictated the types of the music that would be written and performed. Musicians were servants of the royal courts, which were the sole source of funding for artists.

As Mozart's career was developing, however, a new social class was emerging, the bourgeoisie. ("Bourgeoisie" is a French word related to the German "Burgher," which refers to a citizen who is not of the nobility or the lowest working class; the term implies a socially engaged person of some means and standing in the community.) The bourgeoisie included, for example, lawyers, doctors, professors, successful businessmen, and other persons with appreciable wealth and/or education. To establish their credentials as cultured citizens, many members of the bourgeois class supported the fine arts, including classical music.

According to Elias, the problematic nature of Mozart's life reflects the fact that he broke away from patronage at a time when the bourgeoisie's support of classical music was not yet substantial. Mozart was greatly troubled by the humiliation and subordination that he constantly felt at the hands of his employer, the Archbishop of Salzburg. Eventually, his resentment, coupled with a strong desire to pursue his musical interests as he pleased, led to his resignation in 1781, to a break with his patron, and to the adoption of a position as freelance artist. Mozart did not enjoy teaching piano to the children of the bourgeoisie, preferring instead to write operas and symphonies for public concerts that were sold by subscription. Unfortunately, the bourgeois class was simply not big enough to support Mozart's strategy. Moreover, many of them became alienated from Mozart once they realized how much he had antagonized the Viennese aristocracy. Despite his enormous skills and motivation, Mozart spent much of his adulthood struggling to be the success that his talent warranted, only to die in desperate frustration and poverty.

In contrast, consider the subsequent circumstances of Beethoven, whose compositions would not have been viewed as superior to Mozart's. Beethoven left royal patronage in 1794, only thirteen years after Mozart fled the Archbishop, yet he garnered more commissions than he could accept and basked in great success throughout his adult life. While Mozart's and Beethoven's breaks with their patrons were separated by a very short time, the interval was highly significant in that the bourgeois class solidified and created very different market conditions for musical composers. So Mozart was not only a great musical talent, he was also a social trailblazer, among the first of the major classical composers to draw upon the burgeoning bourgeoisie for his livelihood. And like so many social trailblazers, his life was ultimately filled with grief.

Social Change and Social Life: The Sociological Classics
Notice how Elias's sociological perspective directed him to consider how Mozart's life reflected the imprint of society. Much of Mozart's story is the story of his time and place. This is a central and cherished theme in sociology, and can be traced to the discipline's "classics," written mainly in the last quarter of the nineteenth century and the beginning of the twentieth century. The sociological classics are held in great esteem in part because they were among the first explorations of society

based on sociological presuppositions, but also in part because they can be read from so many vantage points. For example, many readers of the sociological classics consider them to be great statements about the nature of inequalities in society, particularly with respect to how social groups arrange themselves in hierarchies, and how they cooperate and conflict with one another. Other readers are attracted to the recurring theme of social change: how the institutions and organization of a society change through history, and how social movements play a role in effecting these changes.

A related theme that is found time and again is how the modernization of societies changes the lives of people. Modernization typically refers to a set of social changes that include industrialization, urbanization, secularization, and the rise of science. Obviously, these aspects of modernization have tended to fit together: mechanization requires advances in science, new factories lead to the emergence and expansion of cities, and the movement of diverse populations from rural areas into the cities leads to a decline in traditional ways of living. Modernization is thus a complex set of phenomena that occur over many years. It has also occurred at different times in different places. For example, England began modernizing by the seventeenth century (if not earlier), while Germany and Russia were still modernizing in the late nineteenth and early twentieth centuries.

Because of its early emergence and its vigorous nature, English modernization stimulated many different reactions from both artists and scientists. For example, facets of modernization inspired authors like Charles Dickens, whose works often reflect how the maladies of factories, cities, and commerce affect the human spirit. One thinks of *A Christmas Carol* with Ebenezer Scrooge representing modernity and Bob Cratchit embodying a more traditional life-style. Other literary works that were reactions to modernization include Mary Shelley's *Frankenstein,* the poetry of William Wordsworth, and the socially engaged novels of George Eliot, Elizabeth Gaskell, and Charlotte Brontë (all women, interestingly enough). In *Frankenstein,* for example, Shelley explores the nature of a monster who is half-man/half-machine, which stands in part as a metaphor for the worker in the factory. Frankenstein's monster suffers from social isolation, crying out, "If I have no ties and no affections, hatred and vice must be my portion. . . . My vices are the children of a forced solitude that I abhor."[5] The link between modernism and the monster is further strengthened by the character of Dr. Frankenstein, who stands in part as a metaphor for science and technology.

On one level, *Frankenstein* is a "scary story" to be enjoyed by teenagers and adults. But on another level, it is an extended exploration of anxieties about modern life, including the rise of science and industrialism and the weakening of people's traditional ties to each other. Indeed, most of the literary reactions to modernism were pessimistic, fretting that modernization would destroy established ways of living marked by a strong sense of community and tradition, and would create social and personal tensions among the newly emerging social classes. The enduring popularity of J. R. R. Tolkien's *Lord of the Rings* trilogy shows that these anxieties about modernism are alive and well. The Hobbits represent an idyllic rural life of simplicity and happiness, as opposed to the empire of Saruman, representing industrialism, the destruction of forests, and indeed the destruction of the traditions and communities of Middle Earth.

Modernization also inspired behavioral science and in fact led to the emergence of sociology. One early sociologist was Karl Marx (1818–83), a German, who, writing at about the same time as Dickens, sought to answer questions concerning how societies change with modernization and the implications of these changes for people. Marx is often looked upon with great suspicion by students. After all, he urged the communist revolutions that would lead to the imprisonment of over 65 million people under Stalin in Soviet Russia alone. And yet, there is a decidedly different way to view Marx, one that appreciates and evaluates his claims about the shortcomings of early industrial capitalism, of which there were undoubtedly many. From this vantage point, Marx was concerned with the emergence of new and hugely unequal social classes of people in industrial societies (principally, factory workers and owners of factories).

Part of early sociological theorizing was directed toward understanding the nature of this social change, inquiring about the origins of critical differences between premodern and modern societies. Another fundamental question of the early sociological thinkers concerned how the changes accompanying modernization affected the lives of ordinary people. Thus, for example, the early German sociologist Ferdinand Tönnies (1855–1936) held that a premodern society (designated *Gemeinschaft* or community) was characterized by, among other things, emotional expression and the importance of tradition.[6] Social status and relationships in the community were heavily based on family ties and other circumstances of one's birth. Individuals were communal in their orientations, sharing many activities and responsibilities. In contrast, according to his analysis, modern societies (denoted by *Gesellschaft,* or society) tend to promote rational systems over traditional ones. Relations between people become increasingly impersonal and devoid of emotional expression. As relationships are increasingly based on contractual understandings, they become much more specific with respect to each person's interests in, and responsibilities toward, other people.

Similarly, French sociologist Émile Durkheim (1858–1917) distinguished between premodern and modern societies by focusing on the distinct types of solidarity that hold such societies together.[7] He argued that premodern societies are characterized by a simple division of labor, which means that people tended to share common tasks (e.g., finding and preparing food, repairing shelters). In turn, a low division of labor coincided with shared ways of thinking, a strong sense of shared values, and a punitive system of justice. Modern societies, in contrast, are characterized by a high division of labor, meaning that people tend to have highly specialized jobs (e.g., brain surgeon, forest ranger). In turn, a high division of labor coincides with a weaker sense of shared values and interdependencies based on contractual understandings. Thus, both Tönnies and Durkheim envisioned fundamental shifts in social relations that would accompany the structural changes associated with modernization.

The sociological classics can thus be read as explorations of how historical change, in the form of modernization, leads to changes in the nature of society, the behavior of people, and the ways in which self and society interact. Unlike literary reactions to modernity, which were largely critical, most early sociology was marked by ambivalence. Tönnies, for example, acknowledged that in modern societies people are free to achieve their status in society, as opposed to the inherited, imposed status of premodern times. And yet, modern societies increase feelings of anonymity and engender forms of living that are not based on tradition. Durkheim thought that premodern societies were excessively controlling and harsh in their punishment of any deviance. And yet modern societies often created a sense of anomie, which refers to a sense of meaninglessness as to one's place in society. Even Marx, for all his disdain for capitalism, admitted that it was a highly efficient way to produce goods and that it generated great wealth.

The idea of a strong connection between social change and behavior was thus well established in the traditional sociological classics. In turn, this theme was subsequently developed in three distinct lines of research. The first line, the "character in society" (sometimes called the "national character") tradition, was very much in keeping with classical sociological theory. Sociologists (as well as anthropologists and psychoanalysts) in this tradition were interested in the nature of society and how it shaped the identities (often referred to as "character" or "personality") of a people. A second line of inquiry focused on intergenerational relations and conflicts and how they produce societal change. The third "social structure and personality" approach addressed linkages between multifaceted social structures and features of the person.

Character and Society

David Riesman's *The Lonely Crowd* (1961) exemplifies the "character in society" tradition.[8] According to Riesman, societies typically progress through three stages, each stage corresponding to a unique character. The first societal stage is characterized by a preindustrialized economy, scarcity of resources, illiteracy, and a fairly stable population in which young people predominate (owing to both high fertility and high mortality rates). Such a society gives rise to the "tradition-directed" person, who is socialized early in life according to rules, rituals, routines, and rigid forms of etiquette that may have endured for centuries. The tradition-directed person has very limited choice in directing his or her life and conducting everyday affairs; rather, such a person is in tune with social institutions and the dictates of the community. (Note that the traditional society and the tradition-directed person are characteristic of Tönnies's *Gemeinschaft* society mentioned earlier.)

The second phase of society is marked by a rapid growth in population, improvements in agriculture and the production of other goods, an increase in the division of labor, and growing inequality. The result is a breakdown in the force of tradition and a shift from the tradition-directed to an inner-directed person. The inner-directed person pursues personal goals and ambitions, maintaining his or her course by way of a "psychological gyroscope" that balances individual objectives with the demands of the external environment, including, but not limited to, tradition. Parents and other authority figures greatly influence this balancing act, but the inner-directed person is aware of more than one tradition and more than one way of viewing one's life. The inner-directed person, while guided by authority figures, is a decision-maker about his or her destiny.

Finally, the third phase of society is characterized by an incipient decline in population growth, the rise of bureaucracies, the increased geographic mobility of the population, and increased contact among diverse peoples. Such a society gives rise to the other-directed person, whose character depends on signals, including those from one's immediate peers and messages from the mass media. The other-directed person spends his or her life constantly attuned to the signals that are sent by diverse people both far and wide. This self is malleable, ready to change depending on perceived and often evanescent criteria for approval, conformity, and success. Riesman could not avoid lamenting the rise of the other-directed person, whom he viewed as superficial, anxiety-ridden, and destined to either a forced conformity or anomie resulting from a failure to conform.

The Lonely Crowd represents a mode of analysis that seeks to interrelate two sets of ideal types, or hypothetical exemplars. The first set describes characteristics of a society. For Riesman, this involves how societies can be characterized by population attributes (e.g., fertility and mortality patterns, geographic mobility), modes of production (e.g., primitive versus advanced agriculture), and technology. The second set describes the character of the persons who inhabit these different societies, notably the tradition-, inner-, and other-directed personalities. By interrelating the two sets of ideal types, Riesman is claiming that societies go through stages of development, each stage with a different "character."

(One can contrast this perspective with that of C. Wright Mills, discussed in the preface. Instead of beginning with attributes of society and asking what types of personalities or characters they might produce, Mills began with people and asked what type of society could "produce" them.)

It is noteworthy, however, that through all of these works, spanning the classical concerns of premodern versus modern societies and the character-in-society tradition, little or no attention is actually devoted to biography. All of this theorizing and research concerns a generic, seemingly ageless adult who is buffeted in predictable ways by the tidal forces of social change. In classical sociology, the capitalist worker *will* be alienated or perhaps deluded (Marx) and the fast pace of social change *will* lead to anomie (Durkheim). In the character-in-society tradition, the upper- and middle-class urban American of the 1960s *will* be other-directed (Riesman) and the citizen of high-tech mass society *will* be sexually repressed (Marcuse[9]). Presumably, the person could be sixteen or eighty-six years old, and their alienation, anomie, repression, and any other experiences of society are unchanging features of their lives.

One commentator, Irving Horowitz, articulates this issue when he notes that the work of C. Wright Mills, as well as of the classical sociologists, is *epochal*.[10] This means that, through the study of social change and its implications for people, they are ultimately concerned with understanding large swatches, or epochs, of social history. Their interest, for example, is in characterizing the capitalist epoch of Western history, including "what people are like" in such a social system. The motivation driving their inquiry is to describe capitalist societies and to explain their workings. Their ultimate unit of analysis, however, is not the person who changes and develops through time. They do not consider how people age, how the phases of their lives are interconnected, how the multitude of social forces that dynamically create the biography lead to many different life stories. Their interest is not in documenting how a child is born in a capitalist society and through a lifetime of experiences may or may not be alienated or repressed. Their focus is the social life of a distinct period in history, not how this history was experienced from birth to death.

Equally significant, most of this classic sociological research had little, if any, empirical basis. That is, sociologists in this tradition were rarely concerned with the sampling and measurement of societies and their inhabitants. Further, though they were interested in the development of theory, in fact they were not trying to organize a clearly articulated set of empirical observations. These works are largely impressionistic and at best they provide accounts of society that resonate with the scientific and lay communities. (Indeed, commentators have marveled at how a book like Riesman's *The Lonely Crowd,* with so little empirical basis, could have captivated a purportedly scientific discipline for so many decades.)

Another shortcoming concerns the theme with which we began this chapter. These works tend to fall short of describing how people in the same society can be both similar and different. Marx's capitalist worker is either alienated or deluded, with no other possibilities. Similarly, Riesman's modern person is simply other-directed. And yet, as Dennis Wrong suggests in his famous essay "The Oversocialized Conception of Man," models such as these fail to appreciate the diverse motives that both inspire and restrain people.[11] According to Wrong, "socialization" refers to two distinct ideas: the process of becoming human through interactions with other people and the transmission of culture. As Wrong observes, "All men are so-cialized in the latter sense, but this does not mean that they have been completely molded by the particular norms and values of their culture [in the first sense]." To varying degrees, people are approval seekers (believed by Wrong's generation of sociologists to be a major human motive), but they are also power seekers, materialists, sensualists, spiritualists, and so on. Given the complex motives that characterize each person, it is unlikely that a given social structure will lead to the same "character" for everyone.

Intergenerational Linkages

If the classics in sociology were concerned with large-scale social structures and their implications from personal experience, a second line of research conceptualized the link between society and behavior as a problem of intergenerational relationships. Sociologists working in the character-in-society tradition, and, one might add, the classical sociologists themselves, rarely considered *how* a society came to produce certain types of personalities. In contrast, other sociologists were interested in the idea of *generations* and sought to understand how cultural heritage is transmitted through history from parent to child and, in turn, how the process of intergenerational transmission creates opportunities for social change.

Much of this work was inspired by Karl Mannheim's influential essay "The Problem of Generations."[12] For Mannheim, each generation is a roughly defined age group located in historical time (e.g., eighteen-to-twenty-nine-year-olds in the mid-1960s might represent one generation) that shares a defining experience. According to his analysis, each generation inculcates and has the potential to transform its cultural heritage. As generations leave childhood, they become increasingly capable of reflection, experimentation, and struggle and, in this state of heightened awareness, they experience a "fresh contact" with the status quo of the earlier generation. Their growing sensitivity to the deficiencies of social institutions and practices, particularly their failure to respond to new social realities and needs, may promote new worldviews and challenges to the existing social order.

Thus, each generation has its status quo, and as successive generations replace one another, both social stability and social change are possible. For social change, Mannheim argued that a generational unit—that is, youth experiencing the same concrete historical problems and viewing themselves as sharing a common destiny—must come to question and actively challenge the received cultural heritage of the previous generation. Written in 1952, Mannheim's essay would find a receptive audience among scholars trying to understand the student rebellions of the 1960s. How could these students turn against the status quo of their parents' generation in such a comprehensive and passionate way? For Mannheim, this historical time would represent a great example of how "fresh contact" with the social order could lead to rebellion. (See Chapter 2 for a detailed discussion of generations.)

The psychiatrist Kenneth Keniston's collected essays on youth in the 1960s are an excellent example of generational analysis.[13] Drawing in large part on Erik Erikson's model of ego development, Keniston argued that "youth" is a period of life marked by tension between self and society. In general, youth are ambivalent about self and society; they are estranged from society; they are filled with a sense of power that comes from how free and malleable they are; and they are resistant to their socialization. Youth seek personal development characterized by movement into a new identity and, in their quest for meaning and identity, they often change both themselves and their society.

Keniston believed that the youth of his own time, by challenging their society's institutions, had attained a "higher level of development," which would in turn lead to a new and improved society. In his essay "Sources of Dissent," Keniston identified "types" of youthful dissenters who were doing the heavy lifting of social change.[14] The "activist" took a stand against injustice, engaged in organized forms of protest, and was committed to improvements in the lives of the less fortunate. Students who participated in Freedom Summer during the struggle for Civil Rights would be good examples of Keniston's "activist."

In contrast, the "alienated" student was too pessimistic to participate in organized dissent, indulging instead in personal forms of nonconformity (especially in dress and behavior). The alienated student was often a hippie, engaged in a loosely defined underground culture that encompassed "love," "turning on," and "human be-ins." Keniston argued that the success of activists was only possible because of their concentration in university settings, coupled with the changing notion of what it meant to be a university student. In his writings, he sought to understand the university-based student protests of the 1960s as both an individual-level quest for meaning and an intergenerational source of social change.

Like research on the character in society, intergenerational research in the tradition of Mannheim was not empirical in any rigorous fashion. Like Reisman, Keniston tells a "just-so" story that resonates with his readership. To anyone familiar with activists and hippies, there is nothing particularly new in Keniston, but his account is prosaic and optimistic in a balanced way (appreciating the activists while expressing reservations about the hippies), recalling the tone of Erikson's work. But it remains unknown how true his account is. More important, however, the typical intergenerational account still did not concern itself with biography. Generational research did not focus on the developmental processes by which cultural heritage is and is not transmitted, but rather took each generation's identity as a given and proceeded to examine points of agreement and slippage between the old and the young.

Social Structure and Personality
Complementing work on character and society and intergenerational linkages, a third line of research was the "social structure and personality tradition." James House describes this perspective as focusing on the relation between macro structures (e.g., formal organizations, social classes), social processes (e.g., urbanization, social mobility), and individual psychological attributes and behavior.[15] In principle, this perspective sounds similar to the character-in-society tradition because both perspectives share an interest in social structure and the individual. In practice, they are distinct because the social structure and personality tradition focuses on specific components of a social structure and specific attributes of the person. It also emphasizes social structure, as opposed to culture, as a causal force. As a result, it is perhaps the first sociological

line of research that attempts to link specific features of society with specific attributes of the person in an empirically rigorous fashion.

One of the most renowned examples of this tradition is Alex Inkeles's and David Smith's *Becoming Modern*, which sought to document how people in societies characterized by various levels of modernity differed in their attitudes, values, and behavior.[16] Reminiscent of the character-in-society tradition, Inkeles and Smith speak of "personality," although with considerably more precision than their predecessors. The premodern–modern continuum is defined in terms of three dimensions, each of which has multiple indicators: an analytic dimension (reflecting, for example, how much the person values calculability and planning and is open to change and new experience); a topical dimension (reflecting, for example, attitudes towards women's rights, exposure to mass media, and the importance of state citizenship over local interests), and a behavioral dimension (reflecting, for example, political activity, arithmetic skills, and verbal fluency).

Inkeles and Smith developed a survey covering these complex phenomena and then administered it to roughly a thousand people in each of six countries representing different levels of modernization (e.g., Chile, India, Israel). The level of modernization of each society was also measured and reflected such things as the rate of infant mortality, newspaper circulation per one thousand inhabitants, domestic mail per capita, and percent of urban population in cities with more than twenty thousand inhabitants.

The authors found that the subjective nature of modernity, the modern personality, is a syndrome. This means that the indicators of individual modernity mentioned above tend to co-occur. For example, a person who is open to new experiences also places great value on planning. As a result, the "modern personality" can be conceptualized and measured. And, as people exhibit varying degrees of modernity in each of the six countries, specific social experiences are linked to their position on the modernity scale. More "modern" individuals tend to have a higher level of education, more months of factory work (as opposed to agriculture), higher exposure to the mass media, more years of urban experience since age fifteen, and own more consumer goods.

To focus on schooling, for example, the authors report that "Those [students] who had been in school longer were not only better informed and verbally more fluent. They had a different sense of time and a stronger sense of personal efficacy; participated more actively in communal affairs; were more open to new ideas, new experiences, and new people; . . . and showed more concern for subordinates and minorities."[17] Schooling did much more than educate the student; it transformed him or her into a modern person. In other words, specific, measurable features of social experience tend to produce specific, measurable characteristics of persons.

The appeal of this work is obvious, elaborating as it does classical sociology's defining theme of the premodern versus the modern. Further, unlike Reisman, Inkeles and Smith set out to measure attributes of society and person and to make empirical claims about how the two are related. There are two important advantages to Inkeles's and Smith's empirical stance. First, they are not merely telling a good story that "sounds right" but may or may not be true. Rather, they are making conceptual claims and then empirically testing them with data from the real world. Second, in developing the empirical measure of "modernity," they were forced to clarify the exact meaning of this concept. In Reisman's case, we are left asking very basic questions: What is character? How do we know when a society is in the second phase of development? And so on. In Inkeles's and Smith's work, their arguments are clear because they are forced to develop measures of all constructs.

Actually, *Becoming Modern* was an unusual piece of scholarship in the social structure and personality tradition, with its emphasis on the nature of societies. Most research in this tradition focuses on social phenomena *within* a society, including, for example, the workplace, schools, and families. A more typical exemplar of the social structure and personality tradition can be found in Melvin Kohn's highly influential *Class and Conformity*.[18] Kohn argued that social class, as indicated by a combination of education and occupational position, affects parenting behaviors by way of values (e.g., the importance of obedience to authority) that parents have for their children. In turn, these values find their origins in class differences in the workplace and the ways in which parents experience class-specific work environments.

To test these ideas, Kohn asked a nationally representative sample of parents to choose three values (from a list of seventeen) that they considered most important for their fifth-grade child. He found that middle-class mothers and fathers placed emphasis on "self-direction," meaning that they valued internally arrived-at standards for behavior. Thus, middle-class parents hoped that their children would be happy, self-controlled, considerate of others, and curious. Lower-class mothers and fathers, by contrast, emphasized conformity to externally imposed rules. Such parents valued obedience and neatness and, in the case of fathers, the ability to defend oneself physically. Kohn also found that while all parents hesitate to punish their children, the factors that trigger punishment, when it does occur, differ by social class. Lower-class parents punish children's misbehavior on the basis of its immediate consequences, while middle-class parents punish misbehavior on the basis of the child's intent. For the former group, punishment is necessary when conformity is obviously lacking. For the latter, punishment hinges on whether the child maintains reasonable intentions and effective self-control.

Kohn was further able to explain the origins of such differences in parenting. Analyses revealed that the higher the father's socioeconomic position, the more men valued self-direction for themselves as well as for their children. Conversely, men lower in the social class hierarchy placed less emphasis on self-directed traits. Further, the value placed on self-direction among higher-class men was associated with high levels of self-direction in the workplace, as indicated, for example, by low levels of supervision. In contrast, the value placed on conformity among working class men reflected their actual working conditions, their greater exposure to higher levels of supervision, and less self-reliance. As Kohn concludes, "occupational experiences that facilitate or deter the exercise of self-direction come to permeate men's views, not only of work . . . but of the world and of the self."[19]

Unlike the character-in-society and the intergenerational traditions, this perspective relied heavily on empirical study. Inkeles and Smith and Kohn, for example, carefully developed hypotheses and then measured people and their settings in the real world to test these hypotheses. Further, research in this tradition was not epochal in its focus, but rather sought to explain variability in actual human behaviors in actual social settings. The unit of analysis was not a time and place in social history, but rather groups of people (e.g., premodern versus modern people, or working-class versus middle-class people). Yet, like the other two lines of research, the social structure and personality tradition typically viewed life (and, indeed, the social system) in static terms. Although much was learned from research in this tradition, by failing to consider how people age in a changing society, many interesting questions were overlooked. For example, in the case of Inkeles and Smith, there is an interest in the level of modernization of the society, but not in its historical development. Likewise, there is interest in people's exposure to modernizing influences, but little interest in how this varied across their lifetime. In the case of Kohn's research program, there is interest in how occupation acts as a source of parental values, in how values (and other psychological orientations) change as jobs change, and in how prior psychological orientations lead to the selection of particular kinds of work. Still, neither the linkages of these dynamic processes to historic changes, nor their intersection with age- or stage-specific life circumstances, were the focus of attention.

THE EMERGENCE OF LIFE COURSE SOCIOLOGY

Thus far, we have considered sociology's classical interest in how people differ in premodern and modern societies and how this interest inspired research in the character-in-society, inter-generational, and social structure and personality traditions.

All of these research traditions contributed to increasing so-
phistication in the study of lives. The character-in-society tradition refined ideas about behavior in modern societies. The
intergenerational tradition drew attention to the succession of
generations as a source of social change. The social structure
and personality tradition showed that detailed empirical studies of context and person were possible. And yet, as we have observed, none of these traditions considered both the changing
society and the aging person.

What was lacking up to this point was a perspective, more
complex than prior conceptualizations, that viewed both the
society and the person in dynamic temporal terms. Life course
sociology arose to meet this challenge in the 1970s. The water-
shed work in this development was the 1974 publication of
Glen H. Elder Jr.'s *Children of the Great Depression*.[20] Elder told
the story of a group of children who grew up during the Great
Depression in Oakland, California. The study began in 1931
with a group of fifth graders from five schools in northeast
Oakland. (The stock market had crashed in October 1929).
The students and their parents were measured on a broad range
of topics through the 1930s, with two data collection points in
the 1940s, a major follow-up in 1954–55 and again in
1957–58, and a survey by mail in 1965.

Dozens of studies had been conducted on these children, focused on phenomena as diverse as physical growth and parenting. But particularly telling about biases in the study of lives is
that until the late 1960s, with few exceptions, scholars had not
thought to study the Oakland families in the context of the
Great Depression. The psychologists studying these children
and following them into adulthood largely ignored the cata-

clysmic events of the Great Depression and World War II. If people from this time were asked to describe their lives, many would undoubtedly talk about the Great Depression and War. Yet for behavioral scientists working from a psychological presupposition, such matters were irrelevant. In contrast, Elder refocused research by distinguishing between families that had and had not experienced serious economic loss, between working and middle-class families, and between boys and girls.

How did the Depression affect families and the children, and what were the long-term consequences of this historic event in the lives of these children as they aged? Deprivation often increased the centrality of the mother in managing the affairs of the household. Hardship encouraged boys to generate income outside the household, which fostered a sense of industry and financial responsibility. Girls frequently helped to maintain the domestic household and likewise developed a sense of industry and financial responsibility. In other words, with the father's unemployment or decrement in wages came a realignment of roles in the family, which developed new economic strategies with new divisions of labor. Further, the Oakland children appeared to have escaped tensions in the household by spending more time with peers and nonrelated adults. In short, though exposed to great hardship, many of these children played constructive roles and avoided bad family experiences.

Although the Oakland boys often ended schooling earlier than they might have, had the Depression not occurred, they eventually experienced reasonable successes in work, owing in large part to their service in World War II, and subsequent reintegration into the booming economy of the 1950s, often by way of the G.I. Bill. As adults, the boys of deprived families placed little value on close family ties, but did view saving money as important. As adults, the girls from deprived families placed great emphasis on kinship ties and domestic values, although they were critical of their mothers. Despite the extreme deprivation of their childhoods, however, the Oakland children grew up to be unremarkable adults in many respects, including, for example, their emotional lives.

The story of *Children of the Great Depression* takes on added significance with a series of studies Elder conducted after its publication. Those papers drew on a related but strategically different data set, the Berkeley Guidance sample, comprised of 214 children born in 1928–29. Though born only a few years after the children in the Oakland sample, members of the Berkeley sample experienced the Great Depression as small children, while members of the Oakland sample were in mid-childhood in 1929 and then grew into late adolescence by the Depression's end. Generally, the Berkeley children were too young to be of substantial help in their families' efforts to deal with the Great Depression. Because of their young age, they were also limited in the extent to which they could escape the tensions at home by spending time with unrelated adults. Further, the Berkeley boys were too young for military service in World War II. At adolescence, the boys were likely to feel personally and socially inadequate and victimized and to have low aspirations for the future. Their grades worsened through the high-school years. This combination of historical and personal experiences cast a long, dark shadow over the lives of the Berkeley boys, who, in later life, showed high levels of dysphoria.[21] Though their births were separated by only eight years, the Berkeley and Oakland children had radically different experiences in the Great Depression and World War II, which in turn shaped their adult lives in very different ways.

The significance of *Children of the Great Depression* and the subsequent empirical studies is obvious: by studying linkages between social change and how people aged, Elder pointed the way for a new mode of analysis in the study of society and biography. In keeping with the intergenerational tradition, he viewed the experience of history as fundamentally the story of parents and their children. But he departed from the Mannheimian tradition in two important respects. First, he focused on both familial generations, parents and their children. Second, he located the children in history by way of their year of birth (called a "birth cohort"), rather than in terms of Mannheim's "generation," a group of people who experience more or less the same historic conditions and develop a shared sense of destiny. By empirically comparing these birth cohorts of children and their parents, he revealed marked differences in their life circumstances that would have been missed by a more general purview of Depression-era conditions.

In keeping with the social structure and personality tradition, *Children* was an empirical study of real people in real settings. Departing from that tradition, however, *Children* mapped out the meaning of the social change for families, and, in turn, for the childhoods, adolescences, and adulthoods of the Berkeley and Oakland subjects. In short, Elder had demonstrated the feasibility and fruitfulness of studying human development in a changing society.

Moreover, *Children* avoided the problem, inherent in earlier works like Riesman's, of assuming that sociohistorical context shapes all people in the same way. This is an important feature that is often overlooked. Elder's and his colleagues' studies of the Great Depression promoted a thoroughly multifaceted and interactive view of aging, which means that they viewed development as contingent on many factors. Thus, for example, the effects of the Great Depression varied by birth cohort; some effects were stronger for girls than for boys; and within cohorts, some effects were stronger for the working class than for the middle class. Rejected was the simplistic view, implicit in classical sociology as well as later work, that social and historical forces have the same effects on all people. In fact, the meaning of broader historical changes like the Great Depression was highly dependent on one's position in society, in the community, in one's organizational affiliations, and in one's networks of significant others. The meaning of such changes further depended on when they occurred in a person's life, suggesting important temporal contingencies that give such events unique biographical meaning.

Like all great works, *Children* had its precedents and is a logical extension of these earlier works. Research had already investigated how the Depression affected household dynamics, familial relationships, and various indicators of adjustment and well-being. Social scientists had also recognized that generations may have very different experiences of the same event, and these differences may have lasting consequences. Yet, the genius of *Children* is in bringing these conceptual strands together and demonstrating their utility in a sustained program of empirical research.

The Life Course as a Concept
In thinking about *Children of the Great Depression* and related works, scholars began speaking of the life course as a concept

that refers to the *age-graded sequence of roles, opportunities, constraints, and events that shape the biography from birth to death.* The use of the term *"age-graded"* means that the roles and events of the life course occur in predictable ways with respect to age. Age-graded roles form sequences and pathways, and people move through these with the passage of time. What are examples of age-graded roles, sequences, and pathways? The broadest roles refer to the phases of life: neonate, infant, early childhood, middle childhood, late childhood, early adolescence, middle adolescence, late adolescence, early adulthood, and so on. For each phase of life, there are unique expectations about how people in these different groups will behave. Each age group is expected to have different capabilities and hence different duties and responsibilities. Accordingly, each age group is provided with unique opportunities and rewards, and distinct limits are imposed on each phase of life.

Other major sequences of roles reflect our various involvements in the domains of family, school, and work. Work roles, for example, progress from informal work (i.e., unpaid, household-based tasks), to paid work while still in school, to the first job of one's career and the sequence of jobs that define an occupational career, including retirement. The life course thus defines the biography as a dynamic social construction. As we pass through the phases of life, social institutions and people provide opportunities and constraints that are tailored to our chronological age and our "social age," reflecting the social roles that we inhabit. Thus, the age-graded social roles of the life course are the fundamental building blocks of biography.

Two important ideas follow from this definition. First, the *age-graded roles that make up the life course are embedded in society's institutions and organizations.* Thus, the sequence of educational roles reflects the structure of the educational system, work roles reflect the structure of labor markets, and family roles reflect a wide range of social influences, including the structures of educational system and labor markets, government regulations, and normative expectations. In this respect, the "life course" is a social structure. The basic scaffolding of biography, to large degree, reflects how society is organized.

Second, *no phase of life can be understood in isolation from the other phases.* Each life phase is intimately linked with past roles and experiences and also anticipates "possible futures." Because the life course is comprised of sequences of interconnected roles and experiences, the phases of life cannot be viewed apart from earlier experiences. In the case of the Berkeley boys, for example, their dysphoria in adulthood is best understood in relation to boyhood experiences during the Great Depression. Many early experiences are known to shape one's adulthood, including, for example, poverty, disruptions in family life, and institutionalization. Does this mean that childhood poverty or parental divorce always leads to a troubled adulthood? Of course not. Still, to say that the phases of life are interconnected and cannot be viewed in isolation means that life experiences are often linked in predictable ways. This is quite different from saying that early experiences dictate or completely determine what will happen later. The goal is to identify likely sequences of experiences that shape the life course.

Especially with the publication and reception of *Children of the Great Depression,* the life course as a concept was born, and rather quickly the life course as a paradigm emerged.

FURTHER READING

Philosophy of Social Science, Social Scientific Theory

Collins, Randall. *The Sociology of Philosophies: A Global Theory of Intellectual Change.* Cambridge, MA: Harvard University Press, 1998.

> Maps out the ways in which ideas, including conceptualizations of societies, changed over time.

Little, Daniel. *Varieties of Social Explanation.* Boulder, CO: Westview, 1991.

> Excellent introduction to basic issues in the philosophy of the social sciences.

Megill, Allan, ed. *Rethinking Objectivity.* Durham, NC: Duke University Press, 1994.

> Thought-provoking essays by historians and sociologists (especially the essays by Daston and Porter) on the social dimensions of "objectivity," the hallmark of scientific knowledge.

Reynolds, Paul Davidson. *A Primer in Theory Construction.* Boston: Allyn & Bacon, 1971.

> Concise, indispensable introduction to the structure of social scientific theories and their relationship to empirical research.

Modernization and the Sociological Classics

Collins, Randall. *Four Sociological Traditions.* New York: Oxford University Press, 1994.

> Accessible intellectual history of the emergence of major classical sociological theories.

Coser, Lewis A. *Masters of Sociological Thought: Ideas in Historical and Social Context.* 2nd ed. Fort Worth, Texas: Harcourt Brace Jovanovich, 2003.

> Portraits of fifteen classical sociological theorists, demonstrating the breadth of sociology's interests and approaches to social structure. Also reveals differing ways that classical theorists attempted to link social structures and the person. Especially helpful is the material on W. I. Thomas, who helped set the stage for the emergence of the life course.

Lepenies, Wolfgang. *Between Literature and Science: The Rise of Sociology.* Cambridge: Cambridge University Press, 1992.

> Advanced intellectual history of connections among natural sciences, literature, and sociology.

Mazlish, Bruce. *The New Science: Breakdown of Connections and the Birth of Sociology.* University Park: Pennsylvania State University Press, 2004.

> Intellectual historian offers brief and highly readable survey of literary and scientific reactions to modernity.

Society and Self: Early Sociological Traditions

Alwin, Duane, and Ryan McCammon. "Generations, Cohorts, and Social Change." In *Handbook of the Life Course*, edited by Jeylan T. Mortimer and Michael J. Shanahan, 23–49. New York: Kluwer-Plenum, 2003.

> Excellent, critical survey of literature on generations and birth cohorts. Discussed further in Chapter 3.

Kertzer, David I. "Generation as a Sociological Problem." *Annual Review of Sociology* 9 (1983): 125–149.

> Good overview of the historical meanings of "generation" and their relation to age, cohort, and life-stage.

McLeod, Jane D., and Kathryn J. Lively. "Social Structure and Personality." In *Handbook of Social Psychology*, edited by John Delamater, 77–102. New York: Kluwer-Plenum, 2003.

> Concise, contemporary description of the social structure and personality tradition. Very nice update of House (1981).

Emergence of Life Course Sociology

Elder, Glen H., Jr., and Michael J. Shanahan. "The Life Course and Human Development." In *Handbook of Child Psychology*. Vol. 1: Theory, edited by Richard Lerner, 665–715. Hoboken, NJ: John Wiley & Sons, 2006.

> Our account in this volume of the origins of the life course is highly simplified. This essay by Elder and Shanahan, however, identifies the major streams of thought that informed the emergence of the life course and cites basic works for each such stream.

Elder, Glen H., Jr. *Life Course Dynamics: Transitions and Trajectories, 1968–1980.* Ithaca, NY: Cornell University Press, 1985.

> An excellent description of the practical issues arising from the collection of longitudinal data on a large sample of Americans and both the methodological relation of such data to key theoretical questions in a life course perspective and the contribution that such data make to improving and extending life course theory.

Marshall, Victor, and Margaret M. Mueller. "Theoretical Roots of the Life-Course Perspective." In *Social Dynamics of the Life Course*, edited by Walter R. Heinz and Victor W. Marshall, 3–32. New York: Aldine De Gruyter, 2003.

> Excellent overview of theoretical models that have informed life course studies.

Chapter Two
THE LIFE COURSE AS A PARADIGM

*I have attempted to write the following account of myself as if I were
. . . in another world looking back at my own. Nor have I found this
difficult, for life is nearly over with me.*

—Charles Darwin

HOW CAN ONE MAKE SENSE of a life in all of its complexity?
Consider Charles Darwin, often considered one of the most influential thinkers of modern Western civilization, having co-
founded (with Alfred Russell Wallace) the theory of evolution
by natural selection. In its broadest contours, Darwin's life has
a surprisingly predictable quality. He was born in 1809 in
Shrewsbury, England; his father was an upper-middle-class
physician, his paternal grandfather was known as a naturalist,
and his mother came from the wealthy Wedgwood family,
makers of porcelain china. Given the times and his lineage, one
might well have predicted at Charles's birth that he would become a physician, a scientist, a clergyman, or perhaps a combination of all of these things. Further, given his financial
resources and family connections, one might have predicted
that he would achieve some notable degree of success. In fact,
both predictions would prove correct. Darwin set out to become a physician (but abandoned this plan while at university),
studied for the clergy, and ultimately became a scientist. As a

naturalist, he made seminal contributions to biology and achieved great renown.

Such a sketch, however, neglects the many twists and turns in Darwin's life, the many challenges that he faced, and a multitude of details that make his biography uniquely his own. Consider the following additional facts about his life: Darwin was not originally chosen to be the naturalist of the HMS *Beagle* (during the voyage of which he would make his crucial scientific observations) and his father consented only when persuaded by an in-law that such a post would not be inappropriate for a prospective member of the clergy. Darwin failed to label his scientific specimens properly, which would have rendered them worthless had they not been supplemented with information collected by an uneducated crew member, Syms Covington. Beginning in childhood, Darwin was incredibly dedicated to his studies of nature and pursued his interest relentlessly. (Once, while collecting beetles in a field, he came upon a much-desired specimen while already holding a beetle in each hand; rather than lose the opportunity, he popped one of the beetles in his mouth and it proceeded to stun him by squirting a "noxious boiling fluid.") In adulthood, his ideas created a firestorm of controversy that created great stress in his life. Finally, while the *Beagle* was exploring South America, he was apparently bitten by the black bug of the pampas and contracted Chaga's Disease, which led to chronic fatigue, intestinal problems, and, generally, physical disability and social withdrawal for the rest of his life.

How do you make sense of such a life, or of any life for that matter? This is a perfectly good question, but there is no *one* answer and hence there are dozens of well-known biographies of Darwin. According to a biography by Adrian Desmond and James Moore, he was a tormented figure, racked with anxiety over the clash between his scientific theories and religion.[1] In another biography, Janet Browne emphasizes that he was a tactician who deftly managed the media and the Victorian institutions of England and marshaled a huge volume of correspondence to develop his ideas.[2] In yet another biography, John Bowlby argues that he suffered from psychosomatic diseases that can be traced to the death of his mother when he was eight years old.[3] There is probably some truth to all of these accounts, each of which focuses on specific themes or sets of variables: ideological, social, and psychological, respectively. Importantly, implicit in each life of Darwin is a perspective about how human lives should be studied and understood.

The life course provides one such perspective, a way of interpreting biographies, by emphasizing people's social circumstances and experiences as they extend from birth to death. Even within a life course framework, there are many ways to describe and attempt to explain biographies. The reason for this diversity, often a troubling feature to students but an attraction to behavioral scientists, is that the life course is a *paradigm*, which means that it is a cohesive set of concepts, principles, ideas, and methods. That is, the life course initially emerged as a concept (discussed in Chapter 1) and now may also refer to a paradigm. As such, it encourages the imagination and often leads analysts to different accounts.

This chapter provides further detail about the life course, exploring many of the principles, mechanisms, and concepts that together constitute the life course as a paradigm. The overarching goal of any paradigm is to create a new way of looking at things and to provide basic tools with which the imagination can work. We then return to the life of Darwin to illustrate how his life would be analyzed with basic imaginative tools of life course studies.

PRINCIPLES OF THE LIFE COURSE PARADIGM, AND TWO CAUTIONARY TALES

Life course principles refer to the intellectual posts that guide the imagination in thinking about social context, social change, and behavioral development, as well as the various contexts and contingencies that link them in unique and important ways. The principles were originally induced from Glen Elder's *Children of the Great Depression*, which means that the many empirical findings from that research were drawn upon to form generalizations.[4] All but the first principle discussed below have a special status as *linking mechanisms:* they identify processes by which transitions and behavioral development are interrelated.

In the case of the Depression studies, the key transition was the sudden and marked decline in household income brought on by the crash of the stock market in October 1929. Other types of transitions reflect broad-scale historical changes, including economic or political collapse, war, natural disaster, famine, and pestilence. Still other examples refer to "person-scale" changes involving families: divorce or marital dissolution, death of a spouse, a geographic move or change of schools, the onset of serious illness of a family member, marriage, parenthood, or retirement. Oftentimes, broad historical change and social changes at the level of the family coincide. In the case of the Depression, the collapse of financial institutions in the United States was clearly linked to the dramatic loss of income experienced by untold numbers of families. Viewed jointly, the historical transition at the societal level and the transition at the familial level tell a story of how an established order is destroyed and new ways of living emerge.

Principles of the life course paradigm help us think about how such changes and the transitions they precipitate affect people's lives. These principles are discussed here with reference to the Depression studies and then illustrated with a hypothetical case study of children immigrating to the United States from Mexico.

First, *the life course takes on different patterns in different historical times and geographic places.* Consider, for example, the issue of education and work. During the Great Depression some people finished their schooling only to find little meaningful employment afterward. Many of these people would experience negative career patterns through their entire adulthood. Other people entered the labor market after World War II, when the economy was expanding as never before and opportunities were plentiful; even men with limited schooling often experienced great successes in their work. Of course these are dramatic examples, but the general principle holds true. Each graduating class encounters a different labor market, characterized by a unique level of opportunity and unique forms of employment. In some cases, differences between graduating classes are minimal since conditions in one year are usually quite similar to those the year before. In other cases, during depressions or recessions, the differences can be vast. Still, the successes or failures accompanying one's first job may have ramifications for the rest of one's career. As historical circumstance changes, so, too, does the likelihood of biographical change.

Time and space differences in the life course can also be studied by drawing on a second principle, the *importance of situational imperatives, which refer to the demands or requirements of a new situation.* The more demanding the situation, the more individual behavior is constrained to meet role expectations. During family emergencies, helpful responses become an imperative for members, as was true for hard-pressed families during the worst years of the Great Depression. In the Oakland sample studied by Elder, the children were old enough in the early 1930s to be called upon to meet the increased economic and labor needs of their hard-pressed families and a large number earned money from paid jobs to help out in the household. This money was often used to cover traditional family concerns, such as school expenses.

In deprived families, girls generally specialized in household chores, while boys were more often involved in paid jobs. This gender difference made girls more dependent on the family and generally fostered greater autonomy among boys. Adolescent jobs in the 1930s typically included clerking, waiting on tables, delivering newspapers, and running errands. Although employment of this kind may seem developmentally insignificant, it mattered. Indeed, project observers rated the working boys as more energetic and efficacious on a set of scales than other boys. The flow of influence was no doubt reciprocal. The more industrious were likely to find jobs and success in work that would reinforce their ambition. With additional chores at home, working boys experienced something like the obligations of adult status. To observers who knew them, they appeared to be more adult-oriented in values, interests, and activities when compared to other youth.

Boys who managed both household chores and paid jobs were most likely to think about the future and especially about the work they would like to do. In adulthood, these youth were more apt to have achieved a measure of clarity and self-assurance in their work careers. They also settled more quickly on a stable line of work and displayed less floundering during their twenties. Apart from level of education, work life has much to do with the occupational success and work ethic of men who grew up in deprived families during the 1930s. The response of these young people to Depression imperatives had enduring consequences for the rest of their lives.

By themselves, however, situational imperatives fail to capture the full importance of social context because they neglect interpersonal relationships and the dynamic quality of social change and aging. A third principle, *linked lives*, addresses the first deficiency. According to this principle, the effects of social change on a person's life greatly depend on his or her network of interpersonal relationships, including, for example, immediate and extended family members, mentors, and close friends. In *Children of the Great Depression*, drastic income losses between 1929 and 1933 were seen to influence the lives of children through changes in family relationships and social roles. Three types of change illustrate the mechanism of interdependent or linked lives. One type of change altered the household economy by shifting it toward more labor-intensive operations. Mothers and children assumed productive roles as earners and more severe limitations were imposed on household expenditures. At the same time, children became more involved in carrying out household duties, from laundry to food preparation. A second type of change modified family structure by increasing the relative power of the mother, reducing the attractiveness of the father as a role model, and undermining the level and effectiveness of parental control. Heavy income loss also magnified relationship tensions and the instability of families, a third type of change. Discord contributed to family disorganization, the loss of control over member behavior, and more erratic, unpredictable actions, such as arbitrary parental discipline. In combination, these changes made children from economically deprived families emotionally unstable and sensitive to others. Early adult responsibilities fostered a precocious pattern of adult self-consciousness. The young who obtained paid jobs developed a more advanced sense of their vocational maturity.

Situational imperatives describe social settings, but a fourth principle directs our attention to how people actively respond to these settings. *Through the exercise of agency, people construct their own life course through their actions, reactions, and choices.* The concept of *agency* is very broad and refers to many different things including, for example, people's values, planful orientation, aspirations and goals, and all of the skills by which these future orientations are formulated and pursued. Despite the complexity of agency, the overarching point is that people are purposive. People act based on past experience and what they have learned from it. People strategize in the present and make decisions based on the options and opportunities they perceive. And people make plans about their futures and work towards reaching their goals. (We develop the significance of agency in the life course to a greater extent in Chapter 4.)

The Depression studies originally suggested the importance of agency because of the control cycles that were observed. *Control cycles* refer to changing relations between expectations and resources that affect a sense of personal control. A loss of control stems from a process in which resources fall below expectations. This change motivates efforts to restore control by adjusting expectations, resources, or both in terms of their relation. During the Great Depression, heavy income loss tended to affect children, sometimes adversely, through family adaptations to such deprivation. These include the reduction of family expenditures, the employment of more family members, and the lowering of living standards. Although agency is commonly conceived as an individual-level process (i.e., the focus is on individuals, who have motives and goals and take strategic actions), people often are part of bigger collectives that have purpose and motives as well.

By itself, the principle of situational imperatives also fails to appreciate the temporal elements that make the life course distinct. A fifth principle, the "life-stage principle," states that *the meaning and consequences of events depend on when they occur in a person's life.* This principle acknowledges that, without locating people with respect to their age and with respect to history, the life course cannot be understood in its full complexity. As the Depression studies showed, the use of birth cohorts proved critical in locating people in history with empirical precision. In fact, it is not chronological age per se but rather "social age" and "social timing" that determine the significance of historical change and social context. Social age refers to age-graded roles and abilities that a person is expected to have or to assume. Social timing refers to the sequence and duration of roles. Thus, for example, the significance of membership in the Oakland birth cohorts was that these youth were old enough to be delegated important economic roles in the family. By knowing when people were born, we also know when they experienced certain historical events and social circumstances. It is the joining of age and date that define what is and is not possible by way of social age and timing.

The Oakland children passed through adolescence during the worst years of the Great Depression, whereas the Berkeley children that served as a comparison group became teenagers during World War II. Consequently, job scarcity, financial pressures, and emotional stress represented defining features of the Oakland cohort's transition from childhood to young adulthood. By contrast, members of the Berkeley cohort were exposed to the "empty households" of World War II when parents worked long days in homefront industries.

By encountering the Great Depression and other historical events at different times in life, the Oakland and Berkeley cohorts have different stories about their childhood, adolescence, and adulthood. It is the particular sequence and timing of prosperity, economic depression, and war that distinguishes the developmental experiences of the two birth cohorts. The concept "goodness of fit" in the match of person-environment is a key feature of the life-stage principle and its implications for human development. The Berkeley males entered the Great Depression when they were highly dependent on family nurturance and vulnerable to family instability. Economic hardship came early in their lives and represented a prolonged deprivational experience, from the Depression of the 1930s to the war years and departure from home. By comparison, the

Oakland males were older and more independent when hardship hit their families. They assumed important roles in the household economy and entered adulthood with a more crystallized idea of their occupational goals. Despite some handicaps in education, they managed to end up at midlife with a slightly higher occupational rank. The life stage of the Oakland males represented a better fit in the match between person and environment, when compared to that of the Berkeley males.

The sixth and last principle, known as the "accentuation principle," relates transitional experiences to the individual's life history of past events, acquired dispositions, and meanings. *When a transition heightens a prominent attribute that people bring to the new role or situation, we refer to the change as an accentuation effect.* Entry into new roles or situations is frequently selective. In this case the accentuation dynamic tends to amplify selection behaviors. Thus, for example, fathers who were ill-tempered before the Great Depression suffered economic loss with great anger, creating many problems with their children and spouses. Times of challenge often amplify people's strengths and weaknesses.

These principles—summarized in Table 2.1—represent conceptual tools that help understand the connections among individual lives, developmental trajectories, and the changing social world. Because they were induced from the Great Depression studies, it is not surprising that they are especially focused on transitions in people's lives. It would be a mistake, however, to think that the principles and mechanisms are helpful only when thinking about historically based transitions like economic crisis or war. The life course is replete with expected and unexpected relatively discrete changes, including transi-

Table 2.1

PRINCIPLES (P) AND MECHANISMS (M) OF THE LIFE COURSE PARADIGM*

Principle/Mechanism	Example from *Children of the Great Depression*
Historical Time and Place (P)—The life course is structured differently through history and across geopolitical units.	Great Depressions markedly altered biographical patterns.
Situational Imperatives (P, M)—Social demands of new situations constrain role-related behaviors.	During economic crisis, each member of household was expected to make role-specific contributions.
Linked Lives (P, M)—Effects of social change depend on one's relationships with other people.	Great Depression increases mother's / decreases father's authority.
Agency (P, M)—People strive to maintain sense of control over their setting and their biography	Control cycles show loss of control with economic deprivation and family-based strategies to regain control.
Life-Stage (P, M)—Effects of social change depend on the age of the person experiencing it.	Differing effects of Great Depression on Berkeley versus Oakland cohorts.
Accentuation (P, M)—Behavioral patterns before transition are magnified with social change.	Ill-tempered fathers fared especially poorly in response to stressors associated with economic deprivation.

*In this context, a "principle" refers to a broadly applicable idea and a "mechanism" refers to a process that links transitions to behavior.

tions between life phases (e.g., to adolescence, to young adulthood), the transition to and then the completion of schooling, perhaps marriage and parenthood, perhaps starting a career with a first job and ending it with retirement, and a wide range of life events (e.g., losing one's job, serious illness, geographic move, divorce or marital separation, death of a loved one). The principles and mechanisms shown in Table 2.1 have proven helpful in thinking about all such changes.

When viewed holistically, the principles have a major though often unappreciated implication for thinking about social context and social change, transitions, and behavioral development: people's lives are likely to reflect very high levels of *interaction,* which means that the effects of social forces on people's biographies are highly contingent. In other words, the many factors that shape a biography operate in concert. Imagine for a moment that your family has just lost everything but the house or apartment that you live in. What would life be like? The answer is likely to be different for each person because the six principles combine in different ways for different people and different families. The power of these principles, however, lies in how useful they are in studying such diversity in a systematic way.

To illustrate the use of the principles, consider a young child emigrating from Mexico to the United States. Millions of Americans identify themselves as immigrants from Mexico, many having began their lives in small rural villages, having left their country to face uncertainty and perils. One could ask a research question like "How well do immigrant Mexican children do in the United States in terms of their stress levels?" One could then conduct a study to answer this question. The most straightforward study might compare three groups on measures of distress: Mexican children who did not immigrate to the United States, Mexican children who have immigrated to the United States, and non-immigrant American children. Such a study, while valuable, would nevertheless provide an overly simple understanding.

In addition to such a study, the life course analyst might ask a series of questions suggested by the principles. Note how the questions direct attention to issue of context and timing, which is totally neglected by the study we just discussed:

- *Principle 1, Time and Place:* What are the historical circumstances of the move? Where does the move fit in the history of immigration from Mexico? Early and later immigrants face unique opportunities and challenges. What circumstances promoted the move? Where, specifically, did the child move in the United States? Was the destination community welcoming and did it provide adequate social supports? Was the child among the first immigrants to an area of the United States, or was there a well-established Mexican community awaiting them?

- *Principle 2, Situational Imperatives:* How did the move change the demands of family, school, and peer group? What were the child's former responsibilities at school and to his family, and how have these changed? How is the child negotiating the challenges of "being Mexican" and "becoming American"? What about the demands placed on the parents and siblings—how have these changed?

- *Principle 3, Linked Lives:* How many people moved with

the child and how are they related to her or him? Who was left behind and why? Does the family know anyone in the destination community? What types of strengths and weaknesses do his other family members have with respect to the demands of the new situation? Are there people in the destination community who will help the child?

- *Principle 4, Agency:* How have the child's goals and ambitions changed in the course of the move? Is the child a "planner," able to make realistic plans in the new setting? How are old values emphasizing the importance of family and community reconciled with new values emphasizing achievement and independence? What are the family's goals and dreams, and how does the child figure into them? Is the family's view of their future the same as the child's view of his or her future?

- *Principle 5, Life-Stage:* How old was the child when the move took place? Chronological age may help us to understand, in broad terms, the types of coping resources that the child has. What about social age (i.e., roles in the family, school, and perhaps in the workplace)? In some cases, children learn English before their parents; is the child assuming adult-like responsibilities by helping his parents adjust to American society?

- *Principle 6, Accentuation:* Before the move, what did the child's behavioral profile look like? Relevant behaviors would include personality, habits, and temperament, as well as psychological and social strengths and weaknesses. Immigration to a new land is undoubtedly stressful and can accentuate antisocial behaviors. On the other hand, such a challenge can also bring out the best in people. What were the child's behaviors like before, during, and after the move? The same questions should be asked of the other family members; their reactions are undoubtedly part of the child's new social world.

These questions are starting points of a life course analysis and are meant to illustrate that emigrating from Mexico to the United States, indeed any geographic move or any transition, does not have a simple, predictable effect on people's lives but rather depends on many considerations of social setting and timing that interact to shape the biography. *Because each life reflects the workings of the principles of the life course, each life is recognizable as human experience. And yet, because the principles come together in untold diversity, every life is different.* It is the interactive quality of the principles that makes each biography understandable and yet unique among all other life stories. Such questions likewise reveal the importance of the "before," "during," and "after" of transitions: the effect of social change on lives depends greatly on processes that start long before and persist long after the change itself.

Cautionary Tale #1
Few people would disagree with a sociological view of the biography and with the life course paradigm, but intellectual resolve is often necessary to keep the sociological perspective in focus. This is not to say that other perspectives are invalid or not useful. The point is that the life course paradigm is a unique way of thinking and care must be exercised to make sure that its distinctive themes are fully appreciated. Consider an example of a biographical orientation that appears very sim-

ilar to the life course paradigm, Erik Erikson's psychoanalytic model of ego development.[5] On closer inspection, however, this model departs from the principal orientation of the life course perspective in an instructive way.

Briefly, Erikson held that life consists of a series of stages, each of which is defined by its own unique "crisis." A *crisis* refers not to a catastrophe, but rather to a turning point during which the person has the opportunity to consolidate and further differentiate his or her identity. If successfully resolved, the crisis leads to "an increased sense of inner unity, . . . an increase of good judgment . . . and an increase in the capacity 'to do well.' "[6] That is, Erikson proposed a theory of how the self develops from birth to death by progressing through a series of challenges.

The crises are psychosocial in nature because they all involve the interplay between attributes of identity and relationships with other people. Thus, for example, the first crisis, experienced during the first year of life, concerns "trust versus mistrust." During this stage, through interactions with the mother and other caregivers, the child unconsciously learns whether people and the world are either trustworthy or untrustworthy. The issue of trust is especially salient given the dependency of the child to be fed and cared for by other people. With sufficient positive experiences, the child unconsciously concludes that trust in others is possible.

According to Erikson, life consists of a series of eight such crises. Further, this sequence is *epigenetic*, which means that the eight crises are an inherent part of what it means to be human. Every human being, regardless of historical time or place, must pass through the eight stages in their specified sequence.

Throughout his studies, Erikson often emphasized the importance of the fifth stage, identity versus identity confusion, which occurs during adolescence. This crisis refers to willful deliberation about the sincere commitment to a core, lasting identity. Erikson held that it is through introspective struggle with identity that youth arrive at their identities, and, in so doing, quite possibly change society.

One of Erikson's great applications of his model to the study of biography can be found in his *Young Man Luther* of 1958, which sought to explain, in terms of the stage model of crises, how Martin Luther successfully challenged the hegemony of the Roman Catholic Church.[7] Martin Luther was one of the first significant leaders of the Protestant Reformation, which led to the establishment of Christian denominations that broke from Roman Catholicism. The intriguing question is how this man could successfully challenge an institution as vast and powerful as the Church at the beginning of the fifteenth century. According to Erikson, Luther was plagued by two father figures who created great doubt and anguish about his identity. The first, his biological father, strongly rejected his son's choice to become a monk and frequently expressed his dissatisfaction. Luther also felt rejected by his second father, his ecclesiastical father in the person of the pope, because of his inability to live a truly pure and sin-free life. These figures created a strong "negative external conscience" that greatly troubled Luther's sense of identity.

In response to these pressures, Luther's uniquely strong sense of conscientiousness led to an affirmation of his inner voice as a valid instrument of both self-determination and religious belief. Even if his biological father wanted him to be-

come a lawyer, through great psychological struggle Luther
came to accept and take pride in his decision to become a
monk. Even if his church father, the pope, frightened him with
visions of hell, Luther came to accept himself as a Christian, albeit in a totally new sense of the word. In the climax to this
struggle, Luther was summoned before the Diet of Worms, a
general assembly of the princes of the Holy Roman Empire
that met in the French town of Worms. Before the emperor, the
electors, dukes, earls, and estates of the empire, Luther was told
to recant his teachings. In fear but with firmness he replied, "I
cannot and I will not recant anything, for to go against conscience is neither right nor safe. God help me. Amen."

With these words, Luther became his own person and an
early and influential model for the modern, autonomous person. In resolving his identity crisis, Luther reformulated Christianity so that salvation was now based on one's inner sense of
faith rather than on obedience to an ecclesiastical (paternal) authority. "In laying the foundation for a religiosity for the adult
man," Erikson wrote, Luther "displaced the attributes of his
own hard-won adulthood; his renaissance of faith portrays a
vigorous recovery of his own [identity]."[8] That is, in struggling
with his own religious identity, Luther changed both himself
and Christianity.

In some respects, Erikson's approach appears to be consistent with a life course approach. His stage model acknowledges
the aging process, the importance of context, and the interdependency of the phases of life. Accordingly, Erikson emphasized the lifelong implications of the fifth crisis of identity
versus identity confusion, and also Luther's family life.

But there is a critical point at which Erikson and life course sociology diverge. For Erikson, the primary force that drives the biography is an inherent quality of the person (the epigenetic sequence of crises). The point of his inquiry begins with an inherent property of the person and then attempts to bring in context. (In fact, lacking strong evidence about Luther's father, Erikson claimed that the relationship must have been contentious—given the identity crisis that Luther must have had!)

Life course sociology, in contrast, maintains that the biography is a social construct, which, taken seriously, implies that there is no universal sequence through which all people must pass. (Indeed, there are numerous examples of groups of people who do not progress through Erikson's stages.) Social context is not a scene or setting through which the person, loaded with a particular set of natural predispositions, must proceed. Rather, social context constitutes the person, which means that it literally makes people who they are. Each person is viewed as highly malleable, as highly capable of change in response to what he or she encounters. People do not develop according to their natures but, rather, they are continually produced, sustained, and changed by their social context. From this perspective, the inquiry begins with social context and asks how it affects the aging process.

While the example of Martin Luther may seem esoteric, the larger point is that Erikson's mistake is pervasive in the study of lives and thus a constant challenge to a life course imagination. Dale Dannefer refers to Erikson's error as the "ontogenetic fallacy," which refers to attempts to explain lives by referring to assumed, inherent properties of people at the expense of a thoroughly social explanation.[9] According to the ontogenetic fallacy, if Luther is in turmoil, it is most likely due to an identity crisis because "all people have one." Or, to take another example, a forty-five-year-old man's strange behavior is due to his "midlife crisis" because "people his age have a midlife crisis." Or: older people are more conservative "because that's the way they are," or again: adolescents may become depressed or moody "because that is a defining feature of adolescence."

As Dannefer notes, the ontogenetic fallacy stops the study of lives just when things are getting interesting. To say that older people are conservative "because that's the way they are" is not a very satisfying explanation. This would be akin to saying that a patient has symptoms "because those are the symptoms you have with that disease" and leaving it at that. (If you were the patient, you would start looking for a new doctor.) The interesting question is *how* such a disease produces the symptoms. Symptoms cannot be understood without reference to the processes that generate them. And, similarly, the interesting question is *why* some older people are conservative. What are the social processes that lead older people to be more conservative? (This is a hypothetical question, since there is very little evidence that people actually become notably more conservative as they age.) A life course view resists the common temptation to explain someone's life by saying "that's the way people are" and presses the inquiry by asking how the social context has shaped the life story.

Cautionary Tale #2

Many theories that describe people's lives speak of developmental stages, which typically refer to specific periods in life when a person has special sensitivities or strengths or weaknesses. As discussed above, Erikson thought that adolescence was a sensitive period with respect to identity formation. A closely associated idea is the *developmental task*. Indeed, developmental stages are usually defined by developmental tasks.

Robert Havinghurst was an early sociologist who was enamored of the idea of the *developmental task*, which he defined as

> a task which arises at or about a certain time in the life of an individual, successful achievement of which leads to his happiness and to success with later tasks, while failure leads to unhappiness in the individual, disapproval by society, and difficulty with later tasks.[10]

For example, between six and twelve years of age, youth must develop wholesome attitudes about themselves, learn to get along with others, and develop concepts necessary for everyday living. In truth, such tasks are not "developmental" (and one could certainly question whether they are even "tasks" in the usual sense of that word). All of these tasks, indeed all of Havinghurst's tasks and virtually all so-called developmental tasks, are life-long endeavors. Clearly, youth must learn to get along with others, but so must children learn to get along with their parents and siblings, adolescents with their first romances and fellow members of their cliques, young adults with their spouses, and adults with their co-workers and children and grandchildren. By situating each task solely within a specified age range, Havinghurst removes the notions of pathways and trajectories from consideration, and relegates to secondary importance all of the relevant experiences before and after the sanctioned age range.

Developmental tasks, while interesting and perhaps even

valid to some degree, are further examples of the ontogenetic fallacy, according to which people behave in a certain way because that is the way people are, that is their intrinsic nature. This is no explanation. Indeed, it is a statement that there will be no explanation. To avoid the ontogenetic fallacy, the analyst must ask what it is about the person's setting that helps account for their experiences and behavior. Answering that question is greatly facilitated by using core life course concepts, which we now discuss.

USEFUL CONCEPTS IN LIFE COURSE STUDIES AND YET ANOTHER CAUTIONARY TALE

Within the broad imaginative framework of life course principles, a set of analytic concepts has proven useful in thinking about social change and development and aging. These concepts are distinctly life course because they provide *ways of viewing or thinking about social context through time.*

Social Pathways

The idea of a "pathway" has enormous appeal in many of the sciences. Pathways are commonly understood as the well-worn routes that people follow when walking, for example, in the woods or across campus. Science uses the word to describe likely chains of events or sequences, as in a "neural pathway" (i.e., interconnected neurons that form a chain of communication) or a biochemical pathway (e.g., enzyme-catalyzed reactions). Sociologists use pathways to refer to likely sequences of social positions within and between organizations and institutions. Examples of social pathways would include progressing through the grade levels of the school system, tracking within schools, leaving the school system and starting a new job, and then conducting one's career within a company and between companies. Pathways are obviously contextual because they refer to sets of positions within a system (e.g., first grader, second grader, etc.) and they are obviously dynamic because they refer to movement through the positions.

But pathways have several other interesting features. First, they generally have specified time boundaries. The legislated ages at maturity for voting and marriage can be viewed as marking off an accepted duration of dependency. Social pathways are generally age-graded and thus identify relatively early, on-time, and late transitions. Children who are held back in school become aware of their lagging status on the educational ladder and company managers talk about the relation between age and grade in prospects for promotion to senior rank.

In addition to their age-graded nature, pathways structure the direction that people's lives can take. In thinking about educational pathways, including tracking within schools, Aaron Pallas observes that pathways have distinct features that govern how strongly people's behaviors are shaped.[11] These include, for example, the number of options a pathway leaves open in the future, the extent of mobility that is likely to be experienced, stigma and extrinsic rewards, and the importance of personal choice. Some pathways provide future opportunities and chances for upward mobility ("getting ahead") based on personal motivation, while others veer away from promising areas irrespective of one's efforts.

Pathways are also multi-level phenomena, reflecting arrangements in place at levels of culture, the nation-state, social institutions and organizations, and locale. To varying degrees, people work out their life course in terms of established or institutionalized pathways. At the macro end of this multilevel system, pathways are generally established by governments. At lower levels, the terms may be set by institutional sectors (e.g., economy or education), by local communities, school systems, labor markets, and neighborhoods. Each level of the system, from macro to micro, socially regulates the decision and action processes of the life course, producing areas of coordination as well as discord and contradiction (e.g., laws governing marriage, divorce, and adoption). At the level of the individual actor, some decision pressures and constraints are linked to federal regulation, some to the social regulations of an employer, and some to state and community legislation.

Multilevel accounts of the life course are well illustrated with cross national studies of the transition to adulthood, particularly in relation to the social pathways from secondary school to work. In Great Britain, secondary school–leavers can follow a path to work that consists of technical training programs or schools that provide credentials for a particular craft. Even with the freedom to make a wide range of choices, students can still miss opportunities and desirable job placements. Far more structure is provided for working-class German youth in a secondary-level system that joins industrial training and education in an apprenticeship system. Placement in a skilled position is virtually assured for youth who complete their apprenticeships if such jobs are available. In Japan, occupational recruitment typically occurs in schools from the secondary-level to higher education, and specific job training is provided by the particular firm, not by schools or craft institutes. American adolescents encounter the lowest degree of articulation between schooling and workplace. Vocational training in secondary schools is not closely linked to specific industries and skill needs. In many less-developed countries, youth are forced to leave school early to support their families. In turn, their curtailed educational attainment results in low wages, which in turn forces their children to leave school early as well. This vicious intergenerational cycle illustrates how pathways from school to work can reproduce across the generations.[12]

Prior to entry into work, however, young people encounter educational pathways. Studies of the educational system in the United States reveal that these pathways begin very early in life and that their effects cumulate to produce marked differences among students and workers. Drawing on data from the Beginning School Study in Baltimore, Doris Entwisle and her colleagues have documented educational pathways that begin to take form in the first grade.[13] In a school where 88 percent of the students were on subsidy, every first grade student received a failing mark in reading in the first quarter. In low-socioeconomic (SES) schools more generally, the average first-grade reading score was 1.64 (below a C), in contrast to scores in high-SES schools, which averaged 2.15 (above a C). Even after accounting for family background and standardized test scores, black children received lower first-grade reading and math scores and such differences were subsequently magnified in later years. While students of all races and socioeconomic groups benefited from schooling to the same degree, low-SES students' reading ability decreased during the summer vacation, while high-SES students' reading improved. Given initial differences in reading and math ability and these downward summer trends, Entwisle concluded that "the long-term persistence of early rankings means that inequities visible in the first grade translate into deficits all along the line."[14]

Alan Kerckhoff has extended our understanding of life course pathways in a series of studies examining the connections between school and work in Great Britain.[15] Drawing upon data collected from virtually every child born in England, Scotland, and Wales in early March of 1958 and again from the same people in 1969, 1974, 1978, and 1981, Kerckhoff was interested in the extent to which placement in the school system was due to personal characteristics versus social position. He further asked whether a student's initial position in the school system predicted the student's later school position, controlling for achievement. In other words, once children are placed in tracks (or starting points of pathways) in the school system, how much of their "educational career line" is determined by their hard work and intelligence and how much is due to their initial position? If one subscribes to the principle of meritocracy (i.e., that people should be treated according to their achievements), then hard work and intelligence should be decisive, not where their pathway started.

To judge these different hypotheses, Kerckoff mapped patterns of grades, test scores, and placements in the school system across the data collection points. Results showed that students in higher tracks learned more than students in lower tracks, even after taking into account initial differences in students' abilities. Further, students in higher tracks were evaluated more highly than their counterparts in lower tracks, even taking into account actual test scores. Early placement in an elite primary school was associated with the "high road" to the university, while a low-status placement was frequently associated with the opposite path. Moreover, at each stage of schooling, differences were magnified, with the transition from junior to secondary school producing the greatest deflection. By young adulthood (age twenty-three), the subjects' occupational prestige reflected a set of cumulative structural influences that originated early in the life course.

Clearly, by taking established pathways into account, we more fully understand the choices and actions that shape individual life courses and their developmental implications. From this perspective, the life course of each person is constructed over time in terms of the general and more specific dictates of social pathways. For the very young child, these pathways often begin, in large measure, with the residential and socioeconomic histories of parents. In turn, small differences can cumulate over time. By young adulthood, significant differences in achievements and prospects are often readily apparent.

Cumulative Processes

Pathways often are associated with cumulative processes that reflect long-term patterns of experiences. Some cumulative processes reflect social experiences of long duration. Howard Becker notes that long periods of time spent in a given social role—such as student, worker, spouse, or parent—tend to increase behavioral continuity through acquired obligations, investments, and habits.[16] That is, the longer someone is a father or mother, for example, the more firmly they are "held into place" by the obligations and expectations of parenthood and the less likely they are to change. Consistent with this, family researchers have long known that the longer the duration of marriage, the greater the chances for marital permanence. Likewise, duration of unemployment also increases the risk of permanent unemployment, which may reflect long-term patterns whereby relationships are made with other unemployed people, skills are lost, and social, psychological, and physical factors create an incapacity to work. Many forms of social class and economic hardship endure. Ingrid Schoon and her colleagues document "a stark chaining, or continuity of risk factors" such that parental social class powerfully predicts material deprivations through childhood, adolescence, and into young adulthood.[17] In sum, such studies lead analysts of the life course both to describe people's settings yet also to consider how long people have been in given circumstances.

Still, the issue is often more complex than a simple sum of years in poverty, unemployment, or marriage. Consider, for example, the duration of children's exposure to poverty. Long periods of time early in life have been linked to numerous indicators of psychosocial adjustment and achievement, including cognitive development, child behavior problems, adolescent delinquency, and even emotional outcomes. Research on child poverty reveals that about one-third of American children will spend at least one year in poverty between the ages of one and seventeen. Moreover, about half of blacks and one-third of whites will fall into poverty in five or more of the next ten years. But studies also suggest that temporal patterns of poverty are often complex. In often-cited research, Bane and Ellwood show that, contrary to much popular perception, most poverty spells are comparatively shorter, owing in large measure to markedly improved earnings.[18] Slightly more than 40 percent of poverty spells ended within a single year, while about 70 percent were over within a period of three years. At the same time, children's first transition into poverty, particularly if unexpected, may be especially damaging for their well-being. Considerations such as these have led several scholars to formulate typologies of longitudinal poverty patterns in people's lives. Some households experience persistent poverty, while others experience transient or recurrent patterns of deprivation, and each of these patterns has unique precursors and consequences. Such findings, in turn, highlight how inadequate it would be to measure household poverty experiences simply by asking about present poverty status or even number of years spent in poverty.

Time spent in various social classes may also be important to well-being and achievement but, once again, temporal patterns may be complex. Peggy McDonough and her colleagues studied a large group of adults in the United States (respondents of the Panel Study of Income Dynamics) from whom information was collected on an annual basis between 1968 and 1989.[19] They examined whether, in any given ten-year period (e.g., 1968–78), patterns of income in the first five years predicted death in the next five years. The results of their study showed that low income (i.e., less than $20,000 per household) that persisted four to five years raised the risk of mortality among adults significantly when compared to households experiencing this income level for a transitory period. Middle-income adults, however, were at increased risk for mortality if they experienced marked income loss (50 percent or more of household income) over a five-year period. This increased risk of death due to income loss was not observed among low- or high-income households. The results are intriguing because they suggest that to fully appreciate the effect of income on mortality, one must attend to issues of both initial level and change through time, as a life course perspective would suggest.

The duration effects for socioeconomic stressors may be nonlinear, in which case a tipping point is reached before an adverse outcome is observed. As McDonough discovered, declines in income may adversely affect only the middle class. Consistent with this, a study by M. E. J. Wadsworth and colleagues of British men who experienced a long period of unemployment (exceeding three consecutive years) showed less healthy profiles in later life, although this effect was not observed for lesser durations.[20]

Many cumulative processes refer not to the duration of a particular social circumstance, but rather to the *triggering of chains of interrelated events (or sequences),* which, in turn, have significant implications for later well-being and attainment. We have already seen evidence of this in Kerckhoff's study of divergence patterns in the British school system (discussed above). His research suggests that institutional pathways have an inertial property. Once a person is "classified" or assigned to an initial position, the system tends to classify or assign that person to subsequent positions along the same pathway, irrespective of performance.

Besides structural inertia, behavioral continuities across the life course are likely to be found in social interactions that are sustained by their consequences (*cumulative*) and by the tendency of these styles to evoke maintaining responses from the environment (*reciprocal*). In studying the life course implications of childhood personality in the Oakland and Berkeley cohorts (described earlier), Avshalom Caspi, Daryl Bem, and

Glen Elder show that both individual dispositions and family values are likely to favor the choice of compatible environments, and this in turn reinforces and sustains the match.[21] For example, antisocial youth tend to affiliate with other problem youth, and their interaction generally accentuates their behavior, producing over time what might be described as *cumulative disadvantages*. Likewise, among problem youth from inner-city neighborhoods studied by Frank Furstenberg and colleagues, those who were most negative toward their life chances also lacked the support of close kin and friends, did not have a supportive older sibling, and were most likely to be involved with deviant friends.[22]

Although Caspi and colleagues emphasized the critical role of personal predispositions in creating and shaping environments that, in turn, reinforce those predispositions, research suggests that socioeconomic differences may act in a similar manner. For example, Matthew Dupre examined differences in age-specific rates of disease incidence (i.e., the number of new cases of disease occurring in a population during a defined time interval), prevalence (i.e., the number of individuals with a certain disease in a population at a specified time divided by the number of individuals in the population at that time), and survival.[23] The basic idea is that people with higher education will shape their environments (e.g., their diet, stress level, health-related behaviors, access to health care) more effectively than people with less education. That is, advantages (i.e., the avoidance of risk factors, the enjoyment of protective factors) accumulate among the better educated and disadvantages (i.e., exposures to risks) accumulate among the less well-educated. If this conceptual model is true, then differences in health corresponding to education level will magnify (or cumulate) across the life course. Consistent with this reasoning, Dupre found that more educated people live significantly longer without the first diagnosis of a major disease, and live significantly longer after the onset of disease, compared to the less educated.

Reciprocal continuity refers to a continuous interchange between person and environment in which action is followed by reaction and then by another cycle of action and reaction. As with cumulative continuity, the net result of reciprocal continuity is the cumulation of experiences that tend to maintain and promote the same behavioral outcome. For example, the ill-tempered outburst of a child may provoke a cycle of parental rage and aggression, a widening gulf of irritation, and, finally, parental withdrawal which reinforces the adolescent's initial aggression. Over time, the interactional experiences of aggressive children can establish attitudes that lead them to project negative interpretations onto new social encounters and relationships, thereby ensuring behavior that affirms the expected behavior. Aggressive children generally expect others to be hostile and thus behave in ways that elicit hostility, confirming their initial suspicions and reinforcing their behavior.

Cumulative processes can explain why childhood experiences matter for adulthood. At the same time, care must be taken not to overestimate the effects of childhood experiences on adult behaviors. Many people believe that childhood experiences are powerful predictors of later life—that, for example, your mother's and father's parenting skills must surely have a big impact on your personality and your own parenting skills. Yet, there is surprisingly little evidence that this is actually true and, in fact, scientific studies tell us that, short of severe trauma in childhood, the links between early and later life are often weak. If mechanisms of cumulative and reciprocal continuity are constantly at work, how could the link between childhood experiences and adulthood generally be weak? In truth, the answer to this question is unclear owing to a lack of good empirical evidence. However, it appears that continuities are often interrupted or neutralized by subsequent experiences.

Michael Rutter and his colleagues' study of institutionalized children is instructive.[24] Children growing up in institutions often experience behavioral difficulties as adults, as reflected in conflictual marriages, poor work records, and problems as parents. This is not always the case, obviously, but what factors "break" such an association? By following the lives of institutionalized children, Rutter and his associates found that friendships with well-adjusted peers, good performance at school, and approval from teachers and other adults often led to higher self-conceptions, which were, in turn, related to higher educational achievements and better family life in young adulthood. Among institutionalized girls, marriage to a supportive spouse was especially important. Such girls tended to know their spouse for longer periods of time before marriage, and not to be pressured to marry because of pregnancy, when compared with institutionalized girls who did not have supportive spouses and often had adjustment problems.

Thus, experiences may cumulate because social circumstances are largely stable or because they lead to functionally equivalent relationships with people (so-called "cumulative continuity") and involvements with organizations and institutions ("reciprocal continuity"). Still, change seems always possible, reflecting the lifelong possibility of new and constructive relationships with other people.

Trajectories and Transitions

Social pathways and cumulations of experience present temporally sensitive ways of describing context. *Trajectories* provide a dynamic view of behavior and achievements, typically over a substantial part of the life span. Social roles extend and evolve over an extended span of time, as in trajectories of work or family. Yet, they may also change over a short time span. The latter may be marked by specific events, such as children entering school for the first time, completing the first grade successfully, and graduating from high school. Each *transition*, combining a role exit and entry, is embedded in a trajectory that gives it specific form and meaning. Thus, work transitions are core elements of a work trajectory, while births are key markers along a parental trajectory.

Trajectories and transitions refer to processes that are familiar in the study of work careers and life events. Career lines, as pathways, refer to sequences of positions, while careers, as trajectories, refer to coinciding behaviors and achievements. Work careers have been defined as disorderly and orderly, and achievement is represented as career advancement, whether early or late, rapid or slow. Aaron Pallas has offered the idea of "educational careers" to capture the varied the pathways by which people move through the increasingly complex web of school institutions.[25] Still others, such as acclaimed family researcher Reuben Hill, use the term "career" in the context of trajectories of marriage and parenthood.[26] All of these usages fall within the more inclusive definition of a life course trajectory, a term that does not prejudge the direction, degree, or rate of change in its course.

A *developmental trajectory* refers to change and constancy in the same behavior or disposition over time, but consistency of measurement may be difficult to achieve in many cases. For example, does a person exhibit constancy of antisocial behavior from childhood to adolescence? To answer that question, we would have to measure very different things in childhood (e.g., temper tantrums, hitting others, biting others), adolescence (e.g., lying, cheating, stealing), and young adulthood (e.g., substance use, stealing). The problem then becomes how to relate these very different things over time.

Developmental trajectories are integral to life course theory, especially when they are studied as interdependent with the changing dynamics of social trajectories. For example, Xiaojia Ge and his colleagues first studied how emotional depression changed over four years among a group of adolescents in the Midwest and then related these changes to various negative life events (e.g., death of a parent).[27] In other words, how do major negative events change the trajectory of depressed feelings? They found that trajectories of depressive symptoms increased sharply among white girls, surpassing those of boys by age thirteen. Moreover, the increase for girls was linked to their increasing exposure to negative events, while initial warmth and supportiveness of mothers minimized the subsequent risk of depressed states and negative events among daughters. Studies such as these inspire further efforts to interrelate developmental trajectories to context, although such studies frequently neglect the changing nature of social circumstance.

Increasing attention is being devoted to the study of classes of behavioral trajectories based on the supposition that people may be qualitatively distinct in their developmental patterns. For example, Terri Moffitt has hypothesized that there are two distinct groups of people when it comes to antisocial behavior.[28] The first is the small percentage of people who are engaged in antisocial behavior at every stage of life, whom she calls "life-course persistent" offenders. This group is characterized by the presence of neurophysiological impairments and a biography of negative reinforcement. In contrast, the larger group of people are physically, psychologically, and socially "normal" and engage in antisocial behavior only during adolescence. When they cease their delinquency as they transition to adulthood, Moffitt labels this group as "adolescence-limited" offenders.

The multiple role trajectories of life patterns call for *strategies of coordination or synchronization.* Various demands compete for the individual's or family's scarce resources—time, energy, money. To cope with simultaneous, linked trajectories, the scheduling of events and obligations becomes a basic task in managing resources and pressures. The needs of children and financial requirements, for example, play important roles in determining work and leisure options.

Transitions

The meaning of a transition has much to do with its *timing* in a trajectory, consistent with the life-stage principle. Early life transitions can have developmental consequences by affecting subsequent transitions, even after many years or even decades have passed. For example, Matthew Dupre and Sarah Meadows use roughly fifty years of marital-history data to examine the long-term effects of marital trajectories on physical health. For females, they find that the timing of first marriage (before age nineteen) and the cumulative number of divorce transitions increase the risk of adult chronic disease. (Among males, it is the duration of divorce and being widowed that are associated with long-term health risks.)

Early transitions can have lifelong implications because of behavioral consequences that set in motion cumulative advantages and disadvantages, with radiating implications for other life domains. Consider the case of parenthood. In a long-term study of adolescent mothers in Baltimore who were studied from 1966 to 1984, Frank Furstenberg and colleagues show that the earlier the event, the greater the risk of social and health disadvantages for mother and child.[29] At the same time, variations in personal resources (e.g., IQ) during adolescence affected their economic success by influencing how they timed and ordered other life events such as marriage, education, and employment. From the vantage point of this study, the quality of transition experiences early in life may foretell the likelihood of successful and unsuccessful adaptation to later transitions across the life course.

Transitions to parenthood during adolescence in the Baltimore panel point to another important general distinction: life transitions can be thought of as a succession of mini-transitions or choice points. The transition from marriage to divorce is not simply a change in state. The process begins with disenchantment and extends across divorce threats, periods of separation, and the filing of divorce papers. Different causal factors may operate at each phase of the process. The influences that increase the risk of disenchantment are likely to differ from those that sustain the process toward marital dissolution. In like manner, we can think of the transition to motherhood in adolescence as a multiphasic process in which each phase is marked by a choice point, with its particular options and social constraints.

Transitions have both an institutionalized and a personal, idiosyncratic nature. In many cases, life transitions are at once an institutionalized status passage in the life course of birth cohorts and a personalized transition for individuals with a distinctive life history. These faces of a transition apply to the normative transitions of life, from birth to school entry, marriage, parenthood, and retirement. Transitions of this kind may seem more predictable and structured than nonnormative events, but all transitions can be thought of in terms of their structuredness or degree of duration, timing, predictability, novelty, and external regulation.

Turning Points

Life transitions into different environments also have the potential to produce dramatic change in both the internal and the external aspects of the life course. Such transitions are typically called "turning points" and allow for new opportunities and behavioral patterns. A good example of a turning point comes from research on desistance from crime. How is it that adults abandon a life of crime? To answer this question, Robert Sampson and John Laub studied a group of 500 male delinquents and 500 non-delinquent controls from Boston matched on age, race, social class, and IQ who were followed from ages fourteen to thirty-two.[30] To understand why some delinquents desist from criminal activity as they enter adulthood, the researchers' guiding hypothesis was that adult social ties create obligations and restraints that make it hard for people with criminal propensities to actually engage in crime. In other words, desistance from criminal activity evolves from a transition into new situations that provide monitoring, social supports, and opportunities for social investment, which the researchers colorfully call a "knifing-off experience." Consistent with the earlier work of Rutter on institutionalized girls, marriage appears particularly salient in the desistance process.

Particularly illustrative are several case histories.[31] Charlie, for example, was arrested ten times as a juvenile, his first arrest at age eight, and he was incarcerated three times. At age eighteen, he joined the U.S. Maritime Service, which severed his ties with delinquent friends and distanced him from the many opportunities for crime in his neighborhood. Removed from these adverse influences, Charlie met, courted, and married a young woman, and they eventually returned to live in East Boston. He acquired a job, was promoted, and was considered an industrious worker. His time in the Maritime Service, his marriage, and then gainful employment all broke the pattern of crime that characterized his earlier life, and he had no involvements with the law as an adult. In looking at such case histories, Laub and Sampson conclude that some men viewed their turning points as quite abrupt (e.g., marriage, which the delinquent person viewed as utterly changing his world), while other men saw their lives turn around very gradually (e.g., moving from Boston, getting married, getting a job, having a son).

A further example of turning points is found in a study of feeder patterns into high school. In the American school system, pathways between middle school and high school are structured in different ways, affecting the proportion of one's middle-school classmates who attend the same high school. Katherine Schiller's study of how differing feeder patterns affect subsequent grades is revealing.[32] Among students receiving mostly C's in middle school, high-school math grades decrease as the proportion of one's former classmates in high school increases. The reverse is true among students receiving mostly A's in middle school: high-school math grades increase as the proportion of one's former classmates in high school increases. As Schiller notes, when middle-school students disperse into many high schools, opportunities seem to open up for students at the bottom, as peer networks are disrupted. As is characteristic of turning points, the old social world is "knifed off" and new opportunities for growth and identity transformation present themselves.

The concept of a turning point also applies to the particular way people view their lives. Here, it is the subjective account of lived experience which involves some degree of change in situation, behavior, or meaning. Shadd Maruna and his colleagues' interview study of desistance among ex-convicts is one of a few research efforts that investigates the changing nature of the self during a turning point.[33] Key themes in the life narratives of desisters include acknowledging past crimes, understanding their genesis, and recasting the self as "in control" and imbued with newfound purpose. Likewise, John Clausen has used detailed analyses of life histories to assess the subjective turning points of people who have been part of a longitudinal study for sixty or more years. On the basis of this work, he concludes that "one's life does not have to take a different direction for a person to feel that a turning point has occurred. But one must have a feeling that new meanings have been acquired, whether or not life experiences are much changed."[34]

The many paradigmatic concepts that we have discussed are summarized in Table 2.2. While Table 2.1 lists principles and mechanisms that tend to useful in the study of transitions, the concepts presented in Table 2.2 provide conceptual leverage in the study of the biography more broadly. The challenge to life course study is to draw upon these concepts to understand the linkages among changing pathways and transitions, life patterns, and developmental trajectories. The implication is clear: people's lives cannot be fully understood by focusing on one point in time or by neglecting their context. Rather, their social settings and their patterns of adjustment and behavior have dynamic qualities and it is these dynamic qualities that determine their meaning.

Another Cautionary Tale

Life course analysis investigates the dynamic features of social contexts and seeks to understand the relevant mechanisms by which time and place shape human development. However, any study of context and behavior encounters the complex processes by which people select and otherwise experience specific environments in the first place.

Consider major life events (e.g., death of a parent, being fired from a job) that occur in people's lives and are believed to be potent forms of stress. Research on life events often views them as causes of distress (e.g., depressive symptoms), with little appreciation that prior experiences may cause both life events and depressive symptoms (e.g., very high levels of stress

Table 2.2

SELECT CONCEPTS DESCRIBING DYNAMIC FEATURES OF PERSON IN SOCIAL CONTEXT

Concept	Example
Social Pathway—Likely sequence of social positions (roles) within and between organizations and institutions	Tracking within schools (Pallas, 2003); career ladders
Cumulation associated with duration—aggregating effects of a context with its increasing duration	Duration of low income increased likelihood of earlier death (McDonough et al., 1997)
Cumulation associated with a sequence—aggregating effects of a sequence of interrelated events	School failure → peer rejection → low self-esteem → unemployment link (Rutter, 1993)
Cumulative Continuity—predisposition tends to select and mold environments that reinforce predisposition	Age of disease onset and survival after onset better for more-educated versus less-educated (Dupre, in press)
Reciprocal Continuity—predisposition tends to create common action-reaction patterns with other people, reinforcing predisposition	Ill-tempered child provokes parental anger/withdrawal, which aggravates child's outburst (Caspi, Bem, & Elder, 1989)
Trajectory—longitudinal pattern of behavior/achievement	Pattern of change in depressive mood during adolescence; pattern of life-events experienced over same period of time (Ge et al., 1994)
Synchronization—temporal coordination of two or more trajectories or roles	Role overload among teen mothers (Furstenberg, Brooks-Gunn, & Morgan, 1987)
Transition—change in social circumstance, social roles	Geographic move; marital separation; transition to parenthood
Turning Point—change in social circumstance associated with marked change in internal and possibly external life course	Transition to middle school associated with becoming a good student (Schiller, 1999)

at work). When these prior experiences are not measured, the effect of life events on depressive symptoms may well be over-stated. Indeed, *exogenous processes* refer to unmeasured things about people that account for an association between specific contexts (like life events) and specific outcomes (like depressive symptoms). In such instances, understanding the true role of life events in the prediction of depressive symptoms is likely to be incorrect. That is, sometimes the "effect" of a specific context on a person's life is not as strong as it appears at first glance, but rather should be viewed as part of a stream of experiences that began long before the person entered the context. While this point is often considered a methodological issue, it clearly refers to life course processes.

In general, differences that lead people to contexts and also promote behavioral outcomes are likely common in the study of human development. Duane Alwin and colleagues show that high-school students tend to enter college environments that "are consistent" with their personal characteristics.[35] Likewise, risk takers in military service are likely to end up in combat units. Transitions of this kind generally accentuate the behavioral effect of the selected dispositions. Psychologists Robert and Beverly Cairns observe that social selection and accentuation go together in peer group formation.[36] Groups are formed in terms of selected attributes (e.g., aggressiveness), and once such groups are formed the selected behaviors are accentuated. This process has obvious social implications when unruly behavior is involved and makes identifying "peer effects" particularly difficult.

Consistent with this idea of exogenous processes, much research has examined the effects of paid work during high school on grades, yet has neglected the possibility that less academically engaged students may choose to work longer hours. Although studies generally show that high hours of work are associated with poorer school performance, more sophisticated studies that adjust for the selection process reveal that the effect of work hours on grades is negligible or insignificant. The issue can also be viewed in experimental terms: when pre-existing differences between people (e.g., differing levels of school engagement) cannot be ruled out by random assignment (i.e., randomly assigning adolescents to more or fewer hours per week of paid work during high school), the "pure effect" of the work intensity on the outcome (e.g., grades during high school) cannot be determined with certainty.

In some instances, the problem of exogenous processes can be addressed with highly revealing randomized trials. What, for example, are the implications of residential change? Perhaps moving from poor urban areas to more advantaged neighborhoods improves the lives of children. Yet, do they really profit from the change? The question is difficult to answer given that certain types of families, typically those possessing more resources, would be more likely to move in the first place. To deal with this problem it is useful to consider the randomized study Moving to Opportunity (MTO), which has operated in five U.S. cities (Baltimore, Boston, Chicago, Los Angeles, and New York) since 1994.[37] In the study, families were eligible to participate if they had children and lived in public housing or Section 8 housing with a neighborhood poverty rate of 40 percent or more. Interested families who applied were randomly assigned to one of three groups: the experimental group (which received rent vouchers for housing in low-poverty areas), a Section 8 comparison group (which received unrestricted rent vouchers), and a control group (which did not receive rent vouchers). The design is especially helpful in learning about how neighborhoods affect well-being because, in normal circumstances, specific types of families live in specific types of neighborhoods, which makes it difficult to disentangle the contributions of families and neighborhoods.

In the typical move to a white middle-class suburb, the black mothers and their children found themselves in a radically different world with higher behavioral expectations and typically with white age-mates. If unemployed before the move, black mothers who moved to the suburbs were more likely to find jobs and to engage in job searches, when compared to the city movers. In the follow-up, the suburban minority students were more often placed on a college track and were attending two- or four-year colleges. If not in college, they were nearly twice as likely as the city movers to be employed full-time with pay greater than the minimum wage and with job benefits. The suburban adolescents were also far more likely to be engaged in daily activities with white students, despite racial threats and harassment.

Before-and-after comparisons show that the transition improved life chances, at least for the females. Four to seven years after baseline, girls' mental health improved. Girls in the experimental group also reported less risky behavior and better educational outcomes, suggesting that important advantages can accrue from higher-quality neighborhoods. Still, the overall tale is less positive. In contrast to females, males in the study actually exhibited more risky behaviors and physical health problems. The lack of advantage for boys in the MTO experimental group is difficult to explain, although researchers Kling and colleagues and Liebman and colleagues speculate that boys in the experimental group may have experienced stereotyping, maintained more ties to their old neighborhoods, and settled into peer groups that exerted negative influences.[38]

The point of this discussion is that a focus on the effects of context on people's lives, while necessary, must account for the processes by which people "come to" a particular context, as well as their reactions to it, both short- and long-term.

The Life of Darwin Revisited

How might the life of Darwin look from a life course perspective? While a "full-blown" biography is beyond our expertise, we can nevertheless highlight some interesting themes based on life course principles and concepts, all of which direct our attention to his social setting and issues of timing, including historical timing and his own aging process. The overarching point of such an analysis is that it is the interaction of these principles that makes Darwin's life understandable and "common to human experience" while, at the same time, uniquely his own.[39]

Darwin's fame rests on his theory of evolution by natural selection, which states, among other things, that organisms differ in their characteristics, and these differences render some organisms better suited to their environments and hence more likely to reproduce than less "fit" organisms. An analysis of Darwin's life must therefore revolve around his discovery and promotion of this idea. His voyage on the HMS *Beagle* was undoubtedly a turning point in his life and in science, although one that took several years. In thinking about any life or the lives of a group of people, however, not all principles and concepts will be equally telling. Thus, our brief consideration of Darwin's life draws on a subset of these principles and conceptual tools.

Principle 1, Time and Place

How did Darwin's historical setting and place facilitate his achievements? Darwin grew up in nineteenth-century England, which was a hothouse of intellectual ideas associated with modernism, including evolution. Jean-Baptiste Lamarck and Étienne Geoffrey St. Hilaire were well-known evolutionists, but several other naturalists had published speculations about how species come into being and change. Darwin's grandfather Erasmus had promoted his own views of evolution (from which comes the word *darwinizing*, which Coleridge used to refer to outlandish conjecture).

The general intellectual climate in Britain also seemed to pave the way for the idea of natural selection. One hundred years before Darwin, the Scotsman Adam Smith held that economic markets work by way of an "invisible hand." Here, shortages of goods raise their prices, which prompt people to produce more of the goods. In contrast, a surplus depresses the price and causes people to produce other goods. Implicit in the analysis is that people are adaptive, responding to the opportunities of their environments, and the aggregate of these adaptations creates a market. By analogy, the sum total of adaptations by all organisms in a place define an *ecology*.

Contemporaneous with Darwin's life, his fellow countryman the Reverend Thomas Malthus, an economist for the East India Company, wrote famously that increases in the human population would eventually lead to wars, famines, and disease, which would precipitate a struggle among individuals and the survival of "the fittest." Darwin read Malthus and was greatly impressed by the idea that populations adjust to the resources of their settings. A final major influence was the Englishman Charles Lyell, a prominent geologist of the time, who argued that geologic processes, including the forming of sedimentation layers, occurred over vast periods of time, an idea that is opposed to the sudden creation of the world suggested by the Book of Genesis. Given that fossils were found throughout these layers of rock, the implication was that species had emerged over vast periods of time as well. Thus, in retrospect, one can tease out several strands that form an intellectual pathway to Darwin's line of thinking.

Care should be observed, however, when interpreting this last, seemingly innocuous, statement. The point is not that Darwin's theory was obvious to him or anyone alive at the time. Our inquiry is retrospective and, knowing how Darwin's life unfolds, we can assemble a set of facts that makes his intellectual quest understandable. But such an account fails to capture the tremendous questioning and puzzlement that characterized the process of formulating the theory. Had we attempted to predict Darwin's achievements when he was five years old, it seems highly unlikely that any predictions would capture the magnitude of his contributions.

The great difference between the seeming certitude of retrospective accounts, on the one hand, and the lived experience and uncertainties of prospective accounts, on the other hand, has been discussed by the historian Joseph Ellis, who notes that histories of revolutionary America are typically colored by the fact that the historian knows the outcome of the Revolutionary War, the process of writing the Declaration of Independence, George Washington's presidency, and so on.[40] Ellis's own telling of these stories attempts to capture the prospective complexity of these events and results in "history with a different feel," an appreciation that things could well have turned out differently, and it was precisely this sense of unease that motivated many of the actors at that time.

There is another point to made about Darwin's time and place in history: he belonged to a privileged class of his society. Darwin's family had considerable wealth and standing, which allowed him the resources to pursue his interests. In truth, a life course analyst could not address why Darwin was so deeply motivated by his studies. Clearly, he had an exceedingly high level of intrinsic motivation and he pursued his research relentlessly. But without the resources of time and money that his family provided, it is doubtful whether these motivations would have amounted to as much as they did in his case. As once was said, bread before science. Darwin was provided plenty of bread, which made science much easier to pursue. Such a speculation is supported by the fact that many, if not most, noteworthy scientists of the time came from socioeconomic privilege.

Not only did his place in society afford him opportunities to study, but it may have allowed his radical ideas more attention and acceptance than they would have received had he been from the unwashed masses of the time. Despite his intentions, Darwin's theory was interpreted as challenging the very existence of a Christian God and suggesting a social order based on domination by superior men and women. Coming from a "proper" family in society, however, Darwin's message may have been given a hearing that would not have been extended to someone, for example, from a background marked by radicalism.

While our discussion cannot be exhaustive, it can nevertheless serve to demonstrate that Darwin was born at a place and time when his line of thinking, while not "dictated" or "caused" by circumstances, was possible and perhaps even probable. His historical circumstances had created an intellectual opportunity, and his place in society allowed him to rise to meet that opportunity by facilitating his studies and perhaps even helping him to promote his ideas. To apply his own theory, his social circumstances included a niche just waiting to be filled by a fit organism like himself.

In some respects, one is reminded of Martin Luther, whose ideas reflected widespread dissatisfaction with the Church in the northern German provinces and could therefore take root. He, too, can be understood as the right person in the right place at the right time. Had he lived a few hundred miles to the south, in Italy, and few years earlier, he may well have been burned at the stake before his message was widely heard (as was the case of Savonarola). And in some respects, one is also reminded of Mozart and Beethoven, discussed in Chapter 1. Mozart was a bit ahead of his time in thinking that the bourgeoisie could support his career and that royal patronage was unnecessary. Coming on the heels of Mozart, Beethoven, on the other hand, was supported by this emerging class and was able to live a very different life. The point is that historical time and place were reasonably conducive to Darwinian thinking, which is to say conducive to both its formulation and acceptance.

Principle 3, Linked Lives

Who were the significant people in Darwin's life, and how did they add to or detract from his achievements? Again, we must be selective and view linked lives as a dynamic principle. Still, can we identify "convoys" of people, persisting relationships, and well-timed, salient connections with others that appear to have made a big difference in Darwin's life? Indeed, several can be easily identified.

First, some of Darwin's associates formed a "convoy of Establishment England." These people were the voices of orthodoxy, who, typically by example and gentle prodding, urged Darwin to remain a faithful Christian and mainstream Whig (a liberal political party of the time). Prominent in this group of people was the Reverend John Stevens Henslow, an Anglican minister and professor of botany at Cambridge. Henslow was a voice of religious orthodoxy and, given his expertise and congenial nature, a great friend of Darwin through the scientist's early adulthood and a respected acquaintance in his later adulthood. Also, Henslow was himself a naturalist and thus knew the "ins and outs" of Lyell and other innovative thinkers, and he often warned Darwin to avoid their "errors."

Darwin's beloved wife Emma was also religious and often shared her anxieties about his apparently bleak view of human nature and God. Hers was a world filled with grace and divine action; his was a world governed by complex and impersonal laws. In 1839, shortly after their marriage, Emma wrote Charles a note in which she worried that he would spend eternity in hell. The letter reduced him to tears. A lesser figure of orthodoxy was the captain of the *Beagle,* the Captain Robert FitzRoy, a direct descendant of Charles II and an enthusiastic

Tory (a conservative party, then and now). Although FitzRoy had little, if any, effect on Darwin's scientific thinking, he was nonetheless Darwin's only "gentleman companion" throughout the voyage and would "pop up" time and again in Darwin's life as a voice urging allegiance to political and religious conservatism. Beyond these prominent examples, Darwin's life was filled with characters, major and minor, who promoted the status quo through their interactions with him.

On the other hand, some of Darwin's associates form a "convoy of modernism." These people were the voices of change, often having disdain for religion (not to mention religious orthodoxy) and an interest in new and often radical scientific ideas. Perhaps the first such association, beyond the example of his grandfather Erasmus, who wrote erotic poetry and proposed a theory of evolution, was to be found in his brother Erasmus, who was a thoroughgoing freethinker and maintained a close and influential relationship with his brother. A second and early example can be found in the Plinian Society, a group of radical students that Darwin joined while a student in Edinburgh. Many of the Plinians were anticlerical and antiestablishment in their politics. Darwin's primary interest was their scientific expertise, however, and he became a close associate with, for example, Robert Edmond Grant, a freethinker and an expert on the local sponges that so fascinated Darwin. In their excursions to collect specimens, Grant undoubtedly pushed Darwin squarely in the direction of "unorthodox" thinking with respect to religion, society, and science. Darwin would part company with Grant in later adulthood (owing to Grant's inflammatory ways), but Darwin was later befriended by a core group of supporters called the "X Club," nine innovative thinkers led by Thomas Huxley. All these and scores of other major and minor acquaintances amounted to a "convoy" of interpersonal relationships that encouraged Darwin in his highly innovative ways of thinking.

What to make of these two, apparently opposed, "convoys" of linked lives? Unlike so many innovative thinkers, Darwin never dismissed or disrespected his Establishment friends. And unlike so many people with Establishment sympathies, Darwin always maintained an open mind. Through his connections to the "powers-that-be" and the "leading-edge thinkers," Darwin was uniquely positioned to appreciate all sides of an argument, to draw upon a wide array of institutional resources and lines of communication, and to uphold a degree of social respectability that allowed him to introduce and spread his theory.

Principle 5, Life Stage
Darwin himself identifies his commission with the HMS *Beagle* as the great turning point in his life, suggesting that without the experiences aboard the *Beagle* he could never have devised the theory of evolution by natural selection. Was the timing of the *Beagle*'s expedition in his life especially important in shaping its meaning?

Many commentators have noted a directionless cast to Darwin's early life. He studied medicine but abandoned it. He studied theology, but rarely with enthusiasm. He also studied the natural sciences, that is, what we now think of as "science," including botany and geology, but after receiving his BA from Cambridge in 1831, his plans were nebulous. He merely hoped to broaden his horizons through fieldwork, reading, and travel, perhaps secure a position at a university, perhaps marry, perhaps become a clergyman.

In August of that same year, however, the opportunity to serve as the naturalist aboard the *Beagle* presented itself. The timing of the voyage in Darwin's life was highly propitious in at least three ways. First, Darwin had acquired considerable field experience and book learning, and was aware of both conventional and innovative theories of the geology and biology of his time. All of his new observations would be made with these big ideas in mind. Second, he had not yet committed himself to adult roles that might have prevented him from accepting such a long and potentially dangerous journey. Doug McAdam has offered the term "biographical availability" to describe people who have not yet committed to adult roles and thus have greater flexibility in their plans and lines of action.[41] This biographical availability would also allow Darwin to return to England and spend several years digesting all that he had seen and done. And finally, he was young enough to endure both the voyage itself and several very arduous trips on land to make observations and collect specimens. The net effect of these advantages of timing was that a notably directionless biography acquired a new and all-consuming purpose: the experiences aboard the *Beagle* would inspire Darwin for the rest of his life.

Darwin: A Coda

It is the combination of all these principles that make Darwin's life uniquely his own. Darwin was born in a time and place conducive to innovative thinking about evolution. His own position in society afforded him every opportunity to do so. His lifelong series of friendships nurtured both his attachment to "proper society" and his appreciation for novel, cutting-edge ideas. His social standing and many diverse friends also created many opportunities for his theory to be spread. While all of these "potentials" are interesting, it was the voyage of the *Beagle* that led to his substantive achievements, and the salience and value of that event very much depended on its timing in his life: young enough to be vigorous and free of obligations, and old enough to have sufficient field experience and to know all of the major theories of his time. It was the right time and place in history, and the right time in his own life.

Yet no life can be explained by such a short, tidy account. For every observation one might make, new questions arise. The main point of this analysis is to illustrate how life course principles and concepts might be used to *begin* explaining the life of Darwin. The example serves to make clear how incomplete a biography of Darwin would be without reference to a detailed consideration of issues of context and timing.

The case study also brings to mind a methodological point: it is not "scientific" in the sense that it cannot be empirically tested. Most life course research is empirical and scientific (a point discussed further in Chapters 3 and 4), but our case study is not, and it seems unlikely that even a thorough case study, by itself, could be scientific. One of the major reasons for this sad fact has to do with *counterfactuals*, which refer to circumstances opposite those that are supposed to be causal. For example, our account suggests that the voyage of the *Beagle* is critical to understanding Darwin's life. Strictly speaking, to prove this would require what the scientific method calls a *control*—in this case, a "photocopy" of Darwin without the voyage of the *Beagle*. In fact, given the "random noise" that characterizes life—that is, given the many little things that happen—it would be most convincing to observe several hundred Charles Darwins who went on the *Beagle* voyage and an equal number of Charles Darwins who did not. We could then compare how the two groups fare throughout their lives. In other words, we would need to perform an experiment in which one group receives a specific treatment (the voyage), one group does not, and then compare the two groups later.

Obviously, this is not possible. Hence, care must be exercised and we must acknowledge that our account of Darwin is, like all case studies of single individuals, an account that hinges on consistency with the facts—but its truth cannot be established according to all of the canons of the scientific method. This and other case studies throughout the book are used to illustrate ideas about the life course. In fact, life course analysts almost never study single people in isolation, but rather focus on groups of people (e.g., young adults in 1890 and 1990, gays before and after Stonewall), as will be illustrated in the subsequent chapters.

CONCLUDING REMARKS

This book began by discussing C. Wright Mills's call for a sociological imagination, a way of approaching biography by asking questions about history and society. While his message has inspired legions of social scientists, he did not propose how this imagination would actually "work." How *would* people engage in the sociological imagination? Several decades would pass before an answer began to emerge in the form of life course sociology. The lessons of these decades is that the life course is a creative paradigm made up of principles and concepts, requiring that biographies be scrutinized to highlight the importance of context and timing. The life course is less a prescription for precisely how lives must be interpreted than a set of tools that are intended to aid in the creative process of discovery and understanding.

We turn now to ways that this imaginative framework has been applied to the study of macro and micro features of the life course.

FURTHER READING

Given the many relevant conceptual and empirical pieces, this is a necessarily brief selection of further readings, with priority given to conceptual pieces and empirical examples.

Principles and Mechanisms

Antonucci, Toni C., and Hiroko Akiyama. "Convoys of Social Relations: Family and Friendships within a Life Span Context." In *Handbook of Aging and the Family*, edited by Rosemary Blieszner and Victoria H. Bedford, 355–371. Westport, CT: Greenwood Press, 1995.

    Dynamic view of the linked-lives principle.

Clausen, John A. *American Lives: Looking Back at the Children of the Great Depression.* New York: Free Press, 1993.

    Interesting approach to agency in the life course by way of "planful competence." The empirical research, combining quantitative and qualitative data, is engaging and provocative.

Drobnič, Sonja. "Ties between Lives: Dynamics of Employment Patterns of Spouses." In *Social Dynamics of the Life Course*, edited by Walter R. Heinz and Victor W. Marshall, 259–278. New York: Aldine De Gruyter, 2003.

    Nice empirical illustration of linked lives viewed dynamically.

Elder, G. H., Jr., and Michael J. Shanahan. "The Life Course and Human Development." In *Handbook of Child Psychology*, Vol. 1, edited by R. M. Lerner, 665–715. New York: John Wiley & Sons, 2006.

    This article maintains a strong distinction between life course principles and mechanisms (which our book does not do, for the sake of brevity).

Elder, Glen H., Jr., Michael J. Shanahan, and Elizabeth Colerick Clipp. "When War Comes to Men's Lives: Life Course Patterns in Family, Work, and Health." *Psychology and Aging*, no. 1 (1994): 5–16.

> Good empirical example of the life-stage principle, showing how the age of entry into World War II service affected later life.

Mortimer, Jeylan T. *Working and Growing Up in America.* Cambridge, MA: Harvard University Press, 2003.

> Excellent example of how situational imperatives (specific working conditions of adolescents) determine the meaning of paid work for their life course.

Silverstein, Merril, Stephen J. Conroy, Haitao Wang, Roseann Giarrusso, and Vern L. Bengtson. "Reciprocity in Parent-Child Relations over the Life Course." *Journal of Gerontology: Social Sciences* 57B, no. 1 (2002): S3–S13.

> Empirical study of linked lives, examining transfers from parent to children, and then from adult children to their aging parents. Excellent examples of linked lives in terms of intergenerational lineages.

Titma, Mikk, and Nancy B. Tuma. *Paths of a Generation: A Comparative Longitudinal Study of Young Adults in the Former Soviet Union.* Stanford University Press, 1995.

> Powerful example of how the biography is shaped by historical time and place (the first principle of life course sociology).

Willis, Paul. *Learning to Labor: How Working Class Kids Get Working Class Jobs.* Farnborough, England: Saxon House, 1977.

> A fascinating study of the life course fortunes of English working-class adolescents and the mechanisms that reproduce their marginal standing over time. A revealing look at accentuating processes in their various dimensions.

The Ontogenetic Fallacy

Dannefer, D. "Adult Development and Social Theory: A Paradigmatic Reappraisal." *American Sociological Review* 49 (1984): 100–116, and subsequent commentary.

Baltes, P. B., and J. R. Nesselroade. "Paradigm Lost and Paradigm Regained: Critique of Dannefer's Portrayal of Life-span Developmental Psychology." *American Sociological Review* 49 (1984): 841–847.

Dale Dannefer. "The Role of the Social in Life-Span Developmental Psychology, Past and Future: Rejoinder to Baltes and Nesselroade." *American Sociological Review* 49 (1984): 847–850.

> These three articles represent an exchange between a life course sociologist (Dannefer) and two life-span psychologists (Baltes and Nesselroade). Dannefer's initial article is an excellent exploration of the ontogenetic fallacy. The subsequent exchange highlights differences between the ways psychologists and sociologists study long-term patterns in people's lives. Indispensable reading.

Life Course Concepts

Dannefer, Dale. "Cumulative Advantage/Disadvantage and the Life Course: Cross Fertilizing Age and Social Science Theory." *Journal of Gerontology: Social Sciences* 58B (2003): S327–S337.

Excellent essay on cumulative processes, with an emphasis on the intellectual history of the concept and also the possible ways that such processes shape the later life course.

Gamoran, A. "The Variable Effects of High School Tracking." *American Sociological Review* 57 (1992): 812–828.

Superb empirical example of educational tracking as pathways. See also Pallas (2004), bibliography.

George, Linda. "Sociological Perspectives on Life Transitions." *Annual Review of Sociology* 19 (1993): 353–373.

Very thoughtful essay on transitions in the life course, with an emphasis on their social psychological aspects.

Johnson, Monica K. "Social Origins, Adolescent Experiences, and Work Value Trajectories during the Transition to Adulthood." *Social Forces* 80.4 (2002): 1307–1340.

Excellent empirical study of entry into adulthood and the changing nature of work-value trajectories in the context of working conditions.

Laub, John H., Daniel S. Nagin, and Robert J. Sampson. "Trajectories of Change in Criminal Offending: Good Marriages and the Desistance Process." *American Sociological Review* 63 (1998): 225–238.

Creative use of trajectories and turning points in the study of how marriage can interrupt continuity in criminal careers.

King, Gilliam, et al. "Turning Points and Protective Processes in the Lives of People with Chronic Disabilities." *Qualitative Health Research* 13 (2003): 184–206.

Great application of the turning-points concept to people living with disabilities. Considers the social factors that lead to turning points, as well as how people experience them.

Macmillan, Ross, and Ronda Copher. "Families in the Life Course: Interdependency of Roles, Role Configurations, and Pathways." *Journal of Marriage and the Family* 67 (2005): 858–879.

An elaboration of the conceptualization and measurement of pathways, trajectories, and transitions, and a discussion of their role's in the life course implications of early parenthood.

McDonough, Peggy, and Pat Berglund. "Histories of Poverty and Self-related Health Trajectories." *Journal of Health and Social Behavior* 44 (June 2003): 198–214.

Empirical example demonstrating the usefulness of dynamic views of context (poverty histories) and the person (self-rated health).

O'Rand, Angela. "Cumulative Advantage Theory in Life Course Research." *Annual Review of Gerontology* 22 (2002): 14–30.

    Thought-provoking discussion of how cumulating advantages/disadvantages alter the later life course.

Pavalko, Eliza K. "Beyond Trajectories: Multiple Concepts for Analyzing Long-term Processes." In *Studying Aging and Social Change: Conceptual and Methodological Issues*, edited by Melissa Hardy, 129–147. Newbury Park: Sage, 1997.

    Generative discussion of life course concepts not considered in this chapter—pattern, sequence, pace, and reversibility—and their application to the study of mental illness careers. Highly recommended.

Rutter, Michael. "Pathways from Childhood to Adult Life." *Journal of Child Psychology and Psychiatry* 30 (1989): 23–51.

    Excellent review of empirical research on the many paths that children at risk can take into adulthood.

Wheaton, Blair. "Life Transitions, Role Histories, and Mental Health." *American Sociological Review* 55.2 (1990): 209–223.

    Superb empirical example of how prior experiences shape the meaning of transitions in the life course. Noteworthy for its highly interactive view of the life course.

Exogenous Processes

Duncan, Greg J., Katherine A. Magnuson, and Jens Ludwig. "The Endogeneity Problem in Developmental Studies." *Research in Human Development* 1.1 & 2 (2004): 59–80.

    Very clear explanation of exogenous processes as they potentially confound causes and effects in developmental research.

Chapter Three
MACRO VIEWS OF THE LIFE COURSE

Forget the messiness of the years and days—every work of human artifice has a proper viewing distance.

—Tracy Kidder

YOUNG ADULTS READING THIS BOOK are likely to have living grandparents who take an interest in their lives and care about their well-being. Further, many of today's grandparents are physically and mentally active and engaged in their families and communities. Perhaps these observations seem trivial but, in historical perspective, they tell a story of dramatic social change that extends from premodern to modern times. When compared to their counterparts in contemporary Western societies, the children and especially young adults of premodern societies had fewer living grandparents and more siblings and cousins to compete with for their elders' attention. Moreover, the premodern aged were less healthy than their counterparts are today and their roles and cultural scripts often did not encourage affectionate, emotionally close relationships with their children's children. The net effect of changes from pre-industrial times to the present is that, in the words of the historical demographer Peter Uhlenberg, "grandparents play a more significant role in the lives of children now than ever before in history."[1]

"Grandparenthood" is a major role in the life course and has clearly changed in dramatic ways. The life course perspective views grandparenthood as an age-graded social category, which means that it is a set of opportunities, limitations, and expectations specific to people within a delimited age group. These categories for the phases of life are subject to modification as society changes. Indeed, all of the age-graded roles and phases of life have changed between premodern and modern times and even within the last few decades.

Just as such historical comparisons are revealing, cross-national comparisons "create variation" in societal forces: different societies are organized differently, and these diverse contexts are often associated with unique life course patterns. Both historically different societies and different geopolitical units (e.g., states, provinces, nations) at a point in time provide opportunities to compare and contrast how different social forces lead to different biographical patterns.

Such research is typical of the macro perspective of the life course, which focuses on the life course as a *socially constructed* phenomenon—that is, the life course *qua* social structure. Attributes of the life course that may be of interest refer to the phases of life (e.g., childhood, middle adulthood, old age), transitions between phases (e.g., the transition to adolescence or to young adulthood), and sequences of roles (e.g., the sequence of roles that defines the educational or occupational careers). Accordingly, the following types of questions are typical of a macro perspective: How are retirement transitions different among the various countries of the European Union and why? Did "adolescence" always exist? Have educational patterns changed in the United States since 1776, and, if so, how and why? Is it really more difficult than ever before to be an American teenager?

These questions can be answered in ways consistent with the life course paradigm by focusing on social experiences as they change over time. They reflect a macro orientation because they are interested in comparing how aspects of the life course differ through history and across geopolitical units. Such comparisons are often complex and the types of data required are sometimes not available. Suppose, for example, that we are interested in how images of the elderly differ across Western and Eastern societies. What types of information would be relevant? Where would we find such information? The empirical study of macro features of the life course is often difficult and, consequently, researchers have employed a wide array of ingenious concepts and techniques to study macro features of the life course.

This chapter examines some of these concepts and strategies and what we have learned from them. We begin with historical comparisons, proceeding from very wide-ranging time frames to comparatively detailed studies of birth cohorts. We then consider cross-national comparisons. Historical and cross-national comparisons have suggested several master trends that describe how the life course, as a whole, has changed with the modernization of societies. These trends are described and evaluated in the final section of this chapter. Our purpose is not to examine all that is known about the macro features of the life course, but rather to highlight basic concepts and strategies that life course sociologists draw upon to study these features.

Social History and Macro Features of the Life Course

Each phase of life (infancy, childhood, adolescence, etc.) brings with it social norms and institutional constraints that specify appropriate behaviors and roles, thus serving as a principal source of identity for people. Whereas we often think of the construction of an identity (what David Snow and Leon Anderson call "identity work"[2]), as an individual task, large-scale social forces set basic boundaries and provide a framework within which such personal efforts occur. To be a white gentleman in nineteenth-century England had many implications for one's identity and life course, including for example, an increased likelihood of higher education, access to financial wealth, engagement in politics, enjoyment of the arts, and little involvement with one's children on a daily basis. To be a black woman in America during the 1950s had different implications: poverty and the lack of opportunity that comes with it, heavy burdens as a homemaker and mother, and a low level of education. In fact, all of us begin life with a social location (a term defined in Chapter One) that serves as a major source of our biographies. As Norman Ryder has observed, "Every society seizes upon the circumstances of birth as modes of allocating status, limiting the degrees of freedom for the person's path through life."[3]

Interestingly, the implications of these social locations (or circumstances of birth) change through time and space. The life of the English gentleman of the nineteenth century differs from the life of an English gentleman of the twenty-first century, just as the life of a black woman in the early twentieth century differs from the life of a black woman in the twenty-

first century. The issue then becomes how institutional opportunities and constraints change, redefining what it means to be
a child, adolescence, adult, or elderly person. One of the best il-
lustrations of how macro features of the life course have been
studied can be found in research on adolescence, a phase of life
that has been studied extensively by social historians.

Changes in Life Phases

One of the first major works to consider changes in adolescence
as a life phase was Philippe Ariès's *Centuries of Childhood*, published in French in 1960.[4] Ariès claimed that adolescence did
not exist in premodern times. Drawing on a diverse array of evidence, Ariès argued that in medieval times children merged
directly into adult roles starting at around seven years of age.
Medieval society distinguished between adults and nonadults
but, in the latter category, distinctions were not maintained between children and adolescents. Most medieval and premodern
children did not attend school but were incorporated into adult
life as quickly as possible by way of daily interactions with
their elders in tightly knit communities. The few youth who
did attend school remained integrated in adult society by way
of a vocational curriculum designed largely to train lawyers and
the clergy.

According to Ariè, beginning as early as the sixteenth century, a wide range of factors—from military conscription to
technological advancements—led to the prolongation of childhood and the emergence of a new phase of life, adolescence. Increasing percentages of youth were educated in age-segregated
settings according to curricula that were less concerned with
vocational training and more focused on the general training of

young minds. With this prolongation of education and the segregation of young people from the adult world, adolescence
emerged as a distinct age-graded identity. Ariès argued that
prior to these changes, however, adolescence did not exist: "as
soon as the child could live without the constant solicitude of
his mother, his nanny, or his cradle-rocker, he belonged to
adult society."[5]

The idea that this or any phase of life "was invented" as
Western societies modernized is intriguing. How did Ariès attempt to prove such an audacious claim? He drew on a wide
range of sources, including, for example, an analysis of terms
that were used to describe the phases of life (e.g., Latin recognized seven phases of life, but French had words for only three
such phases); the material arts (e.g., the absence of depictions of
dead children on tombs until the sixteenth century, how the
young and old were dressed similarly), the graphic arts (e.g.,
how children were portrayed in family portraits), practices of
games and festivals (e.g., after about age four, youth played
adult games until about the sixteenth century), sexual norms
(e.g., immodest behavior was not tolerated after about age four
before the sixteenth century), and the structure of the educational system and its curriculum.

Although many historians criticized Ariès for his use of evidence (e.g., his description of education in medieval and Renaissance) and, indeed, they have largely rejected his thesis,
Centuries of Childhood made three important contributions.
First, it identified phases of life as *social categories* that warrant
historical study in their own right. Many historians have subsequently published histories of childhood and adolescence, and
have echoed Ariès's basic point that the phases of the life course

have undoubtedly changed through history in response to changes in societies. Second, *Centuries* illustrated how social structures and cultural practices determined and reflected the contours of the phases of life. The educational system, dress, games, artistic representations, and labor markets all shaped and continue to shape pathways to adulthood. Although he was criticized in his details, Ariés's types of evidence have been used in subsequent work. Third, cultural representations of youth—the depictions of youth and their families as found, for example, in literature, newspapers, and art—signify the meaning of childhood and adolescence at different times in history. Paintings, for example, should not be thought of as merely pretty pictures, but rather as statements about social arrangements and meanings attached to the people they portray. Whatever the defects of *Centuries*, its analytic strategies and motifs are readily seen in the historical studies of youth and all phases of life that have followed it.

Demographic Patterns and Cultural Practices
John Gillis's *Youth and History* of 1974 is an instructive comparison.[6] Like Ariès, Gillis believed that adolescence, as a social category, could be studied by examining demographic trends and the role of youth in cultural practices. But Gillis also emphasized youth-oriented peer groups and departed from Ariès's central thesis. While Ariès directed attention to how young children were dressed in adult clothes prior to the nineteenth century, according to Gillis, adolescence is not defined by clothing; rather, it is fundamentally a state of semi-independence between childhood and adulthood (which is a great sociological definition of adolescence!). That is, adolescence refers to a life

phase during which youth are neither completely dependent on their parents (like children) nor completely independent (like adults). Rather, their social responsibilities and opportunities afford them more freedoms and choices and autonomy than those experienced by children, but still less than those afforded to adults. Viewed in this way, adolescence did exist in premodern Europe.

According to Gillis, in premodern England, France, and Germany this state of semi-independence extended from age seven or eight, when a child was sent to another household as a servant (called "binding"), until his or her mid-twenties, when marriage or inheritance would establish a person as a head of household. This pattern held for all social classes, rich and poor. Given the high rate of mortality in the early years of life, parents often had as many children as possible and binding was necessary to lessen the burden of so many mouths to feed (among the poor) or to broaden the horizons of the child (among the rich).

In any event, the practice of binding encouraged a new sense of autonomy from the family of origin on the part of the son or daughter. Adolescence ended with marriage and/or inheritance. Often, the oldest son would inherit most or all of the family property, allowing him to marry in his mid-twenties. Particularly among the poor, daughters and younger sons often did not marry at all, instead remaining celibate and entering the clergy, or joining the army or civil service, or becoming spinsters or bachelors dependent on the oldest brother for support. Notice the mode of analysis at work in *Youth and History:* the implications of the demographic patterns governing fertility and mortality suggest that adolescence (as a state of semi-independence) extended for almost twenty years in premodern times.

Characteristics of peer groups were also revealing. In premodern times, village-based youth groups served as sources of moral support, rowdy brotherhood, and social control, particularly in regulating sexual conduct and courtship. Above all, many youth associations were concerned with the prevention of early marriage, which was considered a disaster for the parties involved and the community.

With the beginning of modernization (particularly urbanization and industrialization), the upper class began limiting their fertility and investing in their offspring through prolonged education. The working class, however, maintained its high birthrate. The old arrangement of inheritance and marriage was no longer the rule. Rather, families adopted strategies by which children would take part in household-based factory work (e.g., weaving), or children would enter factories as wage-laborers. Several children in the factory might mean that a later-born sibling could attend school.

Because of wages, the patriarchy of pre-industrial times was weakened in its authority and some young people established their own households at a younger age than was previously possible. The semi-independence of adolescence was now shortened, as wages liberated young people from the restrictions of inheritance and domination by their fathers. This often led to earlier marriage or, in any event, earlier home-leaving.

Youth groups also changed with modernization in several interesting ways. In premodern times, youth groups were largely restricted to unmarried young people. With industrialization and urbanization, many such groups began to realign along class lines. Among the working classes, such groups were still characterized by brotherhood and rowdiness, but their social aim was the redress of class-based injustices, rather than impeding premature marriage or prenuptial sexual behavior. In urban settings, some of the traditional youth-group practices were now viewed as threats to the civil order, and the "juvenile delinquent" emerged as a new social category. Among the upper classes, youth groups formed in secondary schools and universities and often fostered antiestablishment attitudes, including, for example, political disagreement and bohemianism.

Towards the end of the nineteenth century, with modernism firmly taking hold, adolescence continued to change. The working class began to split into skilled and unskilled laborers, with the former group keeping their young in school for longer periods of time than the latter. In this way, the duration of adolescence remained stable for the unskilled working class, but expanded for the skilled working class. Moving into the twentieth century, youth were increasingly removed from factories, and primary and then secondary school became commonplace, lengthening the duration of "adolescence" across social classes.

While specialists could debate the details of Gillis's research, there is little doubt that the rates of fertility and mortality, the nature of the economy and its modes of production, and cultural mores were constantly changing what it meant to be an adolescent. And yet, all of these changes took place around a core, shared understanding of this phase of life, an understanding that encompassed preparation for adult work, movement to some appreciable degree of economic self-sufficiency, and the formation of one's own household.

Representations and Representers

Joseph Kett's 1977 book *Rites of Passage* set out to provide a history of adolescence in the United States from 1790 to about 1960 and, in so doing, emphasized a new way of thinking about macro aspects of the life course.[7] *Rites* begins with the premise that structural social conditions fundamentally shape the contours of adolescence. Like Gillis, Kett places special emphasis on demographic features and economic necessities that shape the experiences of youth in families, school, the workplace, and community organizations. But, shifting emphasis and building on the interest in social class found in Gillis, Kett argued that these forces created different "adolescences" depending on such factors as social class, region, and gender. The theme seems especially appropriate for a study of America extending from the late eighteenth century: as the nation was being settled and communication was often difficult (creating regional variations in the experiences of young people), America was a place of pronounced socioeconomic and regional differences, ranging from the exceptionally rich to slaves and the rural destitute. A first major theme of Kett, then, is that social structures do not map neatly onto one monolithic "adolescence" that applies to all youth, but rather they create myriad experiences and therefore many "versions" of adolescence.

Like Ariès, Kett relied on representations of youth, especially as found in sermons, narratives, and "conduct of life" (or "self-help") books, to discover what it meant to be an adolescent in the past. *Rites* argued that these representations were not entirely true and should not be taken at face value. Rather, such representations have an element of truth that is magnified greatly by the moral concerns of the person making the representation. Representations of youth often said as much (or more) about the preoccupations of middle- and upper-class adults—the "representers"—than they did about the youth themselves. The shift in focus from the represented to the representers, then, is a second significant theme in Kett's work.

Kett observed that between 1820 and 1870 many youth moved from rural areas into rapidly expanding urban areas, a transition that also corresponded with a change from agricultural labor to jobs in business and commerce. The traditional authority of fathers and the pull of family obligations were waning and young people used their newfound wages to become increasingly autonomous from their fathers (as was observed by Gillis). Accompanying these changes were widely selling advice books that promoted "decisions of character" among youth. The authors of such books lamented the loss of rural ways of living and were appalled at the sexual and social liberties that young people might take, given their unsupervised freedoms in the city (concerns that sound surprisingly contemporary). Such books emphasized the need to balance traditional rural values (especially self-restraint) with essential new life skills, especially planning and autonomy.

As the nineteenth century came to a close, however, middle-class parents were increasingly enrolling their sons and daughters in high schools, and, not surprisingly, conduct-of-life books no longer emphasized autonomy, which would now be a threat to the regimented life of the school. With young people in schools, self-initiative, planning, and practical life skills were no longer deemed as important. Rather, the new focus was vocational development and physical vitality. For writers at the time, personal autonomy was a threat to the social order and submission required by schools. In the course of nineteenth-century America, then, "representers" shifted from exhorting independence, self-restraint, planning, and life skills (all valuable assets for young people leaving farms and entering cities) to fostering an interest in preparing for one's future (a valuable focus in the context of prolonged schooling).

As Kett observed, time and again through American history "adolescence" was imposed, not observed. Little was actually known about youth, but the authors of conduct-of-life books, sermons, and newspaper and magazine articles said much about it anyway, typically reflecting their anxieties about what it should be. The flaw in imposing representations on youth was that such sweeping generalizations about them were never truly warranted. In extreme cases, the representations were completely false. (For example, in an analysis of newspaper articles in Scotland, Nancy Falchikov found that the coverage of youth emphasized adolescents as criminals, as victims, as participants in sports, and as unemployed workers—representations which bore little resemblance to the facts.) In fact, because of gender, race, social class, and geographic location, many versions of adolescence existed.

Kett's history of youth is thus highly dynamic and multifaceted. Demographic, social, and economic conditions change, putting pressures on youth to change their roles and their place in society. In turn, adults create images of youth that reflect apprehensions about these changes and that create new pressures for new versions of adolescence. Representations are often not true characterizations of the way things are, but rather reflections of the hopes, aspirations, and anxieties of the adults (typically middle-class) making the representations.

Still, it is important not to get lost in the details: the purpose of this discussion is not to provide a comprehensive review of the history of adolescence, but rather to show how such histories are written and, secondarily, to present the most important findings. In considering the work of Ariès, Gillis, and Kett, the social category "adolescence" reflects a complex web of ongoing exchanges between social structures and representations. More broadly, these works illustrate how the phases of life can be studied by way of demographic patterns (fertility, mortality, household size, etc.), economic modes of production (e.g., agrarian, proto-industrial, advanced industrial), youth groups, cultural practices and artifacts (e.g., games and festivals, statues, painting and drawings), and other representations (e.g., magazine and newspaper articles, published sermons, conduct-of-life books). Such evidence has revealed much about the opportunities and limitations that come with "adolescence" at different points in history. Chiefly, there has never been one, monolithic "adolescence" because of the diverse circumstances of young people.

Moreover, these same types of evidence and research strategies have also been used to study childhood, adulthood, old age, and, to a lesser extent, middle adulthood. Taken as a whole, these studies show that all of the phases of life are in constant flux as they respond to social change. At any point in history, there are multiple "versions" of each phase of life, and representations about life phases (e.g., in the media) interact with people's actual experiences in complex ways, sometimes depicting reality, sometimes expressing warranted and unwarranted anxieties, and sometimes expressing beliefs that become reality. Each person's life course is thus a pathway of socially established categories (fetus, infant, toddler, young child, etc.), but how each category is experienced by the person greatly depends on her or his social location and place in history.

GENERATIONS, COHORTS, AND THE CHANGING LIFE COURSE

Such works of social history are not without their limits. Empiricists may not be completely satisfied with such accounts as they often lack the temporal precision that behavioral scientists expect. For example, reading Gillis, one might wonder when modernization actually began in Britain, or in Germany, or in France. And when did European youth groups begin to realign into class-based groups? And reading Kett, one might wonder when adults shifted from urging independence and life skills to urging physical vitality and vocational development. If social history is ideal for exploring the myriad sources that illuminate the life course of the past, it is less effective in quantifying the patterns that become evident. The social scientist may well seek greater precision in characterizing historical changes and in measuring how these changes affect the macro features of the life course.

Empiricism also requires the possibility of replication (discussed in Chapter 2). A scientific truth must be subject to "rediscovery" by any interested person who repeats a study's procedures. And yet, it is the very richness of social historical studies that renders replication nearly impossible. However detailed such works may be, the reader must trust that the authors have collated and synthesized their data in a valid and reliable manner. For empiricists interested in how the phases of the life course have changed through history, the issue then becomes whether there are methodologies that can provide enhanced precision and the possibility of replication. In fact, two strategies, the study of generations and the study of cohorts, have been used.

Generations and Generational Analysis

In Chapter 1, we noted that sociologists such as Karl Mannheim urged studying social change and biography with special emphasis on the generation, which was defined as a group of people who are roughly similar in age and who share a defining event. Although social historians view "adolescence" at different points in history (e.g., early industrialization in the United States, or the movement of youth into cities in the early nineteenth century), the timing of these "events" is often not clearly delineated. Perhaps, though, the sociologist can identify homogeneous groups of youth (generations) and link their distinctive features with historical circumstances. For example, what social and economic forces created "The Greatest Generation," or "the Baby Boomers," or "Generation X," and how do these generations differ from one another? How has Generation X affected society? Is there a "Generation Y" and, if so, what are its defining features? While such questions certainly seem legitimate, they are, in fact, very difficult to answer with any precision.

To begin, we must first revisit the definition of "generation," which unfortunately has assumed many meanings, as Duane Alwin and Ryan McCammon have observed.[8] Most commonly, "generation" refers to stages of lineal descent in a family (e.g., great-grandparents, grandparents, parents, children, and their children). "Generation" is also sometimes used to refer to those people born at roughly the same time in history. Because such people grow up together, they experience similar social and economic conditions. Mannheim, however, acknowledged that generations are actually comprised of very diverse people. Indeed, to capture this diversity, he proposed the "generational unit," which refers to a subgroup of the generation defined by their distinct reaction to historical events. Thus, the Vietnam War caused some young people to hate war and others to view it as a necessary evil. Each such group constitutes a generational unit, and collectively these units and their ongoing interactions, whether in harmony or in conflict, constitute a generation and its experiences. Mannheim thought that listening to the diverse voices of generational units was critical to understanding social change and biography.

Yet another meaning of the concept of generations is associated with the writings of the Spanish philosopher José Ortega y Gasset (1883–1955), who emphasized the central identity of a generation and its "vital force" in changing society.[9] Although he acknowledged that each generation is comprised of diverse people, Ortega nonetheless viewed generations as having a distinct character, a central identity. Because his central concern was how history changes, he was interested in how this distinct character empowered a generation to change society. This emphasis on the singular, distinct identity of a given generation has influenced contemporary meanings of the concept.

Alwin and McCammon propose marking a special sense of generations with a capital *G,* as in *Generations.* In this sense, Generations refer to a group of people who are similar in age, who share common historical experiences, who develop a unique subculture and/or consciousness, and who come to view themselves as a unique group in society because they differ from earlier groups. This definition conveys what most contemporary social scientists mean when they refer to the concept. Quite commonly, Generations are thought to be defined by the historical experiences of their youthful years, extending from adolescence to early adulthood. For example, the "Greatest Generation" experienced both the Depression of the 1930s and then World War II in their youth, and these experiences are thought to have had enduring effects on their subculture and self-awareness. Table 3.1 lists a few commonly acknowledged Generations of American life, their unique historical experiences, and their roughly defined place in history.

Behind the concept of the Generation is an implicit theory of human development: the experiences of youth have lifelong consequences for a person's identity (sometimes called the "impressionable years hypothesis"). We encountered this idea in Chapter One with Erik Erikson's psychosocial model. Erikson believed that adolescence was a period of identity formation and thus that social experiences during this life phase have lasting implications throughout life. Norman Ryder casts the same idea in a sociological light, noting that "the potential for change is concentrated in . . . young adults who are old enough to participate directly in the movements impelled by change, but not old enough to have committed to an occupation, a residence, a family, or procreation, or a way of life."[10] Thus, Erikson and Ryder both argue in favor of the "impressionable years hypothesis," Erikson because his model of human development holds that adolescents are psychologically malleable and Ryder because youth are old enough to experience the full impact of social change, but not old enough to have previously shaped their identities by way of adult role commitments.

Table 3.1

COMMONLY ACKNOWLEDGED GENERATIONS IN AMERICAN HISTORY

Years of birth	Cohort name	Became young adults (16–30)	Key events at that time	Ages in census year:										
				1900	'10	'20	'30	'40	'50	'60	'70	'80	'90	2000
1976–1985	Millennial Generation	1992–2015	The Information Era: economic growth and global politics											16–24
1966–1975	Gen X	1982–2005	The Reagan Era: economic polarization, political conservatism										16–24	25–30
1956–1965	Late Baby Boomers	1972–1995	The Watergate Era: economic recession, employment restructuring									16–24	25–30	
1946–1955	Late Baby Boomers	1962–1985	The Hippies: social movements, campus revolts								16–24	25–30		
1936–1945	Early Baby Boomers	1952–1975	The Baby Boom and the Cold War / McCarthy Era: family and conformity							16–24	25–30			
1926–1935	Early Baby Boomers	1942–1965	The Baby Boom and the Cold War / McCarthy Era: family conformity						16–24	25–30				
1916–1925	Children of the Great Depression	1932–1955	Hard Times: economic depression and World War II					16–24	25–30					
1906–1915	Children of the Great Depression	1922–1945	Hard Times: economic depression World War II				16–24	25–30						

The concept of the Generation is commonplace in social commentary and literature. Indeed, literature seems especially well-suited to explore the subculture and self-awareness that defines a Generation—as one finds, for example, in the memorable works of the Beat Generation, actually a generational unit comprised of a group of artists active in the late 1940s and through the 1950s and sharing a vision of American society. Iconic works include, for example, Jack Kerouac's novel *On the Road*—typed on a single roll of paper, which sold for $2.4 million in 2001—and William Burroughs's novel *Naked Lunch*. These and related writings captured the "beatniks'" struggles of Generational identity and struggles with the rest of society. Consider Allen Ginsberg's famous lines from his 1956 poem *Howl*:

> I saw the best minds of my generation destroyed by madness,
> starving hysterical naked,
> dragging themselves through the negro streets at dawn looking
> for an angry fix,
> angelheaded hipsters burning for the ancient heavenly connec-
> tion to the starry dynamo in the machinery of night. . . . [11]

Among other things, Ginsburg describes his generational unit's quest for enchantment and ideological freedom, an ultimately futile quest in a society dominated by materialism and conformism. As many reviewers noted at the time that *Howl* was published (and was causing considerable commotion), these famous lines capture the essence of their self-understanding. And, as if to set the beatniks apart from other generational units and age groups in society, many of their own age-mates looked on with disgust and scorn. One commentator, writing in *Life* magazine, described the beatniks as "talkers, loafers, passive little con men, lonely eccentrics, mom-haters, cop-haters, exhibitionists with abused smiles and second mortgages on a bongo drum."[12] Apparently, he didn't like them. But it was precisely such statements that helped to cement the beatniks' Generational identity.

While various Generations and generational units have captured the public and the artistic imagination, the concept's scientific value has been minimal, chiefly because a Generation's boundaries cannot be located with empirical precision. The unique historical experiences of a Generation are thought to lead to a unique culture and/or consciousness. And yet it is very difficult to determine who participates in a subculture or who shares a special self-awareness. Consistent with Mannheim's idea of the generational unit, Generations are not monolithic entities and, in fact, numerous meaningful subgroups can be identified within any Generation. In a society as diverse as the United States, a group defined simply by age and historical experience is not likely to be homogeneous.

These difficulties are brought into sharp relief by considering the simplified example of "Generation X." The example is "simplified" because discussions of Generation X are inconsistent with Mannheim's emphasis on the diversity of generational units, emphasizing instead the characteristics that define what it means to be a member of Generation X. Nevertheless, the popular press discusses Generation X with great frequency. A recent search of the LexisNexis database to determine how many times "Generation X" appeared in major newspapers between 2002 and 2003 stopped after the first thousand references. In contrast, a recent search of the ISI Web of Science database, covering 1980 to 2004, revealed not a single scientific article on Generation X in a major social science journal. (Such an alarming discrepancy certainly recalls Kett's warning that representations of youth in newspapers may have very little to do with what is actually known about them!)

But the discrepancy reflects the empirical problem with the concept of Generations. Who, exactly, belongs to Generation X? An informal review of sources finds that Generation X is said to begin with people born anywhere from 1961 to "the mid-1960s"; similarly, the same sources have Generation X ending with people born as late as 1975—or 1976, or 1977, or 1978, or 1979, or 1980. The many combinations of beginning and start dates make any agreed-upon definition difficult, if not impossible. Moreover, even if Generation X could be defined precisely as an age group, there would still be great diversity within its ranks. Typically, "X'ers" are thought to be characterized by cynicism, sarcasm, hopelessness, and frustration. Obviously, not everyone born between, for example, 1965 and 1977 could be characterized in this way. Indeed, differences among people are a matter of degree: *how much* cynicism would a person born in, say, 1970 have to display to be considered a member of Generation X? What about people who are highly cynical but nonetheless are not sarcastic? These questions are difficult to answer in a scientifically rigorous way.

To explore the example further: suppose that cynicism were measurable on a scale from 1 (low) to 10 (high). Suppose further that the agreed-upon rules for membership in Generation X are that a person must (1) be an American born between 1965 and 1977 and (2) have a value of 8 or higher on the cynicism scale. These rules imply that someone born in 1970 with a cynicism score of 7 is qualitatively distinct from someone else born in 1970 with a cynicism score of 8. They also imply that someone born on January 1st of 1965 with a cynicism score of 8 is qualitatively different from someone else born on December 31st of 1964 with a cynicism score of 9. Either case seems unlikely to be true. Moreover, both cases illustrate an important problem with the study of Generations: although membership in a Generation is thought to mark a person as qualitatively distinct from others within the same society (in subculture and in consciousness), the lines that mark the boundaries of a Generation (concerning year of birth and Generational subgroup) are fuzzy. Thus, Generations are difficult to use to locate people's lives in history with any empirical precision.

Cohorts and Cohort Analysis

A second approach to linking people's lives with historical change is the *cohort*, which refers to a group of people who experience the same event or condition within the same time interval. Thus, a "birth cohort" refers to a group of people born within a specified duration of time, almost always a calendar year. Accordingly, one could describe all of the people born in 1900 as the "birth cohort of 1900." Or "the birth cohorts of the twentieth century" refers to one hundred distinct groups of people—each group born in a single year of the twentieth century. Birth cohorts clearly link people's lives with history because every member of a birth cohort encounters the same society-wide conditions and events at the same age (give or take about eleven months). For example, as noted when discussing Glen Elder's studies of the Great Depression, the birth cohorts of 1928–29 experienced the Great Depression as children, while the birth cohorts from the early 1920s experienced the same events as older children and adolescents. His essential point was that experiencing the Great Depression at these different ages had lifelong implications.

Matilda White Riley developed a conceptual model that helps greatly when thinking about cohorts.[13] Her core insight was that birth cohorts represent strata (plural for *stratum*, meaning a distinct layer or, in this case, a distinct group) in society and as these strata age they both change and are changed by social forces. From this core insight, several interesting propositions follow. For our purposes, two are of special interest.

1. Cohort Flow and Social Change.
Birth cohorts can be used to study social change in ways similar to what Mannheim proposed with respect to generations: as each birth cohort gets older and passes through the social system they are able to effect some degree of change. If Mannheim's model of generational change was somewhat cataclysmic, particularly in the context of the Sixties Generation and their social activism, the cohort-flow model envisions a relatively measured rate of change. For example, Alice Rossi studied women who attended the National Women's Conference in 1977 and found that the participants differed in important ways according to age strata (i.e., birth cohorts).[14] The pioneers of the feminist movement (attendees from cohorts born earliest in the twentieth century) were often characterized by anger directed toward social and political inequalities. These women typically focused on, for example, gender inequality in the

workplace. The second cohort of women (i.e., those from birth cohorts born after the pioneers' birth years) benefited from new freedoms attained by the first group and worked within the system to expand their equality. The final cohort (the youngest women at the conference) was most likely to take political and economic freedoms for granted, but reacted to inequalities with the same anger that was observed in the first cohort. This last group of women was also most likely to strive for sexual freedoms, which had inspired relatively little political action among early feminists. Thus, successive cohorts of women "collaborated" to win first basic and then more broadly defined forms of equality.

Rossi's study is revealing but atypical. Cohort studies tend to focus on how differing social circumstances shape the lives of age groups differently. Most birth cohort studies have a macro focus, seeking to understand how attributes of the life course have changed over appreciable spans of time or distance. Cohort analyses have commonly focused on basic demographic information (e.g., number of people in a household, age of first birth, age of marriage, age of death), descriptions of achievement (e.g., years of education, job title), and health patterns (e.g., age of puberty, mortality due to virtually any disease state). Thus, birth-cohort studies describe basic changes in the life phases, such as how the age of first marriage is changing, how levels of education are changing through time, and how the causes of mortality have changed.

An example of the use of birth cohorts in the study of macro features of the life course can be found in David Featherman and Robert Hauser's 1978 study *Opportunity and Change*.[15] Sociologists have long appreciated that the father's education and occupational prestige positively predict the son's education and, in turn, the son's first and subsequent jobs. That is, as the father's education and occupational prestige increase, the son's educational attainment and the statuses of first and subsequent jobs increase. In studies of American men at mid-twentieth century, the pattern was especially striking for professional men (e.g., fathers who were doctors begot sons who were doctors) and farm laborers (i.e., fathers who worked on a farm that they did not own begot sons who worked on a farm that they did not own). (The discussion focuses on men because, historically, most research in this area focused on them. As women entered the workplace, researchers found that many of the same ideas applied to them, at least to some degree.)

This basic idea—that the father's achievements predict the son's achievements—is referred to as an *ascriptive process,* meaning that a son's achievements are determined by his father's social status. Notice that such a model reflects a micro life course orientation because it focuses on sequences of men's educational and work roles (both between father and son and throughout the son's early adulthood) and the mechanisms underlying these sequences. Of course, to the extent that people would prefer that a son's achievements be based on his merits (i.e., as in a meritocracy), this ascriptive process is troubling.

Featherman and Hauser shifted the focus of this model to the macro perspective, asking how the relationship between father's achievement and son's achievement has changed through history. For example, given that increases in the father's education lead to increases in the son's education, is the magnitude of this effect constant through historical time? To answer this question, the authors examined the model for successive birth cohorts, recorded how much of an effect a father's education had on his son's education in each cohort, and then examined the pattern of this effect through historical time.

Why would the link between fathers' and sons' education change through time? The authors draw on "the thesis of industrialism," which holds that, among other things, modernizing societies shift from ascription to merit. (Indeed, this shift is commonly thought to coincide with the shift from Gemeinschaft's particularism to Gesellschaft's universalism, discussed in Chapter 1.) Ascription implies that the son's education will reflect the family that he comes from, based on its standing in the community, resources, race, and kinship ties. For example, virtually all young men who attended college in eighteenth-century America came from families of substantial means and reputations. Meritocracy implies that a son's (or, for that matter, a daughter's) education will be based on his relevant merits, presumably his intelligence and motivations. The family of origin becomes largely irrelevant, and educational achievements and attainment come to be linked with how well a person is actually suited to schooling. Industrialization, and modernization more generally, are thought to promote meritocracy because modern societies allocate their resources (e.g., educational opportunities) based on merit. These considerations led Featherman and Hauser to state a series of specific hypotheses or expectations. One is especially relevant for our purposes: "The more industrialized a society, the smaller the influence of parental status [including the father's education] on [the son's] educational attainment."[16]

Featherman and Hauser drew upon a nationally representative sample of men to test this idea. Using a statistical model called multiple regression, they estimated the size of the effect of a father's education on the son's education (taking into account other family background characteristics) for different birth cohorts in the United States throughout the twentieth century. A small selection of their findings is shown in Table 3.2.

If the "industrialization" hypothesis is true, then we would expect that the size of this effect would decrease through successive birth cohorts. In other words, the effect of a father's education on a son's education would be greater for sons born earlier in the twentieth century than for sons born later in the twentieth century. By implication, as society modernized, education would become decreasingly based on family background (ascription), and increasingly based on merit (achievement). To examine this possibility in detail, Featherman and Hauser estimated the effect of a father's education on total number of years of a son's completed schooling ("Years of Schooling" in the table), years of schooling up to senior year in high school ("Grades 1–12" in the table), and schooling up to five years of college ("College Education" in the table). The birth cohorts and levels of schooling are shown in the first column; the effects of a father's education are shown in the second column.

What does Table 3.2 tell us about the father's and son's educations? As the father's education increased one grade level, the son's education increased .284 (top of second column) of a grade level for sons born from 1907 through 1911. (The number .284 can be interpreted as the amount of change resulting in a son's education from a one-unit change in his father's education. Importantly for our purposes, these values can be compared across birth cohorts to see how they change.)[17] Note that,

Table 3.2

SELECT FINDINGS ON THE LINK BETWEEN
FATHER'S AND SON'S EDUCATION BY BIRTH COHORT

Birth Cohort & Level of Son's Education	Impact of Father's Education
1907–1911	
Years of Schooling	.284
Grades 1–12	.225
College Education	.060
1912–1916	
Years of Schooling	.222
Grades 1–12	.161
College Education	.061
1917–1921	
Years of Schooling	.243
Grades 1–12	.174
College Education	.070
1922–1926	
Years of Schooling	.249
Grades 1–12	.170
College Education	.079
1927–1931	
Years of Schooling	.231
Grades 1–12	.160
College Education	.071
1932–1936	
Years of Schooling	.230
Grades 1–12	.146
College Education	.084
1937–1941	
Years of Schooling	.208
Grades 1–12	.122
College Education	.086
1942–1946	
Years of Schooling	.219
Grades 1–12	.123
College Education	.097
1947–1951	
Years of Schooling	.174
Grades 1–12	.083
College Education	.092

Adapted from Featherman & Hauser (1978); unstandardized coefficients reported.

at the bottom of the second column, for sons born from 1947 through 1951 the number is .174. Thus, an increase of one grade level for the father has smaller implications for sons born later in the century (from 1947 through 1951). Tracing the corresponding numbers down this column, the effect of a father's education on a son's declines more or less steadily from .284 to .174 for sons born from 1947 through 1951. Thus, Featherman and Hauser's hypothesis finds support. In the course of forty years (i.e., birth cohorts extending from 1907–11 to 1947–51), the effect of a father's education decreased 39 percent (from .284 to .174).

Does this decreasing relevance of the father's education hold for grades of schooling through high school? For the variable Grades 1–12 in Table 3.2, a one-grade increase in the father's education is associated with a .225 increase among sons born from 1907 through 1911, and only a .083 increase for sons born from 1947 through 1951. This is a large decrease (63 percent) and suggests that high-school educations were much less likely to depend on the father's education as modernization progressed. In other words, as high-school educations became common through the early to mid-twentieth century, the father's education became less relevant.

The same may not be said, however, for college education. The effect is .060 for the birth cohorts 1907–11 and .092 for the birth cohorts 1947–51. Thus, the effect of a father's education on a son's college education was small and hardly changed for birth cohorts in the first half of the twentieth century. Taken together, the findings suggest that ascription became much less important for men born later in the century (at least up to 1951), although this change largely applied to grades 1 through 12.

Featherman and Hauser's research is an excellent example of how cohorts are used to study the macro features of the life course. Specifically, their program of research was concerned with how educational pathways and occupational careers changed with industrialization. As a study of macro features of the life course, their scope of analysis is not individual-level data, but rather information gleaned from the aggregation of those data.

The study also reveals, however, a characteristic problem with cohort studies. Cohorts are proxies; they are used because more precise data are unavailable. In Featherman and Hauser's case, industrialization was the hypothesized mechanism of social change that would diminish the effect of a father's education. Successive cohorts served as proxies (or substitutes) for a wide range of measures that could have actually gauged the level of industrialization and modernization in the society. The assumption is that successive cohorts experienced increasing industrialization. Even if this assumption is reasonable, there were many other changes during this period of time, suggesting that we are far from understanding exactly why the effect of a father's education did indeed diminish.

In any event, if good measures of industrialization were available, the cohorts might not have been necessary at all. In fact, for studies interested in the processes that link social change to the life course, the use of cohorts is a gloss on reality, albeit a necessary one. (Featherman and Hauser also lacked data bearing on achievement. That is, strictly speaking, they were able to show that ascriptive processes became less important, but they were not able to show that achievement processes became more important.)

As noted, *cohorts* refer to groups of people who experience the same event or condition within the same time interval, with the "event" usually referring to birth and the "time interval" usually referring to a calendar year. But the event and time interval could refer to many interesting groups of people with distinctive life course patterns. For example, a cohort may be defined as the graduating high-school seniors of 2001, in which case the event is graduation from high school and the interval is the calendar year 2001. Given that some students will repeat a grade or grades, that some students will skip a grade or grades, and that students differ in their year of entry into the school system, a cohort of graduating high school seniors does not map cleanly onto a birth cohort.

An interesting use of this meaning of cohort can be found in research on age of entry into military service during time of war. Glen Elder suggested that older entrants into military service during World War II experienced serious disruptions in their work and family lives.[18] Such men typically had finished their educations and were in the early stages of their occupational careers and marriages. For these men, being drafted into the military disrupted the life course in lasting ways. For example, when these men returned home from war, they often found that their wives and children were estranged from them and that their positions at work were not appropriate for their age but they lacked the work experience for promotions. In contrast, men who entered World War II at an earlier age experienced no such disruptions and, upon returning to civilian life, were actually afforded a social moratorium during which they could acquire more experiences and maturity that, in turn, promoted better decisions about their future lives. This is not an argument about birth cohorts (e.g., a person could be drafted at age eighteen in 1941 or 1945), but rather about age of entry into a system. Thus, cohorts are by no means limited to year of birth and may also refer to age of entry or exit from a social institution or organization.

2. Relations among Cohorts

The preceding discussion considers how cohorts can be used to study social change and the life course. The logic is straightforward: different cohorts have different social experiences, and these different social experiences change the life course, including educational pathways, occupational careers, and family life. There is, however, another way to look at cohorts and their capacity to change the life course that follows from Riley's conceptual model. Age strata (defined by birth cohorts) represent groups in society that may sometimes compete for resources. In such circumstances, cohort size and mobilization can have important implications for life course patterns. Different age groups, or strata, have different needs and interests and the capacity to pursue these interests and needs depends on cohorts' relative sizes.

Two such mechanisms have received considerable attention. Perhaps the best example comes from Richard Easterlin who, in his well-known work *Birth and Fortune* (1980), argues that cohorts can alter biographical patterns because of their relative size.[19] The "Easterlin effect" states that the birth rate of a cohort has lifelong implications for school, work, family, health, and happiness. Specifically, people born in a low-birthrate co-hort will have better experiences in the educational system, se-cure better jobs, have a better family life, and enjoy better health than people born in a high-birthrate cohort. In this in-stance, the focus is a cohort's size relative to other age-groups in the society.

"Age effects" and "cohort effects" must be distinguished to appreciate this argument. Recall that age effects are patterns of change and stability, with age, in the likelihood of a behavior. For example, the likelihood of church attendance decreases in young adulthood, increases with marriage and parenthood in early to mid-adulthood, and increases again in old age. Cohort effects are patterns of change and stability in the likelihood of a behavior because of membership in a given cohort. For exam-ple, the decline of the effect of the father's education on the son's education is a cohort effect.

Age and cohort effects may work in concert. Focusing on criminality, Easterlin would predict that criminality will be lower in a low-birthrate cohort than in a high-birthrate cohort. Simple enough—except that there is also a well-established age effect for criminality, such that likelihood of criminality in-creases through adolescence before declining through young and later adulthood. Thus, according to this age effect, crimi-nality in both low- and high-birthrate cohorts will be highest in young adulthood. And according to Easterlin's cohort effect, young adults in the low-birthrate cohort will be less likely to commit crimes than young adults in the high-birthrate cohort. That is, cohort birthrate changes the likelihood of criminal acts at each age (e.g., twenty year olds) between cohorts (e.g., those born in 1939 versus those born in 1954).

What is the conceptual basis for this cohort effect? Easterlin argues that changes in the birthrate correspond to changes in the number of people entering the labor market roughly twenty years later. (The birthrate and not the number of births is used because the former reflects the proportion of younger to older persons and thus captures the size of the birth cohort relative to the other age groups.) A small birthrate cohort will represent a "smaller supply of workers" who will find it easier to locate well-paying jobs and to advance in their careers. Their ease of success at work translates into further success in their family life. Low-birthrate cohorts are less likely to experience marital dissolution and more likely to have children earlier and more often. In fact, the differences between high- and low-birthrate cohorts are thought to start before entry into work. The high-birthrate cohorts strain the school systems, diminishing the quality of educational experiences. As Gordon colorfully noted in his study of high birthrate cohorts in Romania:

> These poor souls came into a crowded world—crowded by themselves. There was crowding in the maternity wards when they first saw the light of day; there was crowding in the kindergarten classes when they entered the school system. . . . [T]here will be crowding in the universities . . . in the search for jobs and housing . . . and so on until there is crowding in the funeral parlors.[20]

Not surprisingly, differences between such cohorts extend across the life course. Low-birthrate cohorts experience higher, more sharply increasing income trajectories, for example, and fewer and shorter spells of unemployment. Easterlin himself amassed impressive evidence through his studies of American birth cohorts from the twentieth century, showing, for example, that, low-birthrate cohorts of the 1950s married earlier, had children earlier, had more children, and were less likely to experience divorce compared with earlier and later high-birthrate cohorts. Easterlin suggested that American history can be viewed as an ongoing cycle of low- and then high-birthrate cohorts. Small birthrate cohorts will tend to produce large birthrate cohorts, which will tend to produce small birthrate cohorts, and so on. When this happens, the life course patterns of work and family will differ dramatically between parents and their children.

Nevertheless, evidence for the Easterlin hypothesis is mixed. The idea appears to explain some behaviors in some times and places (e.g., fertility between 1945 and 1980 in the United States), but it does not explain a wide range of outcomes in all times and places. The reasons are not fully understood. Clearly, why people marry and have children and make money are complicated matters, and birthrate is but one possible explanation. For example, Easterlin did not appreciate the importance of women's work in aiding the household finances of a large birthrate cohort. Furthermore, the link between birthrate and job competition (within and between cohorts) is complicated by immigration and job growth, which can increase and decrease such competition, respectively. Finally, a strong welfare state can soften the harsh blows experienced by a high-birthrate cohort. Fred Pampel and Elizabeth Peters suggest that the Easterlin effect may only be observed in high-income industrial countries with good control over fertility and relatively weak welfare systems.[21] In the final analysis, then, there is some truth to the Easterlin hypothesis: a cohort's birthrate may affect its prosperity and well-being, but the link is not likely to be as simple as was once argued.

Samuel Preston also focuses on relative cohort size but emphasizes its central role in intercohort cooperation and conflict. As Preston observes,

> In a modern democracy, public decisions are obviously influenced by the power of special-interest groups, and that power is in turn a function of the size of groups, their wealth and the degree to which that size and wealth can be mobilized. . . . In all of these areas, interests of the elderly have gained relative to those of children.[22]

Preston echoes the importance of competition for resources, but focuses on the political arena. He noted a dramatic increase in the relative size of the elderly population and a coinciding decrease in the relative proportion of children in American society. With these changes in cohort sizes came changing fortunes for both the elderly and children. For example, children were more likely to live in poverty and the elderly were less likely to live in poverty. Similarly, suicide rates were down for the elderly and up for children. Preston argued that, in part, the relative cohort sizes and their political power explained these growing differences. Thus, in 1984, per-child federal expenditures on programs for children were 9 percent of per-capita expenditures on the elderly. Preston thus views age-groups as rational actors who use the political arena to achieve their objectives.

As intuitively appealing as this hypothesis may be, the empiricist must once again consider the evidence. As an example, Fred Pampel collected data from eighteen advanced industrialized nations extending from 1959 to 1986.[23] The variables of interest included public expenditures on different age-groups and the percentage of each country's population that was sixty-five years and older (along with some other factors that needed to be taken into account). Pampel's results show that while a large aged population may lead to age inequality in public spending, this is not always the case. In countries with a leftist government and with strong class-based corporatism, increases in the aged population actually leads to *more* spending on children. The author reasons that in such countries, there is a widespread value placed on public expenditures and this value applies to both the elderly and to children. Thus, like the Easterlin effect, Preston's hypothesis has received some empirical support, but, by itself, it cannot account for intercohort differences in the life course. Although both the Easterlin and Preston hypotheses are attractive for their simplicity, they fail to reflect the complexities that surround interrelationships among birth cohorts.

Which Is Best—Social History, Generations, or Cohorts?
In thinking about macro features of the life course in history, it is tempting to ask which mode of analysis is best: social historical, Generational, or cohort analysis? Yet whenever possible, social historians will draw upon cohort and Generational studies, and cohort and Generational studies draw on social historical research, so clearly the three approaches are not mutually exclusive. This "cross-fertilization" undoubtedly reflects the fact that each mode of inquiry has its strengths and weaknesses, suggesting that under ideal circumstances, results from all

three strategies should be juxtaposed to appreciate changes in the life course fully.

Like the "character and society tradition" discussed in Chapter 1, social historical studies are typically epochal. They seek to understand a period of history, with its tendencies and variability. Given restrictions of available data, such inquiries often focus on changing modes of economic production and cultural practices, and how these affect the life phases and transitions among them. Such studies often lack empirical precision, however, and are not typically concerned with how individual people experience social changes in their lives.

Generations are a useful way to explore the special subcultures and self-awareness of age-groups in history. They are, however, deficient at precisely locating people in history. Generations encourage us to think about the experiences of different age-groups, including their struggles as they reconcile the old and new, and their triumphs and successes as they find their way in society. Social and political commentary, literature, music, film, and conjecture are the lifeblood of a Generational analysis. Of the beatniks, the Generational analyst might consider how and why they turned away from their fathers' occupational, financial, and educational achievements, and what were the feelings that accompanied this rejection. And yet such an analysis cannot be precise in its terms and probably cannot be replicated. As noted in Chapter 1, for example, however resonating Keniston's analysis of the Sixties Generation may be, one is hard-pressed to tell how true the account actually is.

Cohorts have the reverse problem. They can precisely locate people in history, but they frequently lead to a skeletal view of age-groups. Cohorts encourage us to find quantifiable data that describes a historical period, but these data typically fall short of the richness of a social historical or Generational account. Thus, a cohort analysis might use a statistical model to document the relationship between the father's occupational prestige score and the son's educational achievement, but we learn nothing about the son's accomplishments and disappointments, about his feelings and interpretive modes. We do, however, learn a great deal that is precise and subject to replication. The difference in the richness of Generational analyses and precision of cohort studies is the difference between Jack Kerouac's *On the Road* and a table showing the number of unmarried writers living with their mothers in the 1950s by birth cohort. Such differences are incommensurable, suggesting that both cohort and Generational analyses are needed to understand macro features of the life course.

Cross-National Comparisons and Variability in the Life Course

Although studies of the biography at different points in history are numerous, cross-national, empirical studies of the life course are also of great value. Of course, a program of research may be both historical *and* cross-national, but such studies are perhaps the least frequent types of macro studies of the life course (notable exceptions include, for example, Gillis's comparative study of adolescents in English and German towns, and Michael Mitterauer's social history of adolescence, which covers a wide range of sources from Middle Europe[24]).

In part, the infrequency of cross-national studies reflects the well-appreciated difficulties that surround creating datasets that include comparable information from different countries. For example, countries often differ in their distributions of income across social classes, which makes comparisons of high-income people in different countries difficult. What are the minimum annual incomes of "rich" people in the United States, Canada, Britain, France, and Germany? The question is complicated by taxation policies, transfer payments that influence people's wealth, and the many forms that wealth takes (e.g., savings, government retirement accounts, home ownership). Thus, even determining a seemingly simple question like who qualifies as "wealthy" in different countries would be problematic and contentious.

In general, cross-national comparisons are difficult because countries often differ in many ways. Understanding and accommodating such differences typically requires a high level of expertise on the part of the investigator, including facility with different languages, knowledge of national histories, and awareness of the intricate details of societies' institutions. Such differences also make focusing on just one or two variables hazardous. For example, studies suggest that German youth (when compared with American or British youth) leave school and enter the labor market with little uncertainty as to the job or jobs that they can fill. Yet such studies typically ignore the possibility that the high degree of structure easing this transition is part of the same labor market inflexibility that may be associated with higher unemployment. Every society is complex, and comparisons between societies must be sensitive to nuance.

Cross-national comparisons are also a relatively recent practice. Strategic comparisons emerged in the years since the end of World War II, when nation-states began regulating aspects of the life course (e.g., retirement provisions). (Prior to that time, nation-states were largely concerned with territorial and macro-economic issues.) As Lutz Leisering has noted, it is only after decades of sustained growth in social legislation and bureaucracies following World War II that the effects of national governments on the life course become apparent.[25]

Nevertheless, cross-national comparisons have generated many insights into and hypotheses about how and why the life course is structured in different ways in different places. The cross-national study of the life course is based on two major suppositions. First, nations differ in their laws, policies, and institutions, and these structural differences produce different life courses. Second, the life course became increasing "chronologized" with modernization, meaning that age became increasingly important as a criterion in organizing the biography.[26] In other words, the age-grading of the biography intensifies with modernization. With respect to the state, Karl Ulrich Mayer has observed that the modern state pervades almost every aspect of social life, stipulating obligations and limitations with respect to the family, schooling, and work.[27] Through their many policies, regulations, and laws, states shape the timing and quality of transitions among the family, school, and work domains as well as their integration. For example, states might stipulate a minimum amount of schooling and a minimum age of entry into the labor force. Through tax incentives and other transfer payments, states also affect marriage rates, the number of children, age of retirement, ease of migration to another country, and so on.

For Mayer, the expansion of nation-states' interests to the regulation of the biography has led to the "periodization" or "standardization" of the life course. These terms both capture essentially the same idea: the timing of the life course's phases and transitions has become more predictable. For example, level of education (i.e., age of school completion) was highly variable in America at the time of the Revolutionary War. And now, as James Rosenbaum notes in *Beyond College for All,* a high-school education is exceedingly common and postsecondary educational experiences typically fall into a few expected paths (e.g., university, vocational-technical).[28]

The nation-state has also been a force behind the institutionalization of the life course. *Institutionalization* refers to how or how much social institutions and organizations structure the life course. For example, while we take for granted that the age of students is closely connected with grade level (e.g., most American first graders are five years old, give or take six months), such was not always the case. In colonial America, grade level had little to do with age, with students of very diverse ages at every level of the educational system. This lack of age-grading reflected the fact that most school-aged children had substantial obligations at home and attended school only when possible. As the historian Harvey Graff notes, school attendance for most youth was highly irregular and the number of students in the classroom might vary on an hourly basis.[29] Such discrepancies created "very early" and "very late" students, the likes of which are seldom found today. For example, Graff reports of a boy who enrolled at Yale University at age eleven, "To his father, he was now a problem child . . . in no way equipped to be much of anything."[30] In truth, though, there has always been a great deal of ambivalence about "off-time" youth in the American context, with precociousness being regarded as a nuisance in some cases and yet expected in the cases of great people (such as Abraham Lincoln). And sometimes the two attitudes collide, as found in the case of Mozart, both celebrated prodigy and pain-in-the-ass.

To ask how differences among nation-states alter the life course is to ask how the biography changes within different institutional structures. While empirical research does not yet provide a definitive answer, Mayer offers a set of intriguing hypotheses that interrelate political economies with life courses. These are shown in Table 3.3. The central premise is that different political economies give rise to different life course patterns because of their distinct educational systems, labor markets, and policies regarding transfer payments (i.e., taxation and other forms of the redistribution of wealth).

For example, a liberal market society such as the United States has, compared to the other political economies, a less stratified school system. Everyone attends elementary and secondary schools, and a substantial percentage of youth receive at least some college education. The United States, however, has poorly developed vocational and workforce training. Experiences in high school and at the university rarely prepare students for the workplace, and relatively few youth attend vocational schools. There is also a high level of flexibility in the movement of workers among jobs because firms typically do not require specific prior training of the workers they hire. The American political economy also has a low level of transfer payments and supports for families, meaning that, for example, the government provides relatively little assistance to students and young families.

What are the implications of these structural features for

Table 3.3

HYPOTHESES INTERRELATING LIFE COURSE REGIMES
AND VARIATIONS IN POLITICAL ECONOMIES

	Liberal Market	Conservative Welfare	Social Democratic
Leaving Home	Early, high variance	Medium, high variance	Early, low variance
Age Leaving School/Training	Medium homogeneous	High stratified	Medium
Labor Market Entry	Early, stop-gap, low skill	Late, integrated, high skill	Early, integrated
Firm Shifts	High	Low	Low
Occupational Shifts	High	Low	High
Income Trajectories	Flat, high variance	Progressive, low variance	Flat, low variance
Careers of Women	High participation, continuous	Medium participation, interrupted	High participation, continuous
Family	Unstable	Stable	Stable
Retirement	High variance	Low variance, early	Low variance, late

the life course in America? As shown in Table 3.3, a lack of vocational training opportunities dictates that many youth leave
home early and enter the labor market immediately following
high school, while other youth may remain in the home of
their parents until the completion of college or until they are
securely employed. This creates a high degree of variability in
when youth leave home. Youth who start working typically
have few, if any, job-specific skills, and their early employment
histories are marked by frequent job changes and spells of unemployment as they attempt to find the "right job." Consequently, shifts between firms and even between occupations are
not uncommon and income trajectories of young workers are
highly variable. Many youth remain at roughly their initial income level, while many other youth experience marked decreases or increases in their income. Women are likely to work
but, because of poor supports for the family, they remain in the
workplace during their child-bearing years with few and short
interruptions. Also because of poor family supports, families
are unstable. Finally, the combination of wide variance in income and low levels of assistance to the elderly makes the age
of retirement highly variable. Differences in the age of retirement can be striking and it is not uncommon to find retirees in
their mid-fifties and workers in their early seventies.

Life course regimes in other politico-economic systems are
markedly different. Germany exemplifies a conservative welfare
state, which has a stratified school system, good training for the
workplace, rigidly segregated labor markets, extensive transfer
payments, and relatively generous family supports. The German educational system is stratified because students are assigned to different types of schools early in life based on their

academic aptitude. Education is free, and young adults still in school often receive assistance from the government or mandatory assistance from their parents. Yet, because education is directly connected to specific occupations (what Americans call "vocational training"), very few youth leave home early and most enter their first jobs with considerable skills. Because of the extensive required training and strong labor unions, there is subsequently little movement between firms and between occupations. Income tends to increase over time and the German system does not produce the extremes of wealth and poverty found in the American system. Because of family supports, women leave the workplace with the birth of their children, often with the guarantee of their job when they return, and families tend to be more stable. Finally, because of strong labor unions and high levels of transfer payment, many workers retire at roughly the same age, which is, by American standards, early.

Social democratic welfare states, such as Sweden, produce still different life course patterns. The school systems are not stratified, but provide work-related skills. Transfer payments are high, as the government provides extensive assistance to young people, families, and the elderly. Although youth tend to leave school early and enter the labor market with skills, income remains fairly flat and many people earn a similar annual income. Women are typically gainfully employed and, because of generous assistance with childcare, their employment histories are continuous. Because of this and other family supports, families are relatively stable. Most people retire at roughly the same age, although this is later than in Germany.

As hypotheses, the patterns described in Table 3.3 are expectations rather than facts, and the present discussion of them has been highly simplified. Evidence of such cross-national variation in the life course will come from detailed comparisons of specific aspects of the life course in different countries. Nevertheless, what is especially striking is how malleable the life course is. Young adults in the United States appear to accept the transition to work as a period of uncertainty that may involve movement between firms and even occupations, and geographic mobility as a natural or "taken for granted" part of the life course. Such is not necessarily the case, though, as the experience in Germany is radically different, with young adults receiving extensive training for work (including on-the-job experiences).

At first glance, the life course pattern of conservative welfare states may seem advantageous when compared with that of the liberal free-market system. Yet caution must be exercised, given that such political-economic systems tend to differ in a myriad of ways. For example, the German system reduces the uncertainty during the transition to work and during the transition into retirement. And yet the German system also generates less wealth, tends to have greater unemployment among young people, tends to keep most people's incomes at a similar level, and is associated with a relatively high rate of taxation. Thus, with respect to the transition to work, American youth face relatively greater uncertainty about what type of job they will have, while German youth face relatively more uncertainty about whether their specific job will actually be available. While each political-economic system has its strengths and weaknesses, the key point is that the basic contours of the biography, including one's education, work, and family, are powerfully shaped by political and economic arrangements that are unique to nations and hard to appreciate without a cross-national view.

MASTER TRENDS IN SOCIAL CHANGE AND THE LIFE COURSE

While historical study of the life course is challenging and cross-national studies are relatively new, macro studies still suggest a number of long-term trends in the timing and sequencing of roles and in the phases that make up the life course. At first glance, the hypotheses offered by these studies may seem like a potpourri, but there is a common theme uniting many of them: the life course has fragmented across social strata such that different groups—defined by combinations of social class, gender, and race/ethnicity—experience distinctly different life course patterns. That is, there are now a growing number of "life courses" in society.

The Destruction and Emergence of Life Phases

Perhaps the most dramatic claims made about the changing life course refer to the emergence of new phases of life, in much the way that Arie's argued that adolescence "was invented" as early as the sixteenth century. Such claims are dramatic because the phases of life are the skeletal system of the biography, and so claims that old phases have been destroyed or new ones created have major implications for the study of lives.

For example, Phyllis Moen argues that societal changes have created a phase of life called "midcourse," which roughly covers ages fifty to seventy.[31] As is characteristic of life course analysis, Moen begins with changes in society and asks how they have affected biographical patterns. She notes several changes. First, the traditional contract between workers and employers (i.e., loyalty to the company in return for lifelong employment) has given way to more flexible arrangements which have, in turn, led many older adults to early retirement or a high risk of being laid off. Second, retirement benefits are a source of ambiguity and anxiety for many workers. Unlike systems involving "defined benefits," where the worker is entitled to a fixed level of benefits in retirement based on each year of employment, the American system relies on "defined contributions," meaning that retirement benefits depend on lifelong deposits into the system. Many workers find this system confusing and are unclear whether their contributions will be sufficient for their post-employment years. The problem is compounded by another trend, the aging of the population. As more people live longer, uncertainty over the solvency of the Social Security system increases.

Moen argues that these changes have introduced a new phase of life characterized by great variability in what people do after retirement. As Moen notes, "midcourse"

> connotes the period in which individuals begin to think about, plan for, and actually disengage from their primary career occupations and the raising of children, launch second or third careers, develop new identities . . . and establish new patterns of [relationships].[32]

Thus, midcourse is a marked contrast to the post-retirement period of the life course in prior decades, when older people were likely to disengage from paid work completely and were not likely to develop new identities.

A new life phase has also been suggested during the transition to adulthood. For many decades, scholars held that entry into adulthood was delineated by five transition markers: completing school, leaving home, beginning one's career, marrying, and becoming a parent. By assuming these roles, youth were thought to relinquish the hallmarks of adolescence, including dependency on parents, "immature" behaviors that reflect experimentation with roles, and indecision about one's identity. In turn, the newly acquired adult roles brought with them strong expectations for "adult" behaviors. Indeed, most adults at mid–twentieth century held expectations about the timing of these transitions and about the inappropriateness of being "off-time." Based on these five criteria, however, the percentage of people in their twenties and thirties who would qualify as adults has decreased significantly in recent decades. As Frank Furstenberg and colleagues have shown, a considerable segment of the population in recent decades has seen the extension of education into the late twenties and early thirties and a postponement of family formation, with many young people remaining single and childless well into their thirties, if not later.[33] At the turn of the new century, most adults do hold expectations about the timing of these markers, but they do not view off-time transitions as particularly consequential.

In light of such observations, Jeffery Arnett argues that "emerging adulthood" now constitutes a phase of the life course that extends between adolescence and adulthood.[34] Emerging adulthood is characterized by relative independence from age-normative tasks, by experimentation with social roles, and by little meaningful commitment to one's relationships and organizational involvements. In the context of emerging adulthood, young people identify individualistic indicators of maturity (e.g., independent decision-making) as the new markers of whether one is an adult, and, according to this view, the demographic markers are deemed substantially less important.

If the routine demographic components of the life course have recently been in flux, even more provocative transformations have occurred at the intersection of gender, race, and incarceration. Pettit and Western argue that time spent in jail is now an almost routine phase of the life course for black American males with no college education.[35] They observe that among black men born between 1965 and 1969, 30 percent of those without a college education and 60 percent of high-school dropouts went to prison by 1999. Equally important, incarceration is more common among this group than more positive roles, such as military service, that were once a noticeable feature of the life courses of African American males. These men are typically incarcerated for 30–40 months during the young adult years, which greatly disrupts entry into conventional roles of worker, spouse, and parent. And because of difficulties getting married and securing stable employment, these men are at increased risk of committing additional crimes and ending up back in prison. The net effect of imprisonment, according to Pettit and Western, is to fundamentally differentiate the life course pattern of less well-educated black men from other groups of men.

These examples are consistent with the thesis that the life course is increasingly variable. Midcourse recognizes that the post-retirement period is now one of great heterogeneity in people's work and family lives, in contrast to the relative uniformity of the retirement years in earlier times. Emerging adulthood seems best suited to describe the experiences of young people who attend colleges and universities. Many high-school graduates, students attending vocational schools, and military enlistees do not have the freedoms and choices associated with emerging adulthood. On the other hand, students attending universities often experience a "moratorium" from adult responsibilities during which they can experiment with diverse roles and relationships with little commitment. Emerging adulthood is, in short, a privilege of one segment of society. In stark contrast, "jail time" applies to a life course pattern that is unique to less well-educated black men. Thus, all of these proposed phases raise the possibility of fundamentally different life course patterns for subgroups in society.

There are numerous other examples of proposed life phases. As Harvey Graff has noted, public discourse supports the contradictory ideas that childhood has been destroyed and that childhood is now expanding into what was once adolescence. Likewise, popular works and the press lead us to believe that adolescence is ending too quickly and is also dragging into what was once adulthood. Indeed, as Arie's was arguing that adolescence had been invented and was a highly desirable phase of life, Edgar Friedenberg in his *The Vanishing Adolescent* was arguing that adolescence had been destroyed and that young people were quickly becoming adults.[36] There is much debate about the boundary or boundaries that separate adolescence and young adulthood, as well as other phases of life.

The often contradictory claims raise a difficult question: how do we know when a new life phase has emerged? Part of knowing if the phases of life have changed is having an accurate understanding of the history of the life course. Consider the claim that many young people are now experiencing "emerging adulthood" during which the traditional transition markers (e.g., starting one's career, marriage) no longer matter and people's sense of adulthood reflects independent decision-making and a sense of personal responsibility. Historical considerations suggest that combinations of individual characteristics and transition markers have defined adult status in many times and places and the contemporary United States would not appear exceptional. Alice Schlegel, for example, observes that significant groups who delayed marriage or simply never married have characterized much of history in Europe and America.[37] These groups include both youth who were financially independent but too poor to marry and youth from aristocratic or patrician families without adequate resources to provide for the marriage of all of their sons and daughters. Given that financial independence might begin as early as age fourteen, the transition to adulthood for a considerable number of older youth who did not enter into marriage was ambiguous and likely hinged on personal maturity.

On the other hand, youth fortunate enough to marry were not likely to be accorded adult status immediately by the community without basic indications of maturity. Thus, the use of individualistic criteria to determine adulthood is probably not new, and it seems that myriad combinations of individual attributes (including decision-making and a sense of responsibility) and transition experiences lead to one's feeling unambiguously like an adult. While it is not possible to adjudicate here whether "emerging adulthood" is legitimately a new phase of life, the discussion illustrates how difficult it is to empirically test claims about new life phases and to situate these claims accurately in history. It is, perhaps, precisely because of these difficulties that this is an exciting area of research.

The Predictability of the Life Course
As noted previously, Karl Ulrich Mayer has argued that the nation state has "periodized" or "standardized" the life course. Within nations, social structures (including the workplace and schools, as well as legal and religious institutions) organize age-groupings through the process of institutionalization. The educational system, for example, sorts students into grade levels largely by age. In turn, the age-grading of social institutions makes the life course increasingly predictable. Concomitantly, the diversity of life course patterns in a population decreases. From this perspective, one finds greater predictability of the life course in modern than in premodern times. This greater predictability, it is thought, includes family formation (marriage, parenthood), education (progression through the school system, age of school completion), and career (entry into the workplace, retirement).

That the life course is becoming increasingly predictable is a complex idea. The question cannot be answered with any finality because society is always changing and because there are many ways to think about "predictability." Nevertheless, empirical research has examined select life course patterns in the United States for about the last two hundred years and provides considerable relevant evidence. One of the first studies of this kind was conducted by Peter Uhlenberg, who examined the prevalence of different female life course patterns (for example, spinster versus widowed mother) among cohorts of women born between 1830 and 1920.[38] If the institutionalization hypothesis has merit, one would expect to observe that specific life course patterns become more prevalent with successive birth cohorts. In support of this idea, Uhlenberg observed a convergence on the "typical" female life course pattern, involving survival to age twenty, marriage, having children, and surviving with husband until age fifty-five. Among women born in 1830, about 21 percent experienced this "typical" pattern in contrast to about 57 percent of women born in 1920. He also observed a narrowing of the age range in which women typically married and had children.

Additional evidence comes from the work of historian John Modell. In one study, Modell and colleagues Frank Furstenberg and Theodore Hershberg compared life course patterns for a large sample of whites in Philadelphia in 1880 and for U.S. Census data from 1970.[39] The authors used these data to determine whether transitions in young adulthood (e.g., school completion, marriage, parenthood) were becoming more or less common and whether the ages at which such transitions tend to occur were becoming less variable. If the institutionalization hypothesis is valid, we would expect to see that the transitions become more prevalent with the passage of time and that people tend to experience them within narrower age ranges.

Modell and his colleagues found that between 1880 and 1970 it took 80 percent of both men and women increasingly less time to leave the household of origin, marry, and establish one's own household, among those who experienced these transitions. In other research, Modell observed greater "compactness" among the transition markers between 1900 and 1960 in both the United States and Britain. This reflected the upward movement of the median age of school-leaving and decline in the median age of marriage. These and related pieces of evidence led him to conclude that the transition to adulthood has standardized, as the time it takes most people to pass through a range of transition markers has increasingly constricted since the early nineteenth century.

Nevertheless, the institutionalization hypothesis is not without problems. Most notably, in its "strong version," institutionalization supposes that modernization increases the similarity of the life course for everyone in a population and for all of the phases of life (e.g., transition to adulthood and retirement from work). When stated so broadly, the thesis is problematic. First, the premodern Western life course was not an entirely random affair. Some age-grading was to be found (e.g., in apprenticeships, in family formation, and in inheritance) and there were typically strong local expectations about how people should live their lives. To some "hard-to-quantify" degree, the life course of times past was indeed institutionalized, at least in terms of work and family. Second, the institutionalization hypothesis does not acknowledge that modernization is a complex process that, historically, involves many factors and works in complex ways. As a result, it is difficult to identify exactly what it is about modernization that matters for the life course.

As was noted in Chapter 1, while modernization often refers to urbanization and industrialization, its full meaning is much broader and includes, for example, the increasing use of mechanization, technology, and mass media. But how do such diverse factors specifically promote standardization of the life course? Different facets of modernization affect different parts of the life course at different times. Uhlenberg suggested that the standardization of the female life course was due primarily to improvements in mortality rates due to the management of contagious diseases such as smallpox, and, one might add, to an improved understanding of the birthing process. As fewer young men and women died in young adulthood, life course patterns involving widowhood and remarriage became less common.

Modell's studies of the transition to young adulthood suggests that premodern life was "predictably unpredictable" because death and disease were common and because most families lived at the very margin of agricultural subsistence. Sudden death (not uncommon for a mother during childbirth), maiming and accidents, illness, bad weather, and other devastating events necessitated that families work together as a flexible team. But because of these events and the flexibility of family roles, people tended to have very different life course patterns. As modern society increasingly compensated for these losses through the provision of health care, pensions, insurance, worker's compensation, and other services, individuals became less dependent on their family members for survival. Once freed from the unpredictable demands of the family, young people could enter schools and factories and other places of work, which all tended to create more uniform patterns of the life course. Still other facets of modernization, working at other points in history, contributed to the institutionalization of retirement.

Third and finally, however true the institutionalization hypothesis may be, the life course is also affected by historical changes not closely associated with modernization. Although many well-documented factors complicate long-term trends in specific transition markers (for example, the sex ratio in a given area influences the local likelihood of marriage), contemporary research has emphasized economic conditions as a source of intercohort variations in the transition to adulthood, including the timing of first births, courtship patterns and marriage, educational continuation, and entry into the labor market. For example, Ronald Rindfuss and his colleagues show substantial increases in births among women over thirty and substantial decreases among women under twenty-five between 1973 and 1988.[40] These trends are thought to reflect economic opportunities: women's work has shifted to career-oriented, white-collar jobs, especially in the professions, which are perceived to penalize workers for time spent out of the labor force and to foster preferences for nonfamilial responsibilities and rewards.

With respect to employment, Martina Morris and her colleagues observe that the transition to full-time, year-long jobs took longer for a cohort making the transition in 1980, than for a 1960 cohort.[41] This difference can be explained in part by a greater likelihood in the more recent group of "switching" from nonparticipation to participation in the labor force. Indeed, the number of switches was greater and the duration of years between the first and last switch was longer for the 1980 cohort. Morris and her colleagues speculate that this increased "career turbulence" is due in part to a shift from jobs in manufacturing and government to the retail and business sectors, which pay low wages and have high turnover. The authors note, however, that changes in the industrial distribution cannot explain all of the differences between the two groups. Further changes within sectors, perhaps at the level of the firm, are also relevant.

As the preceding discussion shows, while the institutionalization hypothesis, broadly stated, suggests that people's lives will look increasingly similar with increasing modernization, the effects of social change on the life course are not that simple. In fact, some scholars argue that modernization has promoted both standardization *and variability* in the life course. Martin Kohli, for example, has argued that the life course has become both more standardized by age and less determined by the family and locale.[42] This latter idea is called the "individualization hypothesis," and it actually refers to two interrelated ideas. First, with modernization, people came to view their biographies as personal projects rather than as the result of pressures from the family and community (an idea which we discuss in more detail below). Second, individualization may refer to increasing variability among life course patterns.

Thus, two forces are simultaneously shaping the life course: social institutions promote age-grading, and freedom from one's origins (e.g., birth family, place of birth) promotes diversity. John Modell's research also shows how the transition to adulthood has standardized, yet simultaneously diversified.[43] The standardization is found in the timing of transitions, while the diversity is found in how they are ordered. (The reader may have surmised that this pattern requires that the time it takes to experience all of the markers is "compact." As this compactness lessens, standardization decreases.)

Demographer Dennis Hogan provides empirical evidence for variability in the sequencing of transition markers (i.e., school completion, leaving home, starting work, getting married, and having children) over time.[44] In studying birth cohorts born between 1907 and 1946, he found that the percentage of men experiencing an "intermediate nonnormative" order of transition markers (one characterized by beginning work before school completion or getting married before beginning work but after completing school) increased from about 20 percent in the cohorts born between 1907 and 1912 to about 30 percent for men born in 1951. Likewise, the prevalence of "extreme nonnormative" ordering, such as marriage before school completion, increased from less than 10 percent among cohorts born between 1907 and 1911 to more than 20 percent for cohorts born between 1924 and 1947. This suggests a trend toward individualization of the life course by virtue of the sequencing and overlap of transitions.

Other commentators argue that the process of individualization has become markedly different or accelerated since the late 1960s. For example, Marlis Buchmann's 1989 book *The Script of Modern Life* argues that the highly standardized trajectories of school, work, and family have been "shattered" by several structural and cultural developments since the 1960s, leading to new levels and forms of individualization.[45] Such developments include weakened links between educational certification and occupational status, a decreased "half-life" of occupational training and expertise, heightened family instability, and increased emphasis on flexibility, choice, and impermanence in cultural representations of love and work. People finished school, married, and had children in the 1950s, but the links between school and work subsequently loosened, as did the bonds between husband and wife and between marriage and parenthood.

The new individualization hypothesis is difficult to test by empirical study as it requires a systematic analysis of the timing and sequencing of adult transition markers, based on data from both before and after the mid-1960s. Although no such study has been conducted, considerable evidence suggests that the transition to adulthood has indeed become more variable. New pathways have emerged and greater variability in the sequencing of markers is now observed. This basic impression has been supported by much research that documents loosening couplings among marriage, parenthood, and home leaving, as well as the increased likelihood of returning to higher education after leaving school, transferring from a community college to a university, mixing employment with schooling and parenthood, and deviating from the traditional marriage-coitus-conception sequence. Activities constituting family formation become further complicated by cohabitation, beginning in the 1980s. Thus, the life course may indeed have experienced heightened individualization since the late 1960s, especially in the emergence of new pathways into adult roles.

This section began with the idea that modernization has made the life course more predictable. In fact, this is a very ambitious idea that, stated so starkly, is too simple. It is much more accurate to conclude that diverse historical changes associated with modernization have (1) simultaneously promoted both standardization and diversity in life course patterns; (2) done so by way of different mechanisms; (3) done so for different groups in society; and (4) done so for different parts of the life course. In other words, the life course implications of modernization have several layers of contingency. Still, despite the fact that modern societies promote age-grading (and thus standardization), they also free people from traditions and from their families. This creates diverse sequences and combinations of events. In this latter respect, the life course differentiates across sociodemographic strata. Moreover, (5) other changes not closely associated with modernization have also affected the diversity of life course patterns.

The Life Course as Subjective Project

Finally, all of the changes considered thus far refer to the structure and timing of phases and transitions in the life course. Other scholars have focused on a different phenomenon: how the life course is subjectively experienced. That is, how have people's understandings of their own biographies changed through history? The answer to this question is necessarily speculative because we have so little evidence about how people in premodern western societies understood their lives. Nevertheless, some very interesting ideas have been proposed and they are closely connected to discussions around the predictability of the life course. These ideas suggest that, with modernity, people came to understand their lives increasingly as "projects" with life goals and purposive behavior. In contrast, premodern people tended to view their futures as "givens" determined by their familial circumstances and the traditions of the locale.

In an essay entitled "The Self and the Life Course," John Meyer has argued that the self became institutionalized (i.e., it became a standard, established way of thinking) with modernization in at least two respects.[46] First, through their religious, legal, educational, occupational, and familial institutions, modern societies instill in each person a sense of personal responsibility and autonomy. This individualism is found, for example, in an individual's intentions, motives, ambitions, and plans. Ultimately, each person is expected to live a life that can be explained as orderly, according to which purposes are pursued and goals are achieved to some reasonable degree.

Second, the life course is a social institution and provides a "legitimated résumé" for each person. Fairly early in life, modern people develop a sense of where their educational career is headed, and then they learn about their realistic possibilities in the workplace and family life. That is, the modern person quickly acquires an understanding of the age-graded rules, expectations, and opportunities that will confront them, and the identities (e.g., "college graduate," "electrician," "stay-at-home parent") that will follow. This mapping of one's life is strikingly illustrated by Paul Almond and Michael Apted's documentary series that follows the life of fourteen seven-year-olds in Britain to age forty-nine (*Seven Up!*, *7 Plus Seven*, *21 Up*, and so on through, presently, *49 Up*). While their ensuing lives are filled with both unexpectedly colorful and depressing turns, many of the seven-year-olds in the first film were able to articulate, sometimes broadly and sometimes specifically, their educational, occupational, and familial circumstances they would face as adults.

Because of the relatively clear organization of the life course, modern people feel a heightened sense of their past and future—and they place a premium on the predictability of the future. As Meyer writes,

> The modern system, on a number of dimensions, provides and requires a résumé for each individual. Many of the elements of the résumé are fixed in advance. . . . Most of them are easy to anticipate, given the long chains of sequencing rules. And most of them, once established, are both fixed and important.[47]

This is not to say that the life course, as an institution, dictates our identities. In fact, the other institutional basis of the self, individualism, requires that each person develop a unique sense of personhood, finding meaning and satisfaction in their situation.

Meyer thus claims that the modern self is unique in its dual institutional bases of the life course and individualism (which may seem, at first glance, contradictory or at least conflicting). Is this historically true? The life course has undoubtedly existed throughout Western history, but it has assumed increasingly elaborate forms. Consider the life of a typical male from sixteenth century England, who would have been an agrarian peasant strenuously working on leased land and always living on the margin of subsistence. Such a person received no formal education and began working as part of his family's economic strategy as early in life as possible, perhaps age four. Courtship was probably highly regulated by the community (by way of peer groups and adults) and the prospects of marriage and the establishment of one's own household were not high. In the event of marriage, a steady stream of children likely ensued. Death of the wife at an early age, due to childbirth, infection, contagious disease, or accident, was not uncommon. Indeed, when historians refer to life in premodern times as "nasty, brutish, and short," they have just such a life course pattern in mind. One can see age-grading in this example, but only in a rudimentary sense. Further, a strong sense of individualism (marked by decision-making about one's self) does not appear to be a prominent theme.

In contrast, the modern person is shaped by age-graded expectations from the moment of birth. Child-care books provide timetables for crawling, walking, various stages of talking, and all manner of social interactions with family members and nonrelated adults. These expectations extend into the preschool, which also adds a set of age-graded expectations about behavioral control and cognitive performance. "Slow" children may have "special needs" because of their "delay" and therefore need "special education," while "accelerated" children are, in some sense, "gifted," may skip grades, and are worthy of special admiration. This age-graded logic follows young people through their school years. And, as we have discussed, schooling is followed by the age-graded institutions of the workplace and family life. Thus, Meyer's claim that the age-grading associated with life course is a largely modern institutional force is entirely plausible.

What about the claim that individualism is a modern phenomenon? In other words, do modern people plan their lives and act purposely in ways that most premodern people did not? This is a difficult question, but historical research suggests that people did not commonly view their biography as a purposive project until perhaps the late eighteenth century. According to this line of interpretation, choices concerning life options were not at all typical of premodern people, who typically followed in the footsteps of their parents and lived their lives according to the standards of the village. One of the first major departures from this rule may have been the doctrine of adult baptism espoused by the Anabaptist Church of the early sixteenth century. Prior to that time, the Catholic Church had held that infants could be baptized into Christianity, in accordance with the belief, for example, that infant baptism represented a pledge by the parents to raise the child a Christian. Some early

Protestants, including the Anabaptists, argued that the New Testament provided no scriptural basis for infant baptism and instead taught that each person must freely choose whether to enter the Christian community. This act of deciding something so fundamental as one's religious identity was a clear departure from the long-established tradition that children automatically follow their parents' example and hence assume their religious identity. Perhaps this break with tradition was one of the first major steps toward people interpreting their lives as deliberate projects that involved choices.

In a fascinating study of biographical materials from 1750 to 1920 in the United States, Harvey Graff argues that an "emergent" life course pattern in the late eighteenth century involved choice-making, life-planning, and risk-taking, particularly with respect to education and one's occupational career.[48] Often this new way of thinking about one's life course was inspired by the widely selling autobiography of Benjamin Franklin, who espoused the minute-by-minute planning of one's day in order to attain life goals. After reading Franklin's book in the early 1790s, one young man wrote in his diary:

> from that time I determined to adhere strictly to Reason, Industry, and good Economy, to Always examine both sides, to keep my mind free from prejudice of any kind, always to practice reason and truth.[49]

Thereafter he applied himself vigorously to his profession (schoolmaster) and eventually extended his efforts to also become a storekeeper and city assessor. Graff's review of hundreds of biographical documents suggests that this emphasis on effort, planning, and achievement was new when compared with the ascription and tradition that tended to characterize how people thought about (or did not think about) their lives in premodern times.

These considerations suggest that the life course of the modern self is uniquely shaped by individualism, which leads people to develop plans about their lives, to pursue these plans with purposeful action, and to place great value on the predictability of their futures. A modern person must have a comprehensible past and future (i.e., seeming orderly, purposive, and cohesive to the person and to other people) and yet, within this broad framework, they must "be their own person." These attributes of the self are undoubtedly taken for granted, but evidence suggests that the premodern self was an altogether different beast. Rather, the age-grading and individualism associated with the life course arose from modern institutions.

Nevertheless, these developments are not without their dark side. Consistent with the foregoing, social theorist Anthony Giddens's 1991 book *Modernity and Self-Identity* argues that the modern self is an ongoing, reflexive project.[50] By this, Giddens means that personal identity is not achieved and finalized but rather is continually being created in response to one's social setting. (The word "reflexive" here means that each person "views" his or her self in its social context, and then adjusts his or her identity accordingly.) In modern society, people are constantly thinking of their futures and making adjustments to their identity based on how well their imagined futures "fit" with their past and present experiences.

But, according to Giddens, this process can go awry. First, the "fit" among the past, present, and future selves may be poor, leading a person to view his or her self as lacking in biographical continuity. Given the self's institutional context of individualism and the life course, such a person is filled with anxiety because his or her life no longer "makes sense." For example, a college student works very hard to become an architect. She views her life as cohesive because she has spent many years planning to become an architect and pursuing that goal through her education. And yet, her application to the school of architecture is rejected. (See our discussion of "Anne" in Chapter 4 for an empirical example.) In an institutional context that places a premium on personal agency and strong connections between past and future experiences, this rejection may precipitate a personal crisis, leading her to view her life as a failure, and instilling a sense of doubt about her own self-integrity.

Another threat to the self that arises in this context is apprehension about the future. Ironically, even as modern people increasingly plan for the future and its predictability increases, so too does their apprehension about what the future will bring. Premodern times were "predictably unpredictable," with people being subject to disease, accidents, death, catastrophic weather, and so on. In such circumstances, people held very low expectations about the predictability of the future and hence were not preoccupied with it. To the premodern mind, the future was God's Providence—mysterious, perhaps, but part of a larger, beneficient design that could only be accepted with a prayer, a laugh, a cry, or perhaps a sigh. In contrast, the modern mind plans rationally for the future, but this planning and predictability create a sense of unease that reasonable expectations may not be met. The mood is one of apprehension, reflecting fear that the future will bring unforeseen difficulty, if not calamity.

All of this is, of course, necessarily speculative, since we lack empirical measures of premodern people's sense of self. But these ideas illustrate how life course sociologists develop hypotheses about subjective understandings of the biography on a macro scale (i.e., differences in how people think about their biographies over large periods of time or across geopolitical units like nations). What is particularly intriguing about such an exercise is that it treats self-understanding as a social process that varies according to time and place. People typically think of their identity as something that was constructed "in their mind" through much personal experience and effort. No doubt this is true. But it is also true that the broad framework for the self is societal in its origins and shows variability through time and place.

CONCLUDING REMARKS

Many diverse topics have been considered in this chapter. Some of the major concepts that proved useful in studying the macro features of the life course are summarized in Table 3.4. Actually, all of these concepts and the preceding discussion are united by one theme: *the basic scaffolding of the biography—the life course as a social structure—is socially organized and hence subject to change with historical time and variation across societies.* Each phase of life, including its timing and defining features, is a social construct, as are the transitions among the phases, and perhaps even people's subjective understanding of their lives. As John Meyer observed, each person passes through a biography that is, to a significant degree, a "legitimated résumé" that is already in place and that reflects social circumstances. Does this mean that society determines your life? No. But it does mean

Table 3.4
SELECT MACRO LIFE COURSE CONCEPTS

Macro Concept	Example
Life Phase—reasonably distinct sociocultural category based on age; *age stratum* (plural: *strata*) similarly refers to a rough division of people on the basis of age	Life Phase: infancy, middle childhood, adolescence, etc. Age strata: people under eighteen years of age and people over eighteen of age
Generation—group of people who are similar in age, share common historical experiences, develop a unique subculture and/or consciousness, and come to view themselves as a unique group in society	Greatest Generation; Baby Boomers
Cohort—group of people (1) born during a specified period of time, or (2) experiencing a social transition within a specific time frame	Birth cohort of 1920; people who entered military the military at age twenty; people who finished high school in 1957
Cohort Flow—process of new cohorts entering a system, moving through age strata, and eventually being replaced by succeeding cohorts; also called "cohort replacement"; the same idea has been applied to Generations, as in **Generational Replacement**	Successive cohorts of feminists change the focus of the feminist movement through history.
Easterlin Effect—Hypothesis that people born in a low-birthrate cohort will have better experiences in the educational system, secure better jobs, have a better family life, and enjoy better health than people born in a high-birthrate cohort	Low-birthrate cohorts of the 1950s married, had children earlier, had more children, and were less likely to experience divorce compared with earlier and later high-birthrate cohorts.
Preston Effect—Hypothesis that in democratically governed societies, public decisions are influenced by the power of special interest groups; often, these groups are defined by age strata, resulting in competition between/among them	In 1984, per-child federal expenditures on programs for children were nine percent of per-capita expenditures on the elderly.
Chronologization—Hypothesis that with modernization, age becomes highly salient in the biography	Concepts like "on-time," "off-time," "delayed," and "precocious" enter popular culture.
Periodization—Hypothesis that timing of the life course's phases and transitions has become more predictable with modernization; also called **Standardization**	"Typical" female life course pattern, involing survival to age twenty, marriage, having children, and surviving with husband until age fifty-five became more prevalent between 1830 and 1920.
Institutionalization—1. Hypothesis that social institutions and organizations structure the life course with modernization 2. Ways in which institutions and organizations structure the life course	Grade levels in educational system became associated with chronological age from the eighteen to early twentieth centuries.
Individualization—1. Hypothesis that, with modernization, the importance of the family and locale decreases and the importance of the person increases for the biography 2. Variability in life course patterns	1. Increasing importance of self as a planned project 2. Prevalence of "extreme nonnormative" ordering, such as marriage before school completion, increased from cohorts born 1907–1911 and cohorts born 1924–1947.

that social forces set boundaries to major facets of your biography, including experiences and achievements in school, work, and family, as well as your psychological and physical well-being. Of course, the same society that sets boundaries also provides opportunities.

Exactly what these boundaries and opportunities are and which social forces created them is typically not well understood. Macro life course studies presently offer less in the way of facts and more in the way of hypotheses about social change and the diversity of life course patterns. The job of the macro life course sociologist is to articulate these hypotheses as clearly as possible, to marshal relevant data, and to propose new data collection efforts to test these ideas.

What is especially impressive when considering biographical patterns through history and across countries is the high degree of malleability of the life course. What is considered a "normal" life in one society may be hardly normal at all in other times and places. This insight, in turn, invites us to think about how societies can be reorganized to create new and, in some sense, better biographies. In the American context, a survey of life course patterns raises many questions that call urgently for answers. What about the American system of retirement? What social forces have led so many elderly people back into the workplace, to bag our groceries and serve as our cashiers? Is this desirable? If not, how can we change the organization of society to make such an outcome less likely? The macro study of the life course invites us to think about such questions.

FURTHER READING

The following suggested readings build on this chapter. Given the very large literatures that have developed around these topics, the listing is necessarily highly selective; it features some excellent conceptual pieces as well as empirical examples not covered in the text of the chapter.

Social History and the Life Course

Haber, Carole. "Old Age through the Lens of Family History." In *Handbook on Aging and the Social Sciences,* edited by Robert Binstock and Linda George, 59–75. Amsterdam: Academic Press/Elsevier, 2006.

 Concise essay, social historical account of the elderly.

Hareven, T. K. *Family Time and Industrial Time: The Relationship Between the Family and Work in a New England Industrial Community.* New York, NY: Cambridge, 1982.

 Excellent social historical studies of intergenerational relations and the life course during a period of industrialization in the United States.

Prude, J. *The Coming of the Industrial Order: Town and Factory Life in Massachusetts, 1810–1860.* New York, NY: Cambridge University Press, 1983.

 Fascinating study of the transformation of two Massachusetts communities from sleepy farming villages to busy industrial towns.

Generations and Cohorts

Cohler, B. J., and A. Hostetler. "Linking Life Course and Life Story: Social Change and the Narrative Study of Lives Over Time." In *Handbook of the Life Course* edited by J.T. Mortimer and M.J. Shanahan, 555–576. New York: Kluwer-Plenum, 2003.

 Excellent discussion of how "generations" can inform life course studies, coupled with an empirical study of narrative life histories of gay men from different generations.

Falaris, E. M., and H. E. Peters. "Schooling Choices and Demographic Cycles." *Journal of Human Resources* 27 (1992): 551–574.

 Highly creative use of cohorts to test the Easterlin hypothesis.

Glenn, N. D. *Cohort Analysis.* Thousand Oaks, CA: Sage, 2004.

Glenn, N. D. "Distinguishing Age, Period, and Cohort Effects." In *Handbook of the Life Course,* edited by J. T. Mortimer and M. J. Shanahan. New York: Kluwer-Plenum, 2003.

 As noted in the preceding chapter, changes in behavior can reflect the unique experiences of birth cohorts (a cohort effect) and aging (an age effect). A third possibility is a period effect, whereby a society-wide change leads to behavioral change across age groups. Our discussion in this chapter has simplified matters greatly in that we ignore the "age-period-cohort conundrum"—age effects are confounded with either period or cohort effects in any study in which age is the independent variable. This is a sticky problem. Glenn (2003) is a concise, superb overview of the problem, Glenn (2004) an extended discussion.

Hendricks, Jon. "Generations and the Generation of Theory in Social Gerontology." *International Journal of Aging and Human Development*, 35.1 (1992): 31–47.

    Thoughtful discussion of how generations have been and could be used in the study of aging.

Kertzer, D. I. "Generation as a Sociological Problem." *Annual Review of Sociology* 9 (1983): 125–149.

Kohli, Martin. "Aging and Justice." In *Handbook on Aging and the Social Sciences,* edited by Robert Binstock and Linda George, 456–478. Amsterdam: Academic Press/Elsevier, 2006.

    Thoughtful essay on competition among the age strata, emphasizing the elderly and children.

Putnam, Robert. *Bowling Alone: America's Declining Social Capital.* New York: Simon & Schuster, 2001.

    Engaging generational analysis of historical trends in social capital.

Uhlenberg, Peter, and Sonia Miner. "Life Course and Aging: A Cohort Perspective." In *Handbook of Aging and the Social Sciences,* 4th ed., edited by R.H. Binstock, Linda K. George, and associates, 208–228. San Diego: Academic Press, 1995.

    Overview of the use of cohorts in life course studies of aging—excellent conceptual and empirical coverage.

Cross-National Studies of the Life Course

Blossfeld, Hans-Peter, and Heather Hofmeister. *Globaliziation, Uncertainty and Women's Careers.* Cheltenham (UK) and Northampton (MA, USA): Edward Elgar, 2006.

Blossfeld, Hans-Peter, Sandra Buchholz, and Dirk Hofäcker. *Globalization, Uncertainty and Late Careers in Society.* London: Routledge, 2006.

    Two of many volumes orchestrated by Blossfeld, a life course sociologist with extensive experience in cross-national research. Highly recommended.

Marshall, Victor, Walter Heinz, Helga Krueger, and A. Verma, eds. *Restructuring Work and the Life Course.* Toronto: University of Toronto Press, 2001.

    An interesting set of chapters that delineate the important ways in which work changed in the late twentieth century and how it was tied to changes in the structure and meaning of the life course.

Evans, K., and W. Heinz. "Studying Forms of Transition: Methodological Innovation in a Cross-National Study of Youth Transition and Youth Labour Market Entry in England and Germany." *Comparative Education* 29 (1993): 145–158.

Interesting use of targeted case studies to examine cross-national patterns in the transition from school to work.

Kertzer, David I., and K. Warner Schaie, eds. *Age Structuring in Comparative Perspective.* Hillsdale NJ: Lawrence Erlbaum Associates, 1989.

Collection of essays with strong emphasis on cross-national study of aging and the timing of transitions in the life course.

Shavit, Yossi, and Walter Müller, eds. *From School to Work: A Comparative Study of Educational Qualifications and Occupational Destinations.* Oxford: Clarendon Press, 1998.

Shavit, Yossi, Richard Arum, Adam Gamoran, and G. Menahem, eds. *Expansion, Differentiation, and Stratification in Higher Education: A Comparative Study.* Palo Alto, CA: Stanford, 2006.

Two of Shavit's many volumes of cross-national studies of the life course.

Master Trends in the Changing Life Course

Buchmann, Marlis. *The Script of Life in Modern Society: Entry into Adulthood in a Changing World.* Chicago: University of Chicago Press, 1989.

Of interest principally for its theoretical model of the life course in modern societies.

Cowgill, Donald O. "Aging and Modernization: A Revision of the Theory." In *Late Life: Communities and Environmental Policy,* edited by J. F. Gubrium, 123–145. Springfield, IL: Charles C. Thomas, 1974.

Furstenberg, Frank F., ed. "Early Adulthood in Cross-National Perspective." *Annals of the American Academy of Political and Social Science.* Thousand Oaks, CA: Sage Publications, 2002.

A thoughtful and comprehensive overview of how early adulthood differs across the globe.

Fussell, Elizabeth. 2006. "Structuring the Transition to Adulthood: An Entropy Analysis of the Early Life Course in the United States, 1880 to 2000." Population Association of America Meeting, Los Angeles, March 30–April 1, 2006.

Exemplary empirical study of the transition to adulthood using synthetic cohorts—clever methods and very broad time sweep. Finds evidence for both standardization and individualization of the life course, as discussed in this chapter.

Giddens, A. "The Nature of Modernity." In *The Giddens Reader,* edited by P. Cassell, 284–316. Stanford, CA: Stanford University Press, 1993.

Although not rich in life course analysis per se, this selection offers a lucid discussion of adult life in modern societies.

Kohli, M. "The World We Forgot: Historical Views of the Life Course." In *Later Life: The Social Psychology of Aging,* edited by V. W. Marshall, 271–303. Beverly Hills, CA: Sage, 1986.

    Classic statement of the role of modernization in the changing life course.

Macmillan, Ross. "The Structure of the Life Course. Standardized? Individualized? Differentiated?" In *Advances in Life Course Research.* Vol. 9. New York: Elsevier, 2004.

    Excellent collection of research articles that examine different ideas about the transformation of the life course over time, across countries, and across groups.

Moen, Phyllis. "The Gendered Life Course." In *Handbook of Aging and the Social Sciences.* 5th ed., edited by R. H. Binstock, L. K. George, and associates, 179–196. San Diego: Academic Press, 2001.

    Thorough discussion of how the life course is gendered and how the gendering of the life course is itself in constant flux.

Chapter Four
MICRO VIEWS OF THE LIFE COURSE

The truth is, part of me is every age. I'm a three year old, I'm a five year old, I'm a thirty-seven year old, I'm a fifty year old. I've been through all of them, and I know what it's like. I delight in being a child when it's appropriate to be a child. I delight in being a wise old man when it's appropriate to be a wise old man. Think of all I can be! I am every age.

—Morrie Schwartz

THE CASE OF "ANNE"

THE PREVIOUS CHAPTER CONSIDERED the life course with respect to populations viewed across large-scale social contexts and expanses of history. In this chapter, we tighten the lens by focusing on the micro dimensions of the life course. Consider the case of Anne,[1] a young woman who was interviewed by the first author as part of a study of occupational careers. Beginning in late childhood, Anne was passionately devoted to becoming a medical doctor. In high school, she volunteered at a local hospital and joined a club that explored careers in the health field. As a college student, she worked at a Girls' Club, continued her volunteer work at the hospital, and studied constantly so that she might excel in her coursework, which she did. Finally, she took the exam for entry into medical school and sent her application to the local university. The decision came back: her exam score was slightly below the cutoff and she was not accepted. While she continued working at the Girls' Club and volunteering, she studied for and took the exam a second time. A letter came in the mail: again, she had not been accepted. Given her intense desire to become a doctor, she arranged to meet with the dean of the medical school. He told her to try a third time. Again, she continued working, volunteering, and studying, and took the exam a third time. A letter came in the mail: she had not been accepted and the dean indicated that it would be pointless to take the exam again—with three scores in her file, she would never be accepted. The foundation of her life, the principle that had given meaning to her biography since childhood, had been pulled out from under her.

Then something unexpected happened: Anne quickly recovered from the shock of her third rejection, began to find joy in her work at the Girls' Club, and claimed that she had in no way failed to meet her life goal. Really, she said, she had always wanted to help people and when she was finally rejected by the medical school she realized that she was a vital, integral part of a community at the Girls' Club. Yes, her family and friends were puzzled and disappointed, but she planned to work at the Girls' Club for the foreseeable future, and greeted every day as a new opportunity to help other people. She had never been happier.

From a micro perspective, this snippet from a life history is thematically rich. First, the micro perspective directs our attention to *agency,* which refers to the processes by which people act and react to produce specific desired goals. Fundamentally, agency reflects the idea that individuals can shape their future experiences. Key questions revolve around how people shape the pathways and experiences of their lives. How does agency "work" in the life course? When and how did the Anne become passionate about becoming a doctor? How did she plan to achieve this goal and how well did she implement her plan? What factors helped and hindered her? To answer such questions we would focus on her social context, including, for example, her relationships, her involvements in organizations, her socioeconomic status and resources. As the preceding chapters have shown, such a focus has clear limits. People are born into social and historical contexts that shape the futures that they may have. Still, it is important to explore the degree to which, the mechanisms by which, and the contexts in which people are able to influence the pathways they take through life and the experiences that they are likely to have.

Second, the micro perspective directs our attention to *subjectivity*, which refers to the ways in which people make sense of their selves in given social circumstances and the role that this understanding plays in guiding their actions. Anne had a very clear image of herself as a medical doctor, the image was shattered, and then she redefined herself with seemingly little turmoil. She refused to think of herself as "failure" or to view her life story as lacking a "cohesive plot line." Actually, research shows that roughly one-third of all graduating high-school seniors fail to achieve their educational and occupational goals, and social science would consider her one such case.[2] How do people react to such turning points? Is her reaction common? Why do some people label themselves "failures" and how do they rise above the label to continue their lives? More broadly, how do we draw upon the many experiences of our lives to create an identity that makes sense to ourselves and others?

While agency and subjectivity are two distinct concepts, the example of Anne also shows that they are inextricably linked: her strong image of self fuels her strivings to be a medical doctor; when that future self becomes impossible, she recasts her self-understanding, and a new sense of purpose and direction is established. Each one of us has a sense of past and future that shapes our motives, informs our plans, and inspires our efforts. The central focus of this chapter is how agency and subjectivity both influence and are influenced by the biography and the life course.

AGENCY AND SUBJECTIVITY IN THE LIFE COURSE

Philosophy and the social sciences have both laid claim to understanding agency, and there are a variety of opinions on what agency is and how it fits into contemporary society. John Meyer and Ronald Jepperson conceive of agency as a "scam" of modern culture.[3] According to their argument, human beings have been increasingly constructed as agents as societies have evolved from simpler and agrarian to complex and modern. As most cultures have moved away from the belief that gods govern the fates of human beings, the notion of a rational, agentic actor has become increasingly prominent. That is, with modernization, people come to believe that they are the masters of their fates although, ironically, the institutional basis of the biography (discussed in Chapter Three) also increases. Thus, modern people perceive themselves as agentic, yet their biographies are highly structured, perhaps to a historically unprecedented degree.

However true this hypothesis may actually be, studying agency in the life course both theoretically and empirically has nevertheless proven useful. What is meant by "agency" as it relates to the biography and how can we measure it? An example will illustrate one straightforward way to proceed. Recall our earlier discussion of the work of Featherman and Hauser on the changing relationship between a father's occupation and education and his son's occupational attainment over the course of the twentieth century (Chapter 3). Such research implies an interpersonal and psychological model that delineates *how* fathers influence their sons. Researchers interested in such questions of social mobility over the life course (i.e., patterns of movement among jobs from one's first to last job) frequently draw upon what is known as the "Wisconsin model" of status attainment in order to elucidate the key mechanisms. To explain social mobility, the model posits a chain of influence that stretches from socioeconomic status in childhood (i.e., the job, income, and education of one's father) and mental ability (IQ of the son) to the son's occupational attainment in early adulthood.[4] This model is shown in Figure 4.1.

A key feature of the model is the inclusion of social psychological measures that intervene (or mediate) between childhood origins and adult outcomes. Two factors that are of particular importance are educational and occupational aspirations (i.e., how far people want to go in school and the types of jobs people want, respectively), which are aspects of agency. The plans and motives of a high-school senior who aspires to graduate school are likely quite different from those of a high-school senior who has decided to leave school and get a job. Empirical tests of the model show that childhood origins including academic performance shape the degree to which people perceive that significant others, notably friends, think they should at-

Figure 4.1

SEWELL-HALLER-PORTES MODEL OF EDUCATIONAL AND OCCUPATIONAL ATTAINMENT

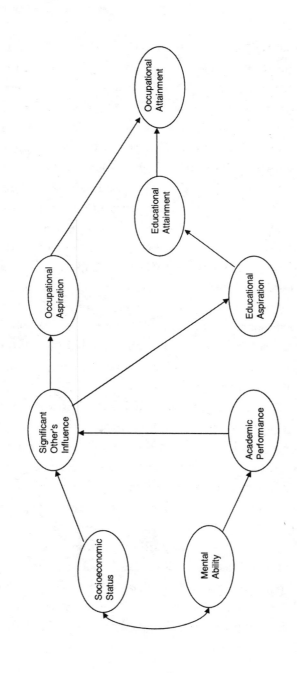

tend college. Such influences further shape both educational and occupational aspirations. Educational aspirations have consequences for later levels of educational attainment, which, in turn, influence occupational attainment.

In this example, agency in childhood has long-term implications for one's educational and occupational careers and is socially embedded, being responsive to the views and expectations of other people. Such aspirations for the future are fundamental expressions of agency in that they provide a model of the life course that guides future actions. This is seen most clearly in the strong relationship between educational aspirations and the ultimate level of education attained, and the relationship between occupational aspirations and the types of jobs attained in later life.

Still, the Wisconsin model takes a limited view of agency (chiefly focusing on aspirations). Mustapha Emirbayer and Ann Mische offer a broader conceptualization that involves three core elements.[5] The first of these, *iteration,* involves the selective use of the past in current activity. The second, *practical evaluation,* is the capacity of actors to make judgments about alternative possible actions that arise in the context of specific demands or ambiguities of a given situation. The third, *projectivity,* is the use of the imagination to generate possible future courses of action. Below we discuss these elements, illustrating each dimension with empirical research and establishing its links with the life course and subjectivity.

THE PAST IN THE LIFE COURSE: ITERATION

In thinking about iteration, the psychologist might consider individual differences in how well people select from past experiences to inform their present situation. How and why do people differ in their capacity to choose relevant past experiences when deciding what to do in the present? The inquiry would no doubt focus on processes like memory and information processing. The life course sociologist asks different questions, which are obviously concerned with context and timing. The life course perspective presumes that past and present experiences are interconnected. The question then arises, how are experiences structured in the past so that actors are enabled in the present?

Schemata and Scripts

There are a variety of ways in which the past can inform our plans and decisions both in the present and with respect to the future. One central idea is that previous experiences serve as schemata for people. A *schema* (plural: *schemata*) is a bundle of knowledge that represents a subset of past experiences. Schemata categorize relationships, scenarios, and events, and we select from these categories (or bundles) when deciding what to do in the present. For example, each adolescent has a schema about what it means to have an occupational career. Such a schema likely reflects observations the person has made of his or her parents' careers. In turn, the schema provides a way of developing a plan of action about his or her future career. In other words, the schema serves as a foundation for how a person thinks about careers, including his or her life course. To complicate matters, each adolescent actually has multiple schemata of occupational careers from the parents of friends and acquaintances, biographies, and so forth.

Iteration, then, involves choosing among schemata to formulate and pursue plans about the future, and schemata are all based on past experiences with other people in social settings. For example, schemata may represent what it means to be an educated person. How would the schemata differ between a boy growing up in a desperately poor neighborhood and another boy growing up in a leafy, gated community? These two boys probably have little in the way of shared schemata about educational careers because of differences in their social settings, with different types of parents, neighbors, and friends of the family. The priviledged boy probably has schemata reflecting interactions with professionals (e.g., lawyers and dentists), scholars (e.g., people with doctoral degrees), business people with MBA's, and people who were able to do well with an undergraduate degree. The boy growing up in poverty probably has schemata reflecting interactions with people who did not complete high school, people who earned GED's (i.e., high-school equivalency degrees) in their late twenties, and people who finished secondary school. During the high-school years, the boys' different schemata will likely be associated with differences in attachment to and engagement with school, in future educational plans, in relationships with teachers, and so on.

Related to the schema is the script. A *script* is generally regarded as a subset of a schema that deals with very specific guidelines for behavior, including, for example, how we dress, speak, and present ourselves in specific circumstances. A schema typically refers to broad and abstract concepts such as what it means to be a family, how one's self-understanding changes with different roles (such as student, mother, etc.), and what a "good retirement" means. Scripts, on the other hand, include such specifics as "how to do my chores," "how to change a diaper," and "how to organize a card game at my retirement community." Thus, schemata and scripts refer to packages of understanding that extend from highly abstract notions like "good career" to more specific routines like "how to speak with the boss at the watercooler."

Education is one of the most salient social experiences that form schemata. Schooling begins very early (typically age four to five) and ends relatively early (by age eighteen for those who do not pursue tertiary education and before about age thirty for those who do). Because current life expectancies in the United States and other western industrial nations are approaching eighty years of age, formal education generally starts and finishes in the first third of the life course. Thus, formal education is typically in one's past through much of the life course even as it continues to inform one's schemata and is connected to iterative agency.

In school, people learn the culture of a society, the rules and norms that serve to guide action. Hence, schools provide a foundation for agentic behavior deep into the life course. In one respect, schooling is connected to agency in a direct and pragmatic manner: it is the arena where skills for a successful socioeconomic future are taught and acquired. Indeed, several decades of research on the Wisconsin model of status attainment reveals that education is the key determinant of the status or prestige of one's first job and consequent income.

But considered in the context of human agency and the life course, the role of education is considerably more complicated. There is no dispute that college graduates on average have "better" jobs and earn more than high-school graduates. Yet how this happens, particularly in American society, is the subject of considerable debate. Excepting vocational, technical, and professional schools, American schools provide a general education, meaning that the curricula do not provide specific skills for specific jobs. Curricula are reasonably consistent across schools, and tracking, as Sam Lucas shows in his book *Tracking Inequality,* is more about the degree of content rather than kind.[6] For example, students in high school typically would choose (or have chosen for them) higher or lower levels of mathematics rather than a completely different subject area. Equally important, there is often little connection between the content of curricula and the world of work. How often, for example, does the average American worker get asked the year in which prehistoric people settled the area around present-day Clovis, New Mexico? Does knowledge of the contentious relationship between ancient Sparta and Athens routinely figure into the average workday? Even knowledge with clear applications, such as the organization of the periodic table, has relevance only to the smallest subset of jobs.

So if school curricula are unrelated to the content of most jobs, why is it that educational attainment is so important for the types of jobs that people get and the types of compensation that they are able to command? Recent research in both sociology and economics suggests that the links between schooling and occupations are less direct than previously considered and are closely connected to issues of agency. Researchers suggest that the reason that schooling connects to later work is not that it provides skills for any particular job but that it teaches people how to be workers. That is, schooling provides schemata and scripts that "transfer" or "generalize" from the role of student to the role of worker in modern economies.

What do such transferable schemata and scripts look like? They describe a whole host of behaviors that characterize both school and work. Schools teach people the value of attendance and punctuality. Schools reward those who show up regularly to class with higher grades and increased likelihood of graduation. At the same time, schools penalize students who do not attend regularly. In extreme cases, they punish them harshly with suspensions or expulsions that dramatically undermine the likelihood of graduation and the earning of a credential. Steady and predictable attendance is thus part of the schemata of rewarded adult behavior in both the school and the workplace. Indeed, a functioning labor market that does not involve the routinized and regular attendance of employees is hard to imagine.

Other schemata/scripts are equally important. Schooling teaches discipline. It teaches people to obey authorities, even when one's interests and views are not respected. It is also an arena where the rewards of discipline and the costs of indiscipline are made extremely transparent. As such, schooling conveys notions of authority, the idea that some people are rule-makers and enforcers while others are subject to rules.

Schooling has two further functions, both less abstract and more focused on the skills required in the modern labor force. First, schooling teaches diligence. Recognizing that the skills taught in high schools do not have many direct applications in the modern workplace ignores the idea that schools teach people *how* to work by requiring them to persevere in mastering varied and often difficult subjects (e.g., calculus). In so doing, schools provide something practically useful to employers: an employee who knows how to learn. This "teachability" is especially useful, as the large majority of occupational skills are actually learned in the workplace. Ultimately, this may be the true value of both high-school and college degrees: they signal the degree to which new graduates are able to learn. "Straight A's" strongly suggest that a student attended class, pursued her studies with energy and determination, and fulfilled all learning objectives with excellence. By implication, she will perform similarly in the workplace.

In the end, schools (and, before one enters the school system, parents) provide fundamental schemata and scripts for later employment that engender people's agentic capabilities (i.e., the "right" schema). From this perspective, a college degree is a credential that signals the possession of schemata. Of course, possessing the right schemata and scripts for success in one's occupational career does not guarantee that a person will necessarily draw upon them and actually succeed. As mentioned above, people are likely to have multiple schemata and they draw creatively upon them to formulate plans of action.

Also, schemata are not restricted to activities that are "good." Consider violent offending, which is clearly undesirable behavior. According to virtually all criminal justice statistics, people convicted of violent crimes receive the most severe penalties. Violence is most subject to imprisonment and violent offenders receive, on average, the longest sentences. So how do schemata of violence play out? Some of the most important work on the topic was conducted by Cathy Spatz Widom, who focused on the "cycle of violence" thesis.[7] In general, this thesis, also called the intergenerational transmission of violence thesis, posits that people who are victims of violence in early life, particularly of child abuse, are more likely to act violently in later life. Victims of child abuse become more-aggressive children, juvenile delinquents, and adult offenders.

In many respects, the cycle of violence thesis is a prime example of iteration. Many people exposed to violence in childhood "learn" violence as a useful, normative, and routine social action. Unfortunately, such people learn that violence is appropriate in interpersonal disputes or conflicts. Exposure to child abuse (or violence more generally) shows people that those who act violently can "win" in disputes and get their way. Further, such exposure may also show people that there are no significant penalties for violent actions (particularly in the case of family violence, which typically escapes the attention of the criminal justice system).

Although the thesis has widespread acceptance, Widom noted that the scientific proof, either for or against, was surprisingly weak. In response to this lack of evidence, she identified all cases of physical or sexual abuse or neglect that were reported to the police and identified as abuse or neglect in a particular Midwestern county in the late 1960s. As the key problem in prior studies was identifying an appropriate comparison group (that is, people who *resemble* victims of child abuse or neglect but *were not* themselves victims of abuse or neglect), Widom painstakingly matched each victim of abuse with an appropriate "control." All abuse cases were matched on sex, race, date of birth, and hospital of birth. For people who were school age, cases were also matched on class in elementary school and neighborhood (i.e., living within a five-block radius of one another). Once the matched sample was generated, the research proceeded to consider the prevalence of different forms of crime and violence in adolescence and adulthood.

In looking at the full sample, Widom reported that people who had been abused/neglected as children were 50 percent more likely to have juvenile records for delinquency, 30 percent more likely to have adult criminal records, and 20 percent more likely to have records for a violent crime. Comparisons by sex and race revealed the same basic pattern: in almost all cases (the exception being comparisons of females with respect to a record for violent crime), abused and neglected children were more likely to have criminal records in adolescence or adulthood. Comparisons across victimization types—comparing victims of physical abuse with those of neglect and with those of sexual abuse, as well as all combinations—revealed that victims of physical violence *only* had the highest rates of arrests for violence, while victims of other forms of victimization had significantly lower rates. (For example, rates for those experiencing only sexual abuse were just 5.6 percent.) Widom thus concluded:

> Early childhood victimization has demonstrable long-term consequences for delinquency, adult criminality, and violent criminal behavior. . . . In a direct test of the violence breeds violence hypothesis, physical abuse as a child led significantly to later violent criminal behavior, when other relevant demographic variables such as age, sex, and race were held constant.[8]

Thus, exposure to violence in childhood, particularly in the form of physical abuse, appears to imbue people with pernicious schemata and scripts for future action, leading to an increased likelihood of committing acts of violence in later adolescence and adulthood.

Still, the relationship between early victimization and later offending is far from exact. Consider this: if all (100 percent) of the abused/neglected sample were victims of abuse or neglect, only one-quarter (26 percent) have records for juvenile delinquency, just over a quarter (28.6 percent) have adult criminal records, and only 11.2 percent have records for violent crime. Further, the intergenerational transmission of violence appears to vary across groups. While almost 20 percent of males have a record for violent crime, only 3 percent of females do and they are really no more likely to act violently in later life than women who were not victims of abuse or neglect (3.4 percent versus 2.4 percent). Similarly, 22 percent of all blacks had a record for violence in adulthood, while only 6.5 percent of whites did. As with women, white victims of abuse or neglect were no more likely to have records for violence in later life than those who were not victims (6.5 versus 5.3 percent).

Although Widom's research is typically cited as evidence of the cycle of violence, a closer examination reveals contingencies in the link between abuse and antisocial behavior. In a life course context, these likely reflect the fact that even within a group of abused children there will be many diverse experiences. Perhaps one abused child is socially isolated, but another spends a great deal of time with a kind and generous friend and the friend's family. Perhaps one abused child has joined a gang of troublemakers, while another has been befriended by a rabbi. Childhood abuse, by itself, offers only one of many possible schemata. Drawing upon a diversity of experiences, abused children will often have multiple schemata and scripts, some of which promote violent behavior and some of which inhibit it.

Autobiographical Memory
In addition to schemata and scripts, iteration also raises the issue of autobiographical memory. The preceding discussion is limited in that it fails to locate schemata and scripts in one's past. Research on autobiographical memory, however, shows that our memories are not randomly distributed in the past. The nineteenth-century English scientist Francis Galton did some of the earliest work on human memory.[9] According to his own description, Galton become interested in memory during a "stroll along Pall Mall," a London street that was the site of gaming and "gentleman's clubs." While walking, Galton would fix his attention on specific objects and then note the associations they brought to his mind. He noted that such associations were quite varied and often referenced things in his distant past (or at least things he hadn't thought much about for a long time).

As a pioneer in psychometrics (the study of the measurement of psychological processes), Galton set about rigorously studying his memory. He began by drawing up a list of seventy-five words. He then placed the list under a book so that he could only see the first word. He would read a word for a few seconds (recorded fastidiously on a stopwatch) and allow some associations to form. He then would make note of his associations and how long they took to form. Galton ended up going through his list several times and generated a total of 505 associations and 289 distinct associations that took just over ten minutes to form. Although unimpressed with the speed and variety of his product, he did note some interesting patterns. For instance, just under half of the associations went back to his youth, while only fifteen percent reflected recent events. The old associations were also much more likely to be repeated, often appearing as many as four times. He was also surprised by the parochial character of his associations. Although he had traveled the world and was a widely accomplished explorer, the associations he developed were decidedly English and were largely confined to the social strata that he inhabited.

Thus, Galton was among the first to demonstrate the intrinsic relationship between biography and memory and the way that the social nature of past and present shapes what one remembers. One of the most intriguing aspects of his findings was the "reminiscence effect"; researchers in subsequent decades have continued to note that as people approach the later years of life their associations tend to turn to youth, suggesting that the schemata formed in youth can endure across the phases of life.

Although Galton's story suggests a certain durability of memory over the life course, more recent research suggests that people are generally not very good at recalling the past. Bill Henry and his colleagues asked a group of eighteen-year-olds to recall various phenomena from their childhood and adolescence; these same young people had already been assessed on the same phenomena earlier in their lives.[10] How much agreement was observed? That is, how accurate are people's memories of their own experiences? Not accurate at all. For example, eighteen-year-olds recalled whether they had moved a lot or a little, but were inaccurate in how many times they had moved. Other findings: the young people tended to overestimate their reading ability earlier in life; and they were not good at recalling family conflict, maternal depression, or behavioral problems. The authors concluded that our memories of psychological states and family processes are poor, and our specific estimates of things like number of moves, reading ability, or the ages at which events were experienced are also poor. Such research is disconcerting, given the centrality of our self-understanding to our identity.

Although research on autobiographical memory has typically focused on individual memories of everyday events, some research on biography and memory has focused on how memory connects to broad-scale historical events. In general, such events provide individuals with a frame of reference for understanding their self and their society. Equally important, there is a general expectation that social location, be it age, gender, race, or class, shapes the salience of different events. As a result, events connect to one's biography in complex ways.

Research by Howard Schuman and colleagues has sought to unravel the complex connections between biography, memory, and history by focusing on the ways in which people understand significant political events.[11] The key question in such work is the issue of collective memory, or the ways in which memories of a historical past are shared by a group of people. Regardless of whether such events are directly experienced or not, autobiographical memories may be linked to collective memories and thus play an important role in identity and identity formation. And whether such events are experienced directly or not, social factors strongly affect individual and group memories.

In an innovative study, people in Lithuania were asked to report on one or two national or world events that occurred in the past fifty years that they considered to be especially important, and then to indicate what it was about the events that made them so important to the individual.[12] Lithuania serves as an important research site for a number of reasons. For much of the twentieth century it was part of the Soviet Union, one of the world superpowers, but it made strong claims for a separate national identity. Not surprisingly, its political history has been rife with conflict. For example, Lithuanian independence prior to World War II gave way to the secret Ribbentrop-Molotov pact, which allowed its annexation by Russia. This led to a bitter period under Josef Stalin characterized by mass deportations and political oppression. Although there was a period of stability after the death of Stalin, the Soviet empire began unraveling in the mid-1980s, with armed conflict in Afghanistan and Mikhail Gorbachev's policy of *perestroika* ("reform"), followed by a declaration of Lithuanian independence in early 1990 and its official recognition in late 1991. Clearly, social and political turmoil was a routine aspect of Lithuanian life throughout the twentieth century.

What implications did this have for biography and collective memory? Schuman and colleagues show that collective memory is a life course phenomenon, one that is shaped by social experience, social timing, and social location. Memories of historical events were quite different for Lithuanians and ethnic Russians. For example, while almost 60 percent of Lithuanians reported the "rebirth of Lithuania" as a significant event, only fifteen percent of ethnic Russians living in Lithuania felt similarly. In contrast, over half of ethnic Russians viewed *perestroika* as a significant event, while less than 15 percent of Lithuanians did. Importantly, although both events deeply affected the everyday lives of Lithuanians regardless of ethnicity, they clearly have variable salience between the groups. Equally interesting, World War II, which had immense significance for Lithuanian society, was referenced by only 16 percent of ethnic Lithuanians but almost 40 percent of ethnic Russians. In general, Lithuanians were also more likely to reference annexation by Russian, deportations to Siberia, and the Ribbentrop-Molotov pact, but significantly less likely to reference manned space flight or the Krushchev era. Lithuanian identification clearly shapes collective memory.

The timing and the experience of such events in the life course also mattered. For example, among Lithuanians, World War II was increasingly salient with age. Memories of the resistance movement were concentrated among those in their fifties and sixties, as were memories of annexation. In contrast, the "rebirth of Lithuania" was decreasingly salient with age: while over 60 percent of those under the age of fifty viewed it as an especially significant event, less than 40 percent of those over the age of seventy felt similarly. Other aspects of social location also mattered. For instance, better-educated respondents, regardless of ethnicity, were more likely to reference annexation and the secret pact with which it was associated. In contrast, the least-educated respondents were most likely to mention the collectivization of farming which, perhaps, they would have been most likely to experience firsthand. Importantly, such research highlights both the complexities of memory and its critical social dimensions. Such work also reveals in stark terms the importance of birth cohort and aging in the mechanisms that link identity, biography, and collective memory.

Summary of Iteration in the Life Course

Past experiences have a profound impact on present understandings of the self. Schemata—which are heavily dependent on one's location in society—enable people to think about the self in terms of such life course phenomena as educational and occupational careers and family formation. Autobiographical memory is likewise based on social context and the timing of significant events—of a personal and societal nature—in a person's past. The past, then, is a construction based on social location and timing.

THE PRESENT IN THE LIFE COURSE: PRACTICAL EVALUATION AND DECISION MAKING

The agentic capacity of individuals to choose and select courses of action falls under what Emirbayer and Mische call *practical evaluation*.[13] Their main point is that people assess the situations they encounter and make decisions to act in particular ways rather than others. As such, no discussion of the micro features of the life course can ignore the role of choice and decision-making.

Practical evaluation involves "the exercise of situationally based judgment."[14] In sociology, this has a long history and has been variously termed "practical wisdom," "prudence," "tact," "discretion," "application," "improvisation," and "intelligence."

Fundamentally, practical evaluation involves the distinct but interrelated processes of "problematization," "decision," and "execution." While it is well beyond the scope of this chapter to discuss these concepts and what differentiates them in detail, the core idea is that people approach given situations, make assessments of their specific circumstances and how they could or should act (i.e., problematization), make decisions about the type of action that is most suitable (typically combining elements of what they hope to achieve and what is expected of them), and then act accordingly (i.e., execution). Obviously, many ideas are subsumed under "practical evaluation."

Within the context of life course research, surprisingly little work actually considers how and why people make the decisions that they do. A wide variety of decisions are made about the broad contours of the biography (e.g., will I get married? how many children would I like to have? when would I like to retire?) both within and across life stages, but research has done little to flesh out who makes what decision and why. (This is particularly apparent when one considers life course research in comparison to the remarkably rich and complex literature in microeconomics, which has used a variety of methodologies, ranging from simple experiments to large-scale surveys to detailed analysis of government data.)

At the same time, life course research has long drawn upon principles and ideas from social psychology to understand what characteristics or capacities of self, often thought of as one's identity, are fundamental in the exercise of agency in everyday life. We will consider two basic features of self-concept that undoubtedly inform practical evaluation and decision-making in the present and have been useful in life course research: subjective age identity and self-efficacy. Before discussing these, however, some background is necessary.

Identity Theory

In the early part of the twentieth century, a social philosopher at the University of Chicago articulated a theory of social development organized around the idea of social interaction. In a series of lectures spanning several years, George Herbert Mead offered a theory of selfhood and identity development through the interactions that people have with one another. Published decades later as the influential *Mind, Self, and Society,* Mead's ideas eventually evolved in the ensuing decades into the theory of symbolic interactionism.[15] According to Mead, the self is a social product in that it arises, is formed, and is maintained through social interactions.

Children, for example, imitate the actions of others, including parents, siblings, agemates, etc., who provide images or symbols of various social roles that children then act out in their routine "play." As children age, such play transforms into "games" incorporating a broader notion of rules and involving role enactments in their fuller and more multidimensional forms. In what Mead called "taking the role of the other," people see their self as other people see it. The "I" is the package of needs, wants, and desires. The "Me" is the social self that results from viewing oneself from the perspective of others, who have socially defined expectations about appropriate behavior. That is, the "I" is constantly monitoring the reactions of other people and changing the "Me" accordingly. Thus, the "I," through interactions with other people, becomes aware of any deviations from schemata, scripts, rules, and other expectations, and then revises "Me."

An important extension of Mead's work is "identity theory." According to Sheldon Stryker, identity theory begins from the premise that identity involves a system linking together a multitude of social roles.[16] Here, Stryker translates Mead's emphasis on social behavior to an individual's "role choice behavior." Identity is characterized by commitments to particular roles (e.g., student, worker, spouse, parent). Identity salience refers to where a particular role exists within a hierarchy of other roles. Identity salience, then, is the engine for behavior. The more salient an identity is, the more likely it is that a person will choose a course of action that conforms to behavioral expectations associated with that role. Identity theory thus provides an intrinsic tie between the self and action, between identity and agency.

From a life course perspective, there are limitations to this view. First, although identity theory is correct in identifying social roles as an organizing principle of self-conceptions, it fails to appreciate that they are developmental and occur with predictability in the life course. Bernice Neugarten and colleagues have shown that people have reasonably well-defined expectations about when a particular role should be adopted.[17] In this respect, people can be "on-time" or "off-time" in their roles with respect to societal expectations. The important point is that roles are inherently a temporal, socially embedded phenomenon. For example, building on the work of Neugarten, Richard Settersten reports that his sample of Chicagoans thought people should leave home between ages eighteen and twenty-five.[18] Thus, there are social expectations about when people should adopt the role of "independent householder."

Settersten asked his respondents, "By what age should a man leave his parents' home?" Generally speaking, a "should statement" like the one used by Settersten is regarded as indicative of a social norm, but herein lies the complexity of age-norm research. A true age norm requires two components: (1) people agree on an age or relatively narrow age range in which something ought to occur, and (2) if this condition is not met, some form of negative sanction will result (e.g., "such a person should be embarrassed").[19] Settersten's results suggest that someone remaining in his or her parents' home after age twenty-five is "off-time," but he also observed that people thought a negative sanction should not be applied to such a person. Of course, this is slightly different from whether they would actually apply a negative sanction (e.g., "look down" upon such a person), but these and other studies suggest that people have rather loose expectations regarding when roles should be adopted, and see little problem when these expectations are violated.

Second, identity theory assumes that people have varying commitments to different roles, which may be overly simplistic. Increasingly, people combine school and work without any clear difference in role commitment. Likewise, work, marriage, and parenthood are combined in complicated ways. Moreover, there are social expectations as to what types of roles can and should go together. Some roles are seen as intrinsically compatible, such as marriage and parenthood. Other roles are seen as largely contradictory, such as school and parenthood. Still other role combinations are contested and their compatibility has as much to do with context and who is occupying them (e.g., work and parenthood). Roles are interconnected both socially and personally in ways that are not captured by simple notions of hierarchy and commitment.

Third, identity theory, although careful to delineate the significance of roles for conceptions of self, has yet to acknowledge the age-grading of roles. As discussed earlier, the life course is characterized by several stages that have unique cultural and structural characteristics. Childhood is distinguished from adolescence, which is distinguished from adulthood, and so on. Yet, how one stage is distinguished from another has both social and psychological facets. In the former case, one life stage is differentiated from another in terms of the types of roles that one can and does enact. Childhood is characterized by limited role enactments, typically including only the "student," "child," and "sibling" roles. In contrast, adolescence opens up role possibilities with the additional possibility of work. Adulthood, in contrast to both, may be seen by the absence of former roles like "student" and "dependent child" and the addition of new roles such as "full-time worker," "spouse," and "parent." In other words, life stages can be defined by the role complexities that characterize them. Such ideas have recently emerged as new avenues of inquiry into self-perceived (or subjective) age.

Subjective Age Identity

When do people conceive of themselves as adults? The first author and his colleagues examined this question in their attempts to understand subjective age identity in the transition to adulthood. Drawing upon data from the Youth Development Study, a survey of a sample of young adults in their mid-twenties who attended high school in St. Paul, Minnesota, they considered factors that influenced the degree to which one "feels" like an adult in a wide variety of situations.[20] The range of situations reflected the various domains of activity and included both roles (e.g., at school, at work, with one's children, with one's romantic partner) and role-related activities (e.g., taking care of the house). It is worth noting that the twenty-somethings they studied clearly see themselves as at least somewhat adult. Only in the contexts of friends, engaging in sports, or with parents do more than a small percentage feel "not at all like an adult."

Still, there is some variability. Seventy percent or more felt "entirely like an adult" at work, taking care of their house, with their children, or with their romantic partner. While this would seem to connote a clear connection between adult-type roles and subjective perceptions of adulthood, more in-depth analysis of the actual associations between objective role transitions and subjective perceptions showed considerable variability. Only becoming a parent had reasonably consistent associations with self-perceived adulthood. Equally important, when all three family transitions—cohabitation/marriage, owning one's own home, and parenthood—were considered simultaneously, they had very strong and consistent effects on perceptions of adulthood. That is, people who had made all three transitions were significantly more likely to see themselves as adults, regardless of context. Interestingly, the same research showed little support for career factors. Finishing school and having a full-time job did not influence whether one felt like an adult.

At the other end of the life span, social gerontologists have long been interested in what factors shape identification as "old." Such inquiry has focused particular attention to movement out of roles, which is such a stark feature of older life. People may leave parenthood by ceasing to be involved in the everyday management of their children's lives, may move out of paid work and into retirement, and may move out of marriage through the death of a spouse (particularly for women). In early work, Arnold Rose suggested an "active resistance towards aging," while other scholars have documented how older people avoid categorizing themselves as "old" or "elderly," even in the face of biological aging and the transition out of the "adult" roles identified by Shanahan and colleagues (as discussed earlier).

Contributing to such work, John Logan, Russell Ward, and Glenna Spitze considered the subjective dimensions of aging in a metropolitan sample from upstate New York.[21] The main focus of their research was to document the nature of age identity in both middle and later life and to distinguish between the two. Importantly, age identity is not divorced from actual age. Those who *are* older are more likely to report that they *felt* older. But the relationship is far from exact. For example, 4 percent of males seventy to seventy-nine years old reported that they were "young" and 44 percent reported that they were "middle-aged." Corresponding percentages among females were 8 and 49. In addition to age, other important factors that differentiated those who felt "old" from those who felt "middle-aged" included self-perceived health (with poorer health increasing the likelihood of feeling old) and marriage (with marriage decreasing the likelihood of feeling old). Do such feelings matter? They apparently do, as those who felt old were significantly more likely to feel distress and were less likely to feel satisfied in life. Much like the work of Shanahan and colleagues on the transition to adulthood, research on age identification in later life showcases the life course context of identity in the present and how individual conceptions of self as adult are shaped both by the role character of situations and by the role content of an individual life.

Self-Efficacy in the Life Course

Although efforts to understand self-perceived age clearly contribute to our understanding of identity formation in the life course, the causal order of social roles and role-related identity is typically assumed rather than identified. For example, while we earlier assumed that movement into family roles increases feelings of adulthood, it is also possible that those who feel more like adults also feel that they are more capable of taking on adult-type roles. Such an idea is entirely consistent with general principles of social psychology that see the self and identity as the ongoing feedback process of action and evaluation. In recognizing a feedback process, we confront the idea of self-efficacy and its relationship to identity and action.

As Victor Gecas notes, the idea of self-efficacy has a long history.[22] Although its prominence in social psychology emerged only in recent decades, the idea's basic core has roots in centuries-old notions of free will, determinism, intentionality, and casuality. One conceptualization focuses on the experience of causal agency, viewing it as a fundamental human need and identifying it as a fundamental element of one's self. A second approach places more emphasis on beliefs and perceptions of causality, agency, and control. Building upon the pathbreaking work of Albert Bandura, this approach focuses on variation in the belief that one can successfully perform some particular action.[23] In essence, it is a judgment that people make about their own competence in a given arena or for a given task. What makes the notion of self-efficacy so useful in empirical research are the early assumptions (and now empirical certitudes) that (1) self-efficacy is a reasonably stable personal characteristic; (2) people differ in their level of self-efficacy; and (3) self-efficacy is a key component in agentic orientations. Put simply, one is more likely to contemplate and invest in some course of action given a higher level of self-efficacy, and hence self-efficacy serves as an important link between self and action.

If self-efficacy plays a key role in linking identity and action, the question arises as to how self-efficacy is formed and how it ties into the various events that characterize the unfolding life course. In other words, how does self-efficacy unfold over the life course? The development of self-efficacy is reasonably well understood. As Gecas explains:

> Self-efficacy, as encompassing the individual's sense of control and beliefs about causality, develops out of the early interactions between individual and environment. Specifically, it is the environment's *responsiveness* to the infant's actions that is critical in the development of a sense of self and a concept of one's world. . . . It is the quality of the individual-environment interaction, primarily with regard to the opportunities it pro-

vides for engaging in efficacious action (e.g., a stimulating, challenging, responsive environment and the freedom to engage it), that continues to be a major condition for self-efficacy throughout a person's life.[24]

Although we have considerable information about the dynamics of self-efficacy in early childhood, less is known about variations in self-efficacy over the life course. While identity theory and symbolic interactionism frame identity around the various social roles that people occupy, research on self-efficacy has typically paid little attention to social roles or efficacy as a role-specific aspect of identity. As alluded to earlier, there are a variety of ways in which efficacy has been conceptualized and measured. Still, a common thread in most prior work is a conceptualization of efficacy as a general and undifferentiated trait. For example, many studies draw upon Leonard Pearlin's concept of mastery, which reflects a general orientation to life situations.[25] People indicate the extent to which they agree with statements like "There is no way I can solve some of the problems I have," "I am being pushed around," "I have little control over the things that happen to me," "I can do just about anything," and "what happens to me in the future mostly depends on me." Such work is clearly useful in that it indexes generalized conceptions of self that (hypothetically) apply in a wide variety of situations. At the same time, the idea that self-conceptions occur in social settings suggests the utility of thinking about efficacy as something embedded in and connected to specific social roles.

The idea of considering self-efficacy in the context of specific role-domains emerges vividly in a study of educational careers by Lorie Schabo Grabowski and her colleagues.[26] The key distinction that Grabowski and colleagues make is between "global self-efficacy" and "economic self-efficacy." While the former is indexed by Pearlin's mastery scale, the latter emphasizes perceptions of the chances (from very low to very high) that one will "have a good job that pays well," "be able to own your own home," and "have a job that you enjoy doing." As social life unfolds in the context of specific, culturally defined social roles, the interrelated processes of "reflected appraisals" of others and self-assessment of one's self in given situations occur in the context of such roles. Thus, Grabowski and colleagues suggest the need to consider the life course contributions of different types of efficacy. Analyzing data from the Youth Development Survey, they find that global efficacy plays only a minimal role in economic attainment in the years between adolescence and early adulthood. Among working adolescents, global efficacy is largely unassociated with economic efficacy. At the same time, however, higher levels of economic efficacy stems from a higher grade point average and successful experiences in adolescent work, suggesting the importance of successful role enactment or "reflected appraisals." Similarly, global efficacy plays little part in processes of educational attainment, but educational efficacy increases both college preparation and overall expectations for educational attainment. Moreover, educational efficacy, both directly and indirectly, influences involvement in full-time work and the extent of postsecondary education. In linking together identity and agency, Grabowski and colleagues show how perceptions of self are both generalized and grounded in particular role domains and how the latter are particularly important in the successful actualization of role behaviors.

Summary of Practical Evaluation

In truth, very little is known from a sociological perspective about how and why people make decisions in the present about their lives. Subjective age identity and self-conceptions like self-efficacy undoubtedly matter, but their exact links to decision-making have not been established. Nevertheless, research suggests a dynamic interplay between the self and social context. People with high self-efficacy are likely to assume new and challenging responsibilities and roles. When these are successfully enacted, self-efficacy is further enhanced. In terms of age identity, efficacious people are likely to engage in activities that solidify their self-perceived age or their desired self-perceived age; when people succeed in these endeavors, their desired self-perceived age solidifies. These considerations suggest cycles of efficacious and inefficacious behaviors through the life course, but this idea has received little attention.

THE FUTURE IN THE LIFE COURSE: PROJECTIVITY

Having discussed subjectivity and agency in the context of the past and the present, we turn now to the future. We may well envision the future and plan for it, and indeed this is central to the study of the life course, but we can never know the future with certitude. Because the future cannot be observed directly, it is a particularly intriguing and complicated realm of human agency.

Emirbayer and Mische conceptualize the future in terms of

projection: people attempt to "go beyond" themselves in the present and construct changing images of their desired and anticipated futures, as well as future-oriented plans. Such images vary both in clarity and how far into the future they project. Some images are very concrete and very clear, and they focus on a fixed point in time. For example, the National Longitudinal Survey of Youth, a large survey of over twelve thousand Americans, asks respondents whether they expect to be married in the next five years. Such a question is premised on the idea that people possess distinct ideas of what roles they wish to occupy within a relatively short period of time. Other aspects of projection are less clear and less bounded in time. Some social research has asked the very general question "where do you want to be" in five years, ten years, twenty years, fifty years. Within a life course context, projectivity may be conceptualized according to four key dimensions.

The Future and Possible Selves

The first such dimension, "anticipatory identification," reflects the reality that alternatives are seldom clearly and neatly presented. As a result, one must attempt to identify patterns of possible developments on the horizon of an often vague and indeterminate future. This aspect of projection is particularly salient in that people need to make sense of what their futures look like. Our knowledge of the social world is not simply grounded in personal experiences and accomplishments but instead often comes to us vicariously through the experience of watching others and through exposure to mass media. The element of subjectivity (i.e., self-understanding and personal interpretation) is especially important during anticipatory identification. A particularly useful concept is "possible selves"—multiple images of who one might want to be, images that bring with them both an orientation towards constructing a particular type of identity and the choice of a self from a range of options.

Hazel Markus and Paula Nurius introduced the idea of possible selves in an insightful article in the *American Psychologist*.[27] Put simply, *possible selves* represent people's ideas of what they might become, and what they are afraid of becoming. Much like studies of the self in the past and the present, in Markus and Nurius's work there is an implicit assumption that people develop a fairly detailed and nuanced understanding of themselves and their place in society—a sense of who they are, what they can and cannot do, what they do and do not want to do, and how they are likely to feel in different circumstances. The foundation for this sense of self rests on how they see themselves in the past and in the present. Yet an additional component of self-identity is who one sees his/herself becoming. This insight ultimately fills out the conception of identity by situating it in an unfolding future life course.

Possible selves are conceptions of the self in future states. While this may initially seem like a relatively simple idea, it actually has several dimensions. In one respect, possible selves might be selves that are *hoped for*. In this case, an individual has formulated an understanding of their current identity but wishes for something different. The identity may be global (i.e., who I am fundamentally) or more role-specific (i.e., student, worker, spouse, parent). In either situation, the possible self represents a specific identity goal that a person orients herself towards. Agency and identity become intertwined as the orientation towards a possible self becomes the basis of action.

While the idea of possible selves easily lends itself to the idea of positive motivations, there is also the case of a possible self being an unwanted self, what Markus and Nurius call the "feared self," that is, an envisioned self in an undesirable future state. Again, identity and agency intertwine, but in this case they forge a course of action that will lead away from such a possible self. An interesting element of the "feared self" is the degree to which it is seen as probable or likely, which resonates with the third form of possible self, the "expected self." In some cases, a wanted or unwanted possible self may be remote. For example, the graduate student who envisions herself as unemployed (or unemployable) and homeless, despite the fact that educational attainment is one of the strongest predictors of socioeconomic success, may fear a particularly unlikely possible self. In other cases, the possible self may be the logical outcome of a given present self. The hardworking and successful student who is heavily embedded in a political and social science curriculum may envision himself as a lawyer or judge in later life, while a person heavily involved in drugs and crime in adolescence may see his possible self as addicted, violent, and aggressive. In both cases, the possible self is logical, possible, and probable. Still, the broader point is that possible selves emerge in self-reflection guided by context: about who one is, where one is heading, who one wants to be, and who one can or could be. Possible selves are ultimately the complex cognitive manifestation of bundles of goals, aspirations, motives, and fears. As such, they have a specific form to them and give direction to the organization of these "bundles" in action.

Social structure shapes the salience of possible selves. Some possible selves may seem remote possibilities given one's social circumstances. Others may seem both tangible and likely. Finally, social position will shape the overall set of possible selves. Possible selves, intrinsically, are cultural products. They derive from an individual's interactions with the social world; they are shaped when one routinely apprehends images of others; and people's socially structured experiences will shape the overall landscape of possible selves.

In their important work *The Ambitious Generation: America's Teenagers, Motivated but Directionless,* Barbara Schneider and David Stevenson attempt to understand how adolescents aspire to particular jobs and how social and psychological factors increase or decrease the likelihood of achieving such jobs.[28] As part of a larger five-year study of more than a thousand tenth and twelfth graders in twelve different parts of the country, the researchers asked adolescents to indicate the types of jobs that they would like to have and then compared the responses with the actual distribution of jobs in the labor force. In the spirit of possible selves, the adolescents indicated what type of worker they wished to become and the researchers assessed the viability of such choices in light of labor market realities.

In no small way, adolescent aspirations are both predictable *and* problematic, as there is a clear discrepancy between the jobs desired and the prevalence of such jobs in the labor force. For example, almost twenty percent of adolescents wanted to become "engineers, architects, or natural or social scientists," yet less than five percent of the labor force involves such work. Likewise, the number of adolescents who wanted to become lawyers or judges is five times the number of jobs, while the fifteen percent who want to become writers, artists, entertainers, or athletes will confront the fact that fewer than *one* percent of jobs involve such work.

At the other end of the spectrum, the jobs that are most prevalent in the labor force, notably in administrative support and clerical work, service work involving food and cleaning, and nonprofessional labor in such fields as farming, machine operation and repair, fabrication, and transportation, have little resonance as possible selves for American adolescents. While the latter account for over half of all jobs, fewer than ten percent of adolescents envision such work as their possible self in adulthood. In the increasingly mass media–dominated world of the early twenty-first century, it should not be surprising that adolescents' possible work selves are inspired by the professionals and entertainers they see on a daily basis. Still, the misaligned ambitions of adolescents are likely to make for a rocky transition into adult work (and by extension other facets of adulthood that are supported by paid employment, such as marriage and parenthood). Indeed, the misaligned ambitions and the various ways this might be remedied are the central themes of Schneider and Stevenson's book.

Even in the context of severe deprivation, envisioning possible selves that are linked to future-oriented agency is fundamental for personal and social change. In the United States and across the globe, recent decades have seen increased attention to the problem of homelessness and its implications for individuals and society. Although definitions vary, homelessness in general refers to a lack of permanent shelter. Social scientists, echoing ideas of "cumulative" advantage and disadvantage (discussed in Chapter 2), view homelessness as a particularly stubborn life circumstance that is very hard to break out of. The key problem is that homelessness undermines the psychological and physical resources that are necessary for securing paid employment and subsequent shelter. Unlike sheltered people whose social networks are typically quite broad, the networks of the homeless are largely constrained to other homeless people, not people who could help secure jobs, shelter, or aid. Equally important, time on the streets erodes social credentials like credit history, rental history, and employment records, which all are important signifiers of suitability for work, mortgages, and leases. Still, there is considerable evidence that people can and do move off the streets, which leads to the interesting question of what factors facilitate or inhibit exits from homelessness.

In a particularly interesting study, Brad Wright conducted interviews with homeless people in Minneapolis, Minnesota.[29] Unlike much prior work on homelessness, Wright's study was longitudinal, interviewing homeless men at two points in time. As part of the interview, respondents were asked whether they planned to live in conventional housing of their own one month after the interview. In the spirit of Markus and Nurius, respondents were being asked to articulate a possible self, a hoped-for self, in that they were indicating where and who they wanted to be in the future. Among the homeless, this possible "sheltered" self was not easy to predict. Regardless of numerous background factors, including sex, race, prior homeless history, skills (i.e., education, employment history), opportunities (i.e., family or friends who would help), and self-efficacy, virtually nothing correlated with plans to leave the street. In fact, the only factor that mattered was the length of the current spell on the street, which had clear implications for identity formation as a "homeless" person.

When respondents were re-interviewed six months later to see who indeed had successfully left the streets, individuals who had previously envisioned a possible self as sheltered were significantly more likely to have done so. Even more striking, the effect of this possible self was much greater than a host of other factors that would logically influence exits, such as employment skills, work history, mental illness, alcoholism, and having family or friends who could help. Ultimately, and in contrast to much conventional wisdom, exiting homelessness appears to have as much to do with envisioning oneself in a different situation as it has to do with the presence of social and psychological resources.

Acting on Images of the Future

In addition to the actual envisioning of future states, the way such visions are used in the construction of action is complicated. Emirbayer and Mische suggest that actors make use of "narrative construction," a second dimension of projectivity according to which future possibilities are situated within more or less coherent causal and temporal sequences. In other words, future possibilities are comprehended in terms of a larger biography that provides a broad map of action by linking what is unknown (i.e., the future) to what is known (i.e., knowledge of one's self and society). For example, the adolescent envisioning a future career as a doctor may locate such an image of the future in relation to both past experiences as a hospital volunteer or as a student interested in anatomy and physiology (just as "Anne," described in the introduction to this chapter, may have done). Similarly, the homeless man may think about various aspects of his past that indicate what a sheltered person looks like and acts like, and what particular experiences may help him get there. Still, the way in which this works is often quite fuzzy, and actors can insert themselves into a variety of trajectories of action and then spin out a variety of means and ends. In doing so, they expand the variety of responses to a given situation.

Equally important, this practice often ignores or "brackets" real-world constraints on action and instead allows one to freely consider the world of possibilities. Although an extraordinarily small percentage of Americans become president of the United States, anecdotal evidence suggests that literally thousands, if not millions, of young boys—and increasingly, young girls— envision themselves as president. Less dramatically, children and adolescents routinely envision a variety of seemingly glamorous occupations, including doctor, lawyer, police office, firefighter, professional athlete, and movie star, even though they may have only a vague knowledge of what such jobs entail, virtually no knowledge of how to obtain them, and ultimately little likelihood of actually getting one of these jobs.

Yet the nature of perceived reality does enter into the process, usually in the form of the third dimension of projection, "hypothetical resolution," which occurs when one's survey of possible actions gives way to the task of envisioning and proposing imagined outcomes. Actors will develop descriptions of what they "want" or what they "intend" to get from a particular course of action. While this may seem simplistic, it is important to recognize that people in the exact same situation will have widely varying desired outcomes. Consider an issue that every student has confronted: what do or did you want to get from your college education? In his influential book *Beyond*

College for All, James Rosenbaum shows that the proportion of the population opting for postsecondary education has steadily increased in recent decades.[30] This should not be surprising. If college graduates earn more over their life course, people will opt for this route. Yet, anyone who has ever evaluated students and assigned grades knows that students vary dramatically in what they want out of their college education. For some, high grades are paramount. Perhaps these students envision going to law school, medical school, or other professional or graduate programs, and they recognize that their undergraduate grade point average is perhaps the most important criterion used for admittance. These students may seek out the professor during office hours, asking for clarification of lecture material or answers to exam questions. These students may also challenge the manner in which their exams were graded and ask for explanations of why they received eight rather than nine out of ten.

Other students don't seem to care, or they care much less. They come to class (or don't), hand in their assignments (or don't), write their exams (or, on rare occasions, don't), and generally organize their educational career by a very different set of criteria. It is not particularly important here to determine which is a "better" strategy, but instead to recognize that agents make decisions about what they wish to achieve from their educational careers and how they organize their behavior and investments accordingly. (This does not deny the potential for inconsistencies: some students may act like they do not care about grades, may put little effort into their school work, yet still ask for extra assistance and/or challenge the evaluations they receive.)

The final dimension of projection is "experimental enactment," in which actors try out hypothetical resolutions in tentative and exploratory ways. The key idea here is that trying out alternatives in a given situation allows one the flexibility of determining what is a more successful and what is a less successful strategy. Again, consider the example of a college student. While it is tempting to conclude that individual students act the same way in all of their classes and throughout their educational careers, logic and evidence suggest otherwise. We are all aware that some students will put more effort into some classes than others, will show up more regularly in some contexts than others, and will assign greater value to some materials than to others. Such behavior makes sense in the context of experimental enactment in that students will try out different ways of being a student in light of what they hope to get out of a given class, how they perceive the system working, and how they strategize the route to their chosen goal.

In the study of the life course and in sociology more generally, there is a long history of research that examines the role of future orientations in various types of life course experiences. As described earlier, the Wisconsin Model of status attainment places aspirations for educational and occupational attainment as the key element linking family origins and occupational destinations. Such work draws upon a rich vein of social psychological research that considers how people's desire for future goals shapes their actual attainment of these goals. While such work does not mimic the detailed, multidimensional process that Emirbayer and Mische describe, it does provide a glimpse into the ways in which future-directed agency operates.

One particularly important example of research into aspirations was conducted by William Sewell and Vimal Shah.[31]

They began with a relatively simple puzzle. Studies have shown that children from higher social-class origins are more likely to aspire to higher educational and occupational goals than children from lower social-class origins.[32] What makes this puzzling is that one might expect that there would be little difference across groups because social achievement, as sociologist Robert K. Merton poignantly emphasized, is a universally valued goal in American society. Alternatively, one might expect that children from lower class origins would have higher aspirations, desiring to improve their standing and consequent life chances—what William Rushing referred to as "mobility aspirations."

In examining survey data from over ten thousand Wisconsin high-school seniors, Sewell and Shah tested the hypothesis that parental encouragement was the key factor that linked social class to aspirations. In other words, children from higher class origins have higher aspirations because their parents are more likely to foster such aspirations in their children. Consistent with their expectations, children from higher-class families were much more likely to report that their parents "wanted them to go to college," and such children had "definite plans to enroll in a degree-granting college or university." Equally important, the effects of parents' aspirations for their children on their children's aspirations were strongest for those who scored relatively high on intelligence and came from families with high socioeconomic standing.

Although again somewhat counterintuitive, there is a certain logic to this process in that the formation of "hypothetical resolutions" and "experimental enactment" would lead parents to align their aspirations for their children's future with their children's actual experiences and the constraints of the world they face. Children with lower intelligence would be less likely to meet the goals of higher educational attainment. Likewise, children from families with lower socioeconomic standing would be less capable of paying for the costs of higher education. As such, Sewell and Shah's model reveals the structural origins of aspirations and the ties between larger social context and the exercise of agency, a point we return to in some depth in the next chapter.

Still, the idea of aspirations and where they come from would be of only passing interest if we did not assume that such aspirations are meaningfully, if not powerfully, connected to later life attainments. Again, researchers in the Wisconsin tradition have done much to examine this issue. For instance, in their research on Wisconsin high-school seniors surveyed both in high school and in early adulthood seven years later, William Sewell and colleagues specifically examined the links between social background, social psychological expectations in adolescence, and later educational and occupational attainment. Beginning by measuring expectations about attending college and the socioeconomic index of the jobs they desired, Sewell and colleagues sought to predict the actual level of education achieved in early adulthood. While the authors admit that the effects of aspirations are not very strong, their work nonetheless shows that those planning on going to college do attain more years of education and those who desire more prestigious jobs do occupy more prestigious jobs later on. Not surprisingly, concordance was greater for educational attainment in light of the more limited range of choices in both aspirations and years of education. Nonetheless, this research stands as a seminal example of future-oriented agency, showing how those who envision themselves in future states are more likely to attain those states in later life.

Complications and Contingencies

From a life course perspective, this type of research has both positive and negative dimensions. A strength of the research is the consideration of how earlier aspirations are tied to later life achievements. Such work highlights the projective dimensions of agency and showcases the important linkages between different stages of life. A weakness, however, is the implicit assumption that aspirations are either fixed aspects of individual lives or that aspirations formed during late adolescence are those most important for shaping later life. In this regard, it is important to situate aspirations in the life cycle as well as within a given biography; both ultimately give meaning to aspirations and both likely condition the role that aspirations play in the life course. Although most research is static and assumes substantial stability of adolescent aspirations over long periods of time, some studies have considered broader life course dynamics.

In one particularly provocative study, Sandra Hanson considered the issue of "lost talent" among over 28,000 American high school seniors who were assessed through the early and mid-1980s.[33] "Lost talent" referred to a reduction of expectations, specifically among people who reported that they expected to receive a college degree in 1980, but then reported in 1986 that they no longer expected to receive this degree. How common is the downgrading of expectations? In Hanson's study, over a quarter of American adolescents experienced a decline in expectations. Although the instability of expectations is significant in and of itself, women and nonwhites were significantly more likely to change their expectations than were males and whites.

From a life course perspective, Hanson's findings make sense. Some social institutions and their concomitant social roles are more apparent and more compatible with certain life stages than with others. Education, for example, is most consistent with adolescence and early adulthood, and the passage of time probably signals to people that their likelihood of both entering and successfully completing college is decreasing.

Of course, contingency in agentic orientations is not confined to educational issues. In fact, if anything, one might expect that educational goals would be easier to meet in light of the relatively clear pathways through education (e.g., getting into college), the dramatic expansion and "opening" of higher education (as shown in James Rosenbaum's *Beyond College for All*), and the limited range of choice (i.e., college or no college).

In contrast, occupational aspirations (i.e., aspirations for a particular type of job) have less clear routes to them and exist in relation to many job possibilities (with over twelve thousand job types in the *Dictionary of Occupational Titles*!). The occupational realm provides an interesting arena to consider the stability of aspirations. Examining data from a sample of over five thousand young American men (ages fourteen to twenty-four in 1966) who were studied annually or biannually through their early forties, Jerry Jacobs and his colleagues examined the patterns of aspirations between ages fifteen and twenty-seven.[34] From a life course perspective, this age range is significant in that it encompasses adolescence, when such aspirations are typically studied, and extends through early adulthood, when most men, particularly men of that generation, would be expected to have entered into paid employment. The research considered aspirations within the context of the transition to adulthood, a central feature of the life course.

In examining survey responses to the question of the occupation in which the young men hope to be employed by age thirty, the work of Jacobs and colleagues is explicit in its critique of focusing solely on adolescent aspirations. First, there is a decline in aspirations with age. For example, while 57 percent of young men at age fifteen aspired to professional jobs, this number declined to 26 percent by age twenty-seven. Interestingly, aspirations appear to align with actual likelihoods of occupations, as only 21 percent of the sample was employed in professional jobs at age 30. So where do former aspirants for professional jobs end up? Interestingly, managerial jobs are not particularly desired in adolescence even though they make up a large proportion of the workforce and are clearly connected to mobility ladders. At age fifteen, only 6 percent of young men aspired for management jobs; by age twenty-seven, 26 percent had similar occupational orientations.

Second, at some point in time the overwhelming majority of American men have high aspirations. In some respects, this is surprising. As people go about their everyday lives, they are typically exposed to a wide variety of occupations. As such, even the most mathematically challenged person should gain some sense of more and less common jobs. Equally important, the occupational hierarchy in Western nations is such that higher status, more prestigious, and better-paying jobs are rarer. Yet even as aspirations ebb and flow over time, they typically move into the high-status terrain.

Finally, as people age, their occupational aspirations tend to solidify. In other words, there is significantly more variability in aspirations in adolescence and less in early adulthood. This pattern may reflect the reflexive character of agency, including the development of "hypothesized resolutions" and the "trying on" of different roles. As adolescents enter their early twenties, they combine school and work, largely part-time, and thus can explore their potential in both domains. In doing so, they may update their aspirations to draw them in line with their education, both completed and potentially completed as well as the accompanying likelihood of both desiring and actually gaining access to given jobs. Not surprisingly, race and class differences in aspirations also grow with age, indicative of the different experiences that people of different social origins have in educational and occupational environments. As Jay McLeod shows in his well-known book *Ain't No Making It,* aspirations of adolescences rise and fall in relation to the social realities they encounter.[35] What exactly those salient realities are remains to be seen.

Summary of Projectivity in the Life Course

Projectivity is a multifaceted process that describes how people think about the future. *Possible selves* refer to images that people have about hoped-for, expected, and dreaded selves in the future and are thus central to projectivity. Possible selves have a strong social basis: the range of images of the future that a person can entertain strongly reflects past experiences with other people, role performances, and experiences in institutions and organizations. Moreover, possible selves are images of one's self in future social roles and relationships. Possible selves also appear to be consequential: evidence suggests that images of the future self are motivational, perhaps powerfully so. People make plans about their future lives, and the anticipation of actually achieving the desired future self impels them to pursue these plans. Yet whether they are successful or not depends to a significant degree on social circumstances, as one finds, for example, in educational opportunities and labor markets. Not everyone can be a medical doctor or lawyer or entertainer, or can earn a doctoral degree in biomechanical engineering. Finally, possible selves have an interesting temporal quality, reflecting exchanges between the person and his or her setting. Possible selves are not static entities but rather are constantly subject to revision because of experiences.

CONCLUDING REMARKS

The major concepts that we have considered in this chapter are summarized in Table 4.1. Common to all of these concepts is a fundamental idea: the way people experience and create their lives is a highly dynamic, socially embedded, ongoing process. A person's memory of his or her past is often highly selective, objectively erroneous, and organized around socially significant transitions and events. And our autobiographical understanding is always undergoing revision based on the known present and the anticipated future. A person's future is a set of possible selves, all with unique social roles and relationships. And the present is the unique intersection of a reconstructed past and multiple future possibilities, creating a sense of self in the moment, a self filled with regrets, pride, motives, dreams, and de-

Table 4.1

SELECT MICRO CONCEPTS OF LIFE COURSE STUDIES

Micro Concept	Example
Agency—processes by which people formulate and pursue goals	Adult planning for retirement and taking steps to realize this plan
Subjectivity—ways in which people make sense of their selves in given social circumstances and the role that this understanding plays in guiding their actions	Self-Conceptions like self-efficacy; autobiographical memories
Iteration—process of selective use of past thought and action in current activity	Drawing on prior experience with personal finances to make a financial decision
Schema (plural: schemata)—bundle of knowledge that represents past experiences, categorizing relationships, scenarios, and events	"Mother," "Female Career," "Boss," "New Worker"
Script—subject of a schema that deals with specific guidelines for behavior	Appropriate colors for a woman or man to wear to the workplace
Autobiographical Memory—construction of a self located in the past, based on autobiographical "knowledge" (which may be true or false). **Narrative self** is a telling of this memory.	Older adult reflecting on life to answer questions about "life satisfaction"
Practical Evaluation—process of making judgments about alternative possible actions that arise in the context of specific demands or ambiguities of a given situation	Deciding a college major; deciding when to retire
Age Norms—expectations about the age-grading of specific behaviors (e.g., the "appropriate age" at which one should leave school), which are largely agreed upon in a group and the violation of which triggers some form of social disapproval	Agreed-upon expectations regarding age for home-leaving; if violated, expressions of disapproval
Subjective Age—a person's self-perceived age identity	Self-perceived adulthood; self-perceived status as "elderly"
Self-Efficacy—a person's self-perceived sense of competence or control	Pearlin's mastery scale
Projectivity—process by which the imagination generates possible future courses of action	Considering the plausibility of different future occupations
Possible Selves—multiple self-understandings of who one might be in the future; images that represent a range of "self-options" for the future	Reflecting on images of the self in the future with different occupations, marital status, number of children
Future Orientations—dimensions of the self that refer, at least in part, to the future	Educational ambitions; occupational plans

spair. We have emphasized agency as both process and practice, and we have situated it within a temporal context. Agency is both shaped by and reflected in the past, the present, and the future. Similarly, we have highlighted the subjective side of the life course with specific attention to identity—its formation and its dynamics.

The image that we have presented, however, is decidedly partial. In particular, thus far we have separated the life course into the macro and the micro dimensions and have not sought to explore the connections between them. Although we have alluded to such connections in our emphasis on the importance of context, particularly in this chapter, and also to the importance of understanding psychological orientations as embedded within social structures and historical times, the next chapter explores macro-micro linkages in the unfolding life course.

FURTHER READING

The following suggested readings build on this chapter. Given the scope of issues covered in this chapter, the suggested readings are highly select and feature conceptual pieces and excellent empirical examples.

Clausen, John. "Adolescent Competence and the Shaping of the Life Course." *American Journal of Sociology* 96 (1991): 805–842.

    A classic statement on agency with a focus on the idea of "planfulness" as a variable characteristic of adolescents that plays a significant role in the shaping of behavior, experience, and identity through the life course.

Cohler, Bertram J., and Andrew Hostetler. "Linking Life Course and Life Story." In *Handbook of the Life Course,* edited by Jeylan T. Mortimer and Michael J. Shanahan, 555–576. New York: Plenum-Kluwer, 2004.

    Concise overview of the "life story method" and empirical application to generations of gay men.

234 BIOGRAPHY AND THE SOCIOLOGICAL IMAGINATION

Elder, Glen H. "Time, Human Agency, and Social Change: Perspectives on the Life Course." *Social Psychology Quarterly* 57 (1984): 4–15.

Nice overview of the place of agency in life course research, as well as some classic empirical examples.

Giddens, Anthony. *Modernity and Self-Identity: Self and Society in the Late Modern Age.* Stanford, CA: Stanford University Press, 1991.

Broad and largely conceptual, provides an interesting framework for understanding identity in the context of late modern social change.

Johnson, Monica K. "Social Origins, Adolescent Experiences, and Work Value Trajectories during the Transition to Adulthood." *Social Forces* 80 (2002): 1307–1340.

Excellent empirical example of how work values (i.e., the importance attached to various rewards as work, which are integral to practical evaluation and projectivity) change with experiences during the transition to adulthood. Findings suggest the dynamic interplay between person and social experiences discussed in this chapter.

Macmillan, Ross, ed. *Constructing Adulthood: Agency and Subjectivity in the Life Course.* Advances in Life Course Research, vol. 11. New York: Elsevier, 2006.

A collection of chapters that provide a variety of different views on what agency is and how it can be envisioned in a life course context. Each chapter showcases different methods and approaches and provides unique and interesting empirical examples. Essays by Hartmann/Schwartz and Hitlin/Elder are especially helpful in the context of this chapter's topics.

Rubin, David C., ed. *Remembering Our Past: Studies in Autobiographical Memory.* New York: Cambridge University Press, 1996.

Excellent collection of essays on autobiographical memory. Chapters by Barclay, Bruner/Feldman, and Conway are especially interesting, offering social and psychological insights into the constrained nature of such memories.

Chapter Five
FROM MACRO TO MICRO

All actual life is encounter.

—Martin Buber

EVERY LIFE IS DIFFERENT and every life is the same. Having covered fundamentals of life course research, we are now able to explain this seemingly self-contradictory statement, which began Chapter 1, with added precision. In any given time and place, *every life is the same in that it*:

- comprises socially and culturally defined phases with their age-graded roles, responsibilities, and opportunities;
- reflects ongoing life course mechanisms and principles (Chapter 2);
- is structured by life course concepts like transitions and pathways (Table 2.1);
- is subject to macro forces that institutionalize and standardize biographies (Table 3.3);
- and reflects socially embedded processes of agency and subjectivity that extend across the phases of life to shape the character and content of the life course (Table 4.1).

Yet, in any given time and place, *every life is different because all of these principles, concepts, and mechanisms come together in singu-*

lar ways for each person. In other words, the principles and mechanisms interact to create a seemingly infinite set of biographical combinations. Indeed, modern cultures are characterized by the tension-filled imperatives that each person has a "legitimate résumé" and an individualized personal biography, that each person's life is recognizably part of the group's biographical experiences and yet speaks on its own terms. An appreciation for the many ways in which the mechanisms of the life course interact requires that we consider links between macro and micro phenomena. Mainly for pedagogical reasons, we have thus far maintained a clear distinction between these categories. We now turn to bridging them and, in so doing, we hope to illustrate how the concepts and mechanisms discussed thus far can be combined to illuminate "the same but different lives."

At its finest, life course research bridges the macro and micro to consider how changing societies, changing biographical patterns, and the subjective experiences of the person all come together. Such studies are rare. Moreover, just as there is no one right way to draw upon the life course paradigm to study lives, there is no one right way to bridge the macro and micro. In this chapter we consider studies that bring the macro and micro together in fascinating ways. In addition to exploring substantive questions about the life course, we offer these studies as examples of how scholars draw upon concepts and hypotheses to uncover new findings and generate still more ideas. All of these studies are exemplary but nevertheless fall short of the ideal. Thus, we include with each study a series of further avenues of inquiry that the life course analyst might wish to pursue, and hypothetical vignettes that illustrate how lives are patterned and yet unique due to contingencies of context and timing.

We also consider issues that represent important frontiers for future inquiry. For instance, the behavioral sciences are increasingly drawing upon technological innovations in the study of biology to consider the influence of genetic factors in human behavior. From a life course perspective, the key issue is not whether genetics matter but how genetic factors interplay with social experience to shape behavior and experience. In other words, what are the contexts that translate genetic predispositions into lived experiences? What biographical contingencies complicate such processes?

Traditional research on agency and the capacities of actors to select and choose, to cognitively and behaviorally invest in different courses of action, also calls for further conceptualization and empirical study. In particular, how do cognitive orientations and social and historical contexts interact in the shaping of the life course? And how does agency contribute to the changing life course? Thus far, we have focused almost exclusively on how social structural features change the life course. Very little is known about how people—collectively and individually—change the life course. At the macro level, the globalizing world is increasingly characterized by intersecting cultures, economies, and polities. This process of globalization has immense implications for the life course. Thus, we consider phenomena ranging from distinctly micro aspects of human life (genetics) through the social actor (agency) and finally to the emphatically macro (globalization).

THE LIFE COURSE AND GENETIC EXPRESSION

Many people are under the impression that genes dictate intelligence, key features of one's personality, and complex behaviors like the consumption of addictive substances (e.g., alcohol). This idea is not true, however, and indeed there is no evidence to support it. Instead, evidence suggests that genes and the environment combine in complex ways to make specific behaviors more or less likely. One such form of interplay is the *gene-environment interaction,* which refers to situations in which either the effect of genetic variation depends on the social context or the effect of the social context depends on genetic variation. For example, children who have a genetic predisposition for good verbal skills and parents with more than a high-school diploma are more likely to have good verbal skills than children with the same genetic predisposition but poorly educated parents. In other words, the effect of the genetic variation depends on something in the social context (parents' educations).

Consider four hypothetical children: two children (A and B) have identical high genetic potential for verbal ability; two children (C and D) have identical low genetic potential for verbal ability. Now suppose that A and C have parents with less than high-school education and B and D have parents with college degrees. Because genes and environment interact, B's verbal ability is much higher than A's, even though A and B have the same genetic potential. At the same time, B's verbal ability is much higher than D's even though B and D both have parents with college degrees. In fact, B has by far the highest verbal ability, C has by far the lowest, and A and D are essentially the same. The genes, by themselves, do not explain the ultimate differences in verbal ability, but rather it is the *combination of genes and the children's social context* that is decisive. Because the genes themselves are fixed over the life span, the role of the changing environment in translating genes into behavioral outcomes is the principal point of interest for the life course sociologist.

In what ways could social context matter for how genes are linked to behaviors? One mechanism is called *social control*, which refers to any social process that maintains the social order. Through ties to significant others and social institutions, people are socialized to engage in behaviors that tend to promote the stability of social arrangements and socially desired outcomes. Studies of social control typically focus on behaviors like delinquency and crime, alcohol and drug abuse, and other forms of antisocial behavior (e.g., tax evasion). Ideally, societal forces make such behaviors less likely.[1]

In fact, many studies suggest that as social control increases, the effects of genetic differences on behavior lessen, whereas in contexts marked by low levels of social control, the effects of genetic differences on behavior increase. In other words, in circumstances marked by high levels of social control, a large percentage of people, irrespective of their genetic diversity, exhibits similar "socially controlled behavior" (e.g., they do not smoke cigarettes as teens). In contrast, settings marked by low social control will show people's choices and behaviors that are more apt to reflect their genes (e.g., with people genetically predisposed to addictive behaviors being more likely to smoke cigarettes as teens). To simplify matters, one can think of three groups of people: (1) a relatively small group of genetically similar people who will exhibit a behavior in either high- or low-control settings (e.g., they will always smoke cigarettes as teens), (2) a relatively small group of genetically similar people who will not exhibit the phenotype (or behavior) in either setting (i.e., teens who will never smoke), and (3) a larger group of genetically similar people who will exhibit the behavior (smoking) only under circumstances of low social control.

Age of First Intercourse

One of the more interesting arenas of social change with respect to social control is sexual behavior. Specifically, many people believe that social control has declined in most Western societies with respect to sexual mores and behaviors, reflecting the sexual liberation movement that became prominent in the 1960s, in addition to the weakening of family ties, urbanization, and other factors. If this hypothesis is true, then we would expect that the effect of genetic variation on sexual behavior would increase through the twentieth century. And in fact, this pattern is basically what has been observed.

For example, Dunne and his colleagues examined how much variation in age of first sexual intercourse reflected genetics and how much variation reflected social context among Australian youth born in the period 1922–65.[2, 3] Among women, they found that genetic variation accounted for almost a third (32 percent) of the variation in age of first intercourse among those born 1922–52, yet almost half (49 percent) of variation among those born 1952–65. Even more striking, genetic variation accounted for none (0 percent) of the variation in age of first intercourse among men born 1922–52, yet almost three quarters (72 percent) of the variation in men born 1952–65. In general, the effect of genetic variation on age of first intercourse increased through the historical time studied. As the cohorts differed substantially in their mean levels of age of first sexual intercourse (18.9 years among the later-born cohort and 21.1 years for the earlier-born cohort), Dunne and colleagues conclude that young people defer first sexual intercourse when social control is high, regardless of their genetic predisposition. Conversely, as social control lessens, people with a genetic propensity for early sexual intercourse are particularly likely to engage in intercourse earlier than people without such a propensity. The authors suggest that earlier-born cohorts were constrained by levels of social control higher than those en-countered by youth in later-born cohorts.

The study by Dunne and colleagues obviously has life course appeal with its emphasis on birth cohorts and the puta-tive social changes associated with them. Yet, the study is more provocative than definitive and ultimately raises as many ques-tions as it answers. The life course analyst might, for example, ask a series of follow-up research questions. First, what broad historical changes were associated with a lessening of social control and, hence, an increase in expressed genetic propensi-ties? (Note that a life course analysis typically begins with questions about societal changes.) What changes took place be-tween the periods 1943–74 and 1972–84? Changes may be episodic (e.g., World War II), but the design and results of the study suggest that the changes were more ongoing across the cohorts. We can only speculate. The data refer to Australian youth but anyone acquainted with the American experience would probably suspect historical changes such as the sexual revolution of the 1960s and 1970s, an increase in single-mother-headed households, and a decline in involvement in religious institutions. To isolate the relevance of such factors, the life course analyst would ideally become acquainted with the social history of Australia during this period.

Second, in what ways did specific social controls dictating sexual behavior change between the earlier and later historical periods? This question concerns the repercussions of broader social change for people's more *proximal settings.* The essential meaning of the word "proximal" is "nearest"; in the present context "proximal setting" refers to how social changes are linked to changes in people's immediate social contexts. It may be, for example, that when compared with the later period, the earlier period's proscriptions against precocious sexual behavior were more uniformly observed; that adult monitoring of youth was more thorough; that engagement in nonfamilial adult socializing agents (e.g., school, extracurricular activities, voluntary associations) were more commonplace; and that religious affiliations more steadfastly constrained such behaviors.

Related questions would reflect an interest in the timing of lives. For example, if changes in family structure are fundamental features of social control, what temporal patterns are associated with high and low social control? A stable household with few children and two parents who practice a warm and loving form of discipline is likely a situation of high social control. What about a household that experiences a divorce when the children are three and five years old, with remarriage two years later? What about a household characterized by divorce when the children are fifteen and seventeen, with subsequent remarriage? Such questions reflect an interest in the timing of experiences. These questions focus on the dynamic nature of context, and we should also ask questions about the developmental nature of sexual experiences. What other dimensions of courting and sexual behaviors should we consider? Across time, what did each person's sexual history look like?

Finally, the life course analyst would wonder about agency and the subjective experiences of the different groups of youth. What was it like, in terms of subjective meanings, to have a strong genetic predisposition for early intercourse in the 1930s, when social controls exerted strong influences to delay such behaviors? We have seen evidence that such predispositions likely did not translate into behavior, yet we know less about how individuals felt in such circumstances. With strong prohibitions against sexual intercourse, would those with strong genetic predispositions feel sexually aberrant? Would their identities be clouded with a view of themselves as deviant? Would they see themselves as "outsiders" in their own societies? Ultimately, we do not know—but such questions have considerable importance.

All of these "layers" of analysis—*societal, proximal, developmental, and interpretive*—come together in unique ways for each person, creating the sense that each life is the same but different. Consider two hypothetical cases, both involving young men with a strong genetic predisposition for early intercourse but with very different life course outcomes:

> Case 1: One young man is born into a society characterized by high levels of social control, but still engages in intercourse on multiple occasions. The strong norms of the time limit access to contraception and sex education, and by age eighteen he has impregnated his girlfriend. Not surprisingly, there are very few

supports from societal institutions or from his or her social networks. The early entry into parenthood introduces an earnings imperative which forces him to curtail schooling and select from a range of low-wage jobs. Without a solid financial base, both parenting and the maintenance of a spousal relationship is difficult. Thus, his later life involves both a turbulent family life and a constant struggle to maintain steady work patterns.

Case 2: Another young man is born into the same society but his proximal setting is marked by high social control (e.g., deep integration into his church's youth group). He abstains from intercourse until after he has finished his education. With completion of a university degree he is able to select from a range of higher paying jobs. Equally important, his involvement in church provides an introduction to his future wife. At age twenty-four, with work well established, he marries and initiates his sexual life. Although he felt sexually frustrated as a teenager, he is now filled with satisfaction at his "orderly" life. He is respected by family and friends as a faithful, committed husband and a good provider. The resulting life course pattern is marked by economic prosperity and happiness at home.

Note that Cases 1 and 2 are distinguished solely by their proximal settings, with Case 2 living in a household and neighborhood with a high level of social control. The difference between the boys' settings leads to remarkable differences between them throughout their lives, despite our assumption that they are genetically identical. The overarching point, however, is that we are presented with two lives, both recognizable yet both unique. While these cases begin with genetic similarity, proximal variations produce unique and different outcomes. That is, the outcomes are unique, but reflect recognizable combinations of social elements.

Migration and Alcohol Consumption
Substance use tends to run in families: Spouses tend to resemble one another; children tend to resemble parents; siblings show similar levels of consumption. In light of this, it is not surprising that those interested in genetic influences on behavior have focused considerable attention on substance use, particularly the drinking of alcohol. Much like sexual debut, alcohol consumption likely reflects the powerful role of social context and social control combined with genetic predispositions. For example, Richard Rose and his colleagues observed that genetic factors were more prominent in urban than in rural settings for youth from age sixteen to eighteen and a half years old.[4] Following up on this finding, Danielle Dick and her colleagues examined whether it could be accounted for by specific dimensions of the urban-rural difference, including percentage migration into and out of urban municipalities.[5] The authors reasoned that as migration in an area increases, community monitoring and personal accountability decreases. For the area with the highest migration, the additive genetic effect was .60, basically meaning that 60 percent of variation in drinking was attributable to genetics.[6] In contrast, for the area with the lowest migration, the additive genetic effect was only .16 or 16 percent. As expected, in circumstances of high social control, in this case low migration, the additive genetic effect is much lower when compared to the areas marked by low social control (i.e., high migration). In other words, the level of migration in a community changes the degree to which genetic

variance is associated with the likelihood of drinking in a population.

This research stimulates the life course imagination because of its emphasis on context, specifically migration. The results imply that geographic areas of high migration will experience higher levels of alcohol consumption among adolescents. Again, we are interested in expanding upon these findings by asking a series of questions that reflect an interest in context and timing. What broad social factors are associated with increasing migration? That is, what changes in society set the stage for a specific pattern of genetic expression? Migration is often prompted by socioeconomic circumstances, with people migrating to areas with more opportunities for education, jobs, and a higher standard of living. Improvements in transportation, the opening of national borders, and the emergence of social networks that span national borders or geographic regions all represent macro factors that facilitate and encourage migration. It is certainly intriguing to speculate that such societal changes ultimately increase the likelihood that specific genes will be associated with drinking alcohol in some people!

A second question is how social control is altered in areas of high migration. This question focuses on the link between broad societal changes such as those just mentioned and the more proximal settings of people in areas of high and low migration. What is it about migration that affects social control? As in-migration (i.e., people coming into an area) increases, a diminishing number of the inhabitants know each other, which would lead to increasing anonymity. If law enforcement and social service resources do not keep up with in-migration, surveillance and monitoring of potentially dangerous people also decreases. A consideration of these factors, however, raises the issue of whether in- and out-migration have the same implications for social control. The loss of people in a community disrupts social networks, while an influx of migrants may be associated with people who have few, if any, social network ties. Also, are the migrants and non-migrant populations affected equally?

Third, the intersection between the proximal factors and timing requires consideration. The study was conducted with a sample mainly of youth aged sixteen to nineteen. Do the findings apply to young adults, older adults, etc.? What are the implications of this study for children? Other studies show that alcoholism is related to child abuse and child abuse before roughly five years of age interacts with a gene (called "MAOA" because it is associated with monoamine oxidase, an enzyme that metabolizes neurotransmitters) to increase chances of anti-social behavior.[7]

Consider a hypothetical chain of events: a large automotive plant is built on the outskirts of a small town (i.e., economic opportunity) in a rural area, attracting a major influx of job-seeking migrants; the large in-migration loosens social controls and leads to the expression of genes associated with alcoholism in some people in the town; a subset of these people abuse their children; in turn, these children are at heightened risk for anti-social behavior (including criminality) in young adulthood. Timing plays a major role in this scenario: the "perfect storm" of genetic and environment factors requires that the timing of dramatic migration coincide with the time frame of birth to age five for the child, which suggests a parent within a certain age range as well. If the children of the abusive parents are old enough, they may escape the long-term adverse effects of the abuse (e.g., by avoiding their parents). And if the parents are old enough, perhaps they have developed coping skills to deal more successfully with the social dislocations associated with migration.

We should also pose questions about agency and subjectivity. Alcohol can be a major impediment in one's life, standing in the way of plans, decreasing motivation, increasing depression, and threatening one's sense of self. Among migrants, how does alcohol interfere with one's sense of agency and self? How do people who do not drink alcohol and yet are at high genetic and social risk for alcoholism interpret their experiences?

Once again, the interaction among these multiple levels of analysis can be illustrated in part with hypothetical vignettes, all of which feature women with a high genetic predisposition for excessive consumption of alcohol. The case studies are designed to juxtapose the societal, proximal, developmental, and interpretive elements:

> Case 3: A woman in her early twenties migrates from her rural village of 250 inhabitants to a large urban area characterized by high in-migration. She is married with two children, and the family has moved because of economic opportunities for both her and her husband. Both drank in the village, on occasion heavily, and would sometimes have arguments and fights. In the city, their lives are increasingly organized around work and their children. With both the larger community of working parents and each other acting as social controls, they almost never drink since their move. Through the ensuing years, they have a reasonably stable marriage, good income, and good health.

Case 4: A woman, also in her early twenties migrates from her rural village of 250 inhabitants to a large urban area characterized by high in-migration. She is single, has no relatives in town, and has moved to further her studies. She drank socially in the village, typically at a moderate level. Being single with no family, most of her activities involve other students and a general atmosphere of "partying." Since the move she has significantly increased her drinking. Throughout her schooling her social life becomes more and more prominent, resulting in problems in her studies. The woman is eventually dismissed from her educational program without a degree and now works as an assistant in a card shop in a town near her village.

Cases 3 and 4 are very similar in that the women came from small villages and had similar drinking histories. Once again, we assume that they share the same genetic propensity to drink alcohol excessively and are now residing in an area of high in-migration. The decisive difference between the two women is their social embeddedness, which represents a form of social control. The older woman has children, a husband, and a job, and is embedded in a network of other working parents. These social connections compensate for the low social control (due to high in-migration) of her immediate setting. The younger woman with no family lacks social connections and has an abundance of opportunities for drinking. Her sense of rootlessness is magnified by the high in-migration in the area. The nature of the environment leads to drinking patterns that interfere with her performance and curtail her education. A very different life course pattern follows.

Agency and Contextual Contingencies
in the Life Course

There is a popular saying that if you want to make God laugh, make a plan. Let us recast this darkly humorous sentiment as a scientific question: what is the connection between life course agency and society? As discussed in the last chapter, people exercise agency with respect to the broad contours of their lives. Sometimes these plans come to fruition and sometimes they do not. Expressions of agency are likely to have different meanings and different implications in different contexts. Such a thesis clearly links macro phenomena, which focus on the cultural and social setting of the person, with micro phenomena such as the self, identity, and action. Yet how such macro and micro elements come together has been addressed by surprisingly little research. The first author and colleagues' analysis of agency in the context of the Great Depression and World War II provides some unique evidence on this issue.[8]

The Great Depression was indisputably one of the most significant events in the twentieth century in the United States. At its worst, almost one quarter of American males were unemployed. Yet the nature of the Great Depression, particularly its duration and the social conditions that followed, gave it distinctly different biographical meanings for different cohorts of Americans. For example, some cohorts confronted the Depression as they moved into (or tried to move into) paid labor, while others experienced the Depression in early life and were effectively shielded from its impact by schooling. Still others confronted the Depression during the pivotal years between adolescence and adulthood, when life decisions were still in play. It is such variation that provides the framework for the study.

To begin, what is "agency" and how can it be measured? The authors drew upon a concept developed by John Clausen called "planful competence," which refers to the thoughtful, assertive, and self-controlled processes by which people formulate and pursue goals (e.g., a specific occupation).[9] According to Clausen, at midadolescence (around fifteen years of age), differences in planful competence become especially important to the later life course, since it is at this time in life that people begin to make choices about schooling, work, and family. Young people with high levels of planful competence have a fine-tuned awareness of who they are and what they are good at, and consequently they can make realistic plans about the future. In contrast, people with low levels of planful competence have a poor sense of who they are and what they are good at, and consequently they are likely to make unrealistic choices about school, work, and family. These different types of choices, realistic in the case of planful youth and unrealistic in the case of less planful youth, have lifelong implications. Planful youth tend to realize their goals and live more prosperous, stable, and contented lives, while less planful youth often fail to meet their goals, leading unstable, less prosperous, and less contented lives. That is, differences in planful competence at around fifteen years of age have profound and long-lasting effects in the life course.

Building upon Clausen's pioneering work, the first author and colleagues measured planfulness in terms of "conscientious," "perseverance," "desire to excel," and "cognitively committed." That is, youth high in these measures of planfulness reported that they reflected often on their situation, persevered in the face of difficulties, wanted to succeed, and valued learning. Such planfulness should promote a sense of agency in the pursuit of higher education and greater occupational standing in later life.

To what degree do expressions of agency matter, given a structure of opportunity and constraint? Shanahan and colleagues hypothesized that agency matters most when individuals have realistic opportunities that present a range of viable options. When such opportunities do not exist, the ability to make choices is limited, regardless of differences in agency. To examine this issue empirically, Shanahan and colleagues drew on the Stanford-Terman data, which have a particularly interesting feature: they include numerous birth cohorts and have reasonable measures of human agency. Two sets of birth cohorts proved particularly important. Members of the "older cohort" were born between 1904 and 1910; these men were in college during the Great Depression. Members of the "younger cohort" was born between 1911 and 1917; most of these men were in high school or just starting college during the Great Depression.

Thus, the older cohort was attempting to finish school and start paid work when there were very few opportunities for paid work. Many men simply stayed in school, prolonging their educations in the hopes that the labor market would improve. Soon, World War II came and these men were likely to serve in the military, leaving behind their young wives and perhaps young children. In many instances, these men returned from war to find a wife and children who could not reconnect to their husband and father, creating considerable familial tensions. In contrast, the younger cohort typically was in college and entered the military during World War II before joining the workforce during the postwar economic boom. Many of these men postponed marriage and parenthood until after their military service. These men enjoyed unprecedented economic opportunities and had immediate economic incentives to leave school.

This pattern leads to two interesting predictions. First, because the older cohort stayed in school to avoid the job market, planfulness had little connection to their educational attainment. That is, whether these men were planful or not, they all stayed in school. In contrast, the younger cohort could choose between prolonging their educations or starting paid work. The more planful of these men would choose more school, all other things being equal, and thus maximize occupational options in later life. Second, because of the timing of marriage and military service, planfulness had little connection to marital stability for the older cohort. Whether planful or not, men from the older cohort often returned from war to an estranged household. In contrast, more-planful members of the younger cohort postponed marriage and parenthood until after the war and then made good choices with respect to their spouse and parenthood. That is, the more planful members of the younger cohort enjoyed great marital stability than the less planful members. This is a captivating pattern of predictions because it suggests that agency simply did not matter for the older cohort's educational attainment or marital stability. Whether highly planful or not, they prolonged their educations and experienced marital stresses. For the younger cohort, planfulness mattered in terms of education and marriage.

So how does planfulness interact with historical context? For the younger cohort in the Stanford-Terman data, planfulness at age fourteen had a strong and significant impact on educational attainment by age thirty. More planful adolescents had significantly more education. In contrast, planfulness among the older cohort had no effect on educational attainment. When examined in terms of educational attainment at age forty, planfulness mattered for both cohorts, but the effects were more pronounced among the younger cohort. Equally important, education proved to be the gateway to socioeconomic attainment and significantly increased occupational status at both age thirty and age forty. By implication, planfulness indirectly influenced occupational standing through midlife by influencing educational attainment. Also consistent with expectations, planful competence decreased the likelihood of divorce, but only among the younger cohort. Finally, the study found that the effects of adolescent planfulness were predictive of these outcomes early in adulthood, but not later.

These analyses of the Stanford-Terman data highlight two issues in the study of agency-environment interactions. First, they show that social context (i.e., macro phenomena) can enable or disable agentic orientations (e.g., macro phenomena). The conceptual model and empirical evidence suggest that in times of very little choice, agency matters little, if at all. Second, such cohort interactions are age-graded and vary according to where they fit into the overall biography. In the Stanford-Terman data, the effects of planfulness are early, occurring before age thirty, and later ages show less influence. That is, agency matters at certain times in history for certain segments of the life course, depending on one's age. Timing and context thus play a major role in how salient personal agency is to the life course.

As intriguing as these results may be, very little is actually known about the connections among agency, social context, and timing. From a societal perspective, what types of changes are associated with the severe restriction of choices that characterized the Great Depression? In other words, were the results of the planfulness study unique to a catastrophic economic collapse, the likes of which are exceptionally rare? The question really concerns social changes that severely restrict choices about school, work, or family. Certainly sociopolitical collapses such as those experienced in the former Soviet Union and its satellites would likely result in similar disruptions of life course patterns. However, one wonders whether lesser social changes could also alter the effects of planfulness on educational and familial outcomes. For example, could macro economic changes that increase the poverty rate alter the planfulness-education and planfulness-occupation connections? Could changes in educational funding that alter the number of positions available in higher education alter the planfulness-education connection? Could policies that affect the male-female ratio in a society affect the planfulness-marriage connection?

Thinking more proximally, what was it about the Depression that altered people's immediate settings "to turn planfulness on or off?" This is an especially interesting question because, although planfulness "was turned off" for the older cohort as a group, there were in fact some members of the older cohort whose planfulness mattered. What distinguished members of the older cohort whose planfulness did matter from those for whom it did not? The less planful men who left school for work and those less planful men who did not would be strategic groups to study. Did the former have better social networks that helped secure employment? What other social factors helped them?

In thinking about these proximal factors, a developmental perspective is essential. The older and younger cohorts clearly differed in how planfulness operated in their lives, yet cohorts, as studied here, imprecisely locate biographies in history. Ideally, one would like to examine men of different grade-level/calendar-year combinations. For example, one could study men who were seniors in college each year from 1929 to 1939 inclusive. In 1930, which men decided to prolong their educations and which men were able to join the labor market? (The stock market had crashed only six months earlier.) In 1938, which men stayed in school and which men joined the labor force? The lowest point of the Depression had passed by then. Planfulness undoubtedly played a role, but what other factors from the men's lives made a difference?

Finally, a focus on planning clearly raises issues of agency and subjectivity. Of special interest is how men interpreted their lives when, despite talent and a high degree of planfulness, they nevertheless failed to achieve their goals because of societal constraints, while on the other hand some men of low planfulness seemed to "fall into" a good job and a stable, happy marriage. How does the former group make sense of their lives? Did their sense of agency remain largely intact? Did they view themselves as failures? With whom did they compare themselves when thinking about their biographies?

The issues of social change, proximal factors, development, and subjectivity can be highlighted by way of hypothetical vignettes. Consider three young men with high levels of planfulness and talent:

Case 5: A chemistry major works extremely hard and graduates at the top of his class at an elite university. He has several attractive job offers but continues his education with graduate school. His studies are difficult, his salary low, and he postpones marriage and children until graduation four years later. He graduates, lands an exceptionally fine job, marries, and starts a family. Because of his additional education, he is promoted quickly.

Case 6: An engineering major works extremely hard and graduates at the top of his class at an elite university. Expecting to land a good job, he decides to marry and start a family. Shortly after graduating, the country enters a deep recession and the only job offer he gets is far below his expectations. He decides to pursue a graduate degree, which takes six years to complete. Although he excels, the length of the program, the long hours spent studying, and the low pay and unstable work that come with being a research assistant all place great stress on his relationship. Even after graduating, he finds stiff competition for work due to the backlog of engineers who similarly opted to "warehouse" themselves in higher education. He ultimately secures a job that is better than the first job offer but still below expectations. The accumulating stress of the years in school without a significant payoff heighten tensions within the family. His wife ultimately leaves him a year later, taking their two children.

Case 7: Same as Case 6, but the man marries in his third year of graduate school, after the recession has ebbed. Although graduate school is still difficult, his wife has a well-paying job that she enjoys and she is able to contribute to the family finances. The year that he graduates with his doctoral degree, they become parents. With his advanced degree and better economic conditions, he has a wide range of options and chooses a job that allows him to work part-time and be a stay-at-home dad for a year before their son enters daycare. Family life is stable and good, and the two parents jointly earn a solidly middle-class wage.

Clearly, Cases 5 and 6 correspond to the findings of Shanahan and his colleagues. Case 5 involves a highly planful young man who graduates from college during a time of viable choice between school and work. He chooses additional education and postpones family formation, two good choices that have life-long implications. Case 6 involves a highly planful man who graduates from college during a time of little choice. He chooses additional education but it does not translate into a clearly better job. Moreover, he does not postpone family formation, which ultimately results in marital separation. Case 7 shows an exceptional pattern: a man who chooses more education and only partially postpones marriage. Because of the flexibility of their work lives, this man and his wife are able to support each other and they function well as a team. Case 7 illustrates how a focus on cases that do not correspond to the general pattern can help elucidate life course processes: in this case, a spouse with an excellent career is able to compensate for the man's delayed career and their close, mutually supportive relationships puts the family on an excellent trajectory.

BECOMING ADULT IN A GLOBALIZING WORLD

As noted in Chapter 3, life course sociology has a long-standing interest in the transition to adulthood because, in part, how young people move from adolescence into adulthood has major implications for their later lives and for society. Also as noted in Chapter 3, the transition to adulthood is of interest because the pathways that youth can take into adulthood are often shaped in significant ways by broad societal forces. One major force altering the transition to young adulthood today is globalization, which refers to the increasing integration of economic, cultural, social, and political systems across national and geographic boundaries. Not surprisingly, scholars of globalization draw attention to the increased homogenization of societies, with Western norms and institutions playing significant roles in non-Western nations. John Meyer and colleagues have documented processes of "institutional isomorphism" whereby institutions of schooling, work, medicine, politics, and even family become increasingly similar across nations.[10] While the processes that produce this phenomenon are cont inually being studied scientifically, comparative cross-national research highlights a "world society" that is shaping, if not transforming, social environments across the globe. We now focus on two major facets of globalization and consider how they are related to the life course.

First, the "demographic transition" is widely regarded as a global phenomenon during which forces of modernization, including both economic and cultural change, reduce the average number of children born in a population. The theory of the demographic transition suggests that societies are initially characterized by high fertility and high mortality but gradually shift (or transition) to low-fertility/low-mortality regimes. Western nations underwent such a transition through the latter part of the nineteenth and early part of the twentieth centuries.

Non-Western nations have shown such a transition in more recent decades, and many lesser-developed countries are still experiencing it today.

The demographic transition is an important facet of globalization, and yet an equally important and perhaps linked phenomenon is the expansion of formal education. In an insightful study, Evan Schofer and John Meyer document the remarkable expansion of formal education across the globe.[11] Importantly, they show that population-growth patterns are similar in all types of countries but are especially high in countries linked to the "world society." The nature of formal education is central to life course inquiry in that it represents one of the central markers of the transition to adulthood and is a central source of socialization and attainment with lifelong implications. Naturally, then, the intersection of the demographic transition and the expansion of education is a central feature of globalization.

Second, efforts to understand the implications of globalization for the life course clearly need to confront the issue of social change. Yet, the forces of globalization often bring with them different dimensions of social change that are really not seen in the American context. If anything, these forces have greater resonance with classical sociological works focusing on the social implications of industrialization and the transition to capitalism, albeit with numerous unique features. A particularly important issue is how aspects of an individual's biography in one sociopolitical context translate into another, quite distinct, context. Such questions have an interesting legacy in life course scholarship in that Thomas and Znaniecki's *The Polish Peasant in Europe and America,* a book that many regard as an intellectual starting point of life course scholarship, was fundamentally about what it was like to live in a society into which one had not been socialized.[12] The case of Soviet Russia and it satellites provides an interesting arena for considering the implications of this feature of globalization for the life course.

Demographic Transition and Education in Brazil

Brazil's demographic transition was pronounced. Between 1940 and 1960, Brazil's total fertility rate (i.e., the average number of children born per woman) was around 6.2. It dropped to about 4.3 by 1980 and to 2.7 by 1990. At the turn of the twenty-first century, the total fertility rate was 2.3, approximately one-third of what it had been four decades earlier. Although it may seem counterintuitive, the decline in the fertility rate simultaneously produced *increases* in cohort sizes. Between 1950 and 2000, the size of birth cohorts increased from under 2 to approximately 3.5, with the largest cohorts for those born between 1980 and 1985. (In this context, increases in cohort size result from rapid declines in infant and child mortality.) Equally important, Brazil's integration into the global economy has been stressful, characterized by both rapid economic growth and economic crisis. With economic uncertainty looming large for Brazilian adolescents, school enrollment is an increasingly significant factor, as it provides a life course buffer against poor economic prospects.

Close examination of both patterns of schooling and the demographic transition in Brazil, as well as the factors that both increase and decrease the likelihood of enrollment, provides a unique perspective on the nature of the life course in the modern, globalizing world. In a report for the National Research Council's *The Changing Transition to Adulthood in Developing*

Countries, David Lam and Letícia Merteleto note that the average length of schooling in Brazil increased moderately over time, with the most significant increases occurring in the 1990s.[13] The number of years of schooling is moderate, averaging between six and seven years for teenage boys and girls. About 85 percent of Brazilian teenage girls and 80 percent of similarly aged Brazilian boys attended school in the late 1990s, indicating considerable participation. Although years of schooling and enrollment rates increased during the last quarter of the twentieth century, the severe economic depression of the 1980s, sometimes referred to as the "lost decade," saw little growth. Moreover, despite recent increases, educational attainment in Brazil remains low, at least in comparison to Western nations.

Consistent with general principles of context and contingency, general trends towards increased education have not been uniform. Why not? First, the social context of declining fertility and increasing cohort size directly shape enrollment. Specifically, cohorts who experienced high growth rates in the population ages seven to fourteen (a good proxy for the school-age population) have significantly lower enrollments. This is consistent with Easterlin's hypothesis (discussed in Chapter 3) that larger cohorts can overwhelm social institutions and place unique pressures on the people experiencing them.

At the same time, there are important age contingencies as enrollment varies across the teenage years. In Brazil, enrollment increased linearly between ages seven and twelve before beginning to stagnate. Those age fifteen were actually no more likely to be in school than those age seven, and those age sixteen and seventeen were significantly less likely to be in school.

Unlike in North America and most European countries, in Brazil schooling during the teenage years is considerably less regimented and institutionalized, with the consequence that other institutions, such as family and the labor force, are much stronger competitors for Brazilian adolescents' time. The growth rate of the population has also interacted with age to suppress school attendance. Older adolescents are particularly less likely to be in school in times of rapid growth.

Lam and Meteleto suggest that older students are more likely to be at the margins of dropping out and therefore more affected by factors such as school crowding. Part of the problem seems to be grade repetition. Grade promotion is not automatic in Brazil and as a result educational attainment is less regimented and age-variance is greater with increasing grade levels, much more so than in North America and Europe. As such, older teenagers are also more likely to be behind in school and thus face cost-benefit calculations that reflect declining returns from schooling and increased rewards from more-rapid entry into the labor force (i.e., before the rest of the large cohort makes similar decisions).

A second important contingency is parents' education. Research across several nations shows that parents' education exerts strong effects on children's involvement in schooling, both socially and psychologically. Brazil is no exception: children whose parents, either mothers or fathers, have higher educational attainment also have a greater likelihood of enrollment, although there appear to be thresholds beyond which increased parental education has diminishing returns. Perhaps even more important, demographic realities condition the effects of parents' education: cohorts who experienced high growth rates were especially influenced by their parents' education. In such contexts, the effects of a father's education more than tripled. One interpretation of this pattern, consistent with a multilevel and multidimensional conceptualization of the life course, is that children from better-off households are less affected by large cohort sizes as they are better able to take advantage of educational opportunities.

Once again, the life course analyst would wish to examine societal, proximal, developmental, and interpretive levels of analysis. Societal change requires relatively little exploration in this instance because the model is essentially macro: globalization has put a premium on education; larger birth cohorts associated with the demographic transition have lower enrollment levels; and better-educated parents buffer the effects of large birth cohorts and greatly promote educational attainment. How this model operates more proximally and developmentally, however, remains unexplored. What is it about higher parental education that promotes the child's educational attainment and acts as a protective factor against a large birth cohort? Perhaps parenting behaviors? Social networks? On the other hand, specifically what is it about large cohorts that leads to lower enrollment levels? Presumably the answer relates to crowding, but how does crowding translate into higher percentages of children not being enrolled? In thinking about such issues, our imagination turns to "unexpected cases." What factors promote youth from larger birth cohorts who have parents with little education? On the other hand, what factors in the early life course detract from educational attainment among youth in smaller birth cohorts who have highly educated parents?

In turn, what are the implications of these patterns for subjective experience? The question is especially interesting against the backdrop of the planful competence cohort study (discussed above). In that instance, economic collapse virtually eliminated choice between school and work, and it rendered planfulness inconsequential for the older cohort. In the case of Brazil, larger cohorts decreased the likelihood of educational continuation, but only incrementally. Do the planful orientations of young Brazilians matter for their educational and work careers regardless of their birth-cohort membership? If not, are the planful orientations of Brazilians from larger cohorts diminished by the increased likelihood of leaving school earlier more than for those born in a smaller cohort? In larger cohorts, do planful orientations differ between young adults with well- and those with poorly educated parents?

Consider three hypothetical case studies, all of which involve young women of equal talent and educational aspirations:

Case 8: One young Brazilian woman has highly educated parents. She earns a master's degree in electrical engineering, marries a school classmate, and they both join a start-up firm that will supply specialized testing equipment to companies throughout the world. The firm enjoys great success, and the couple becomes wealthy and has three children. A nanny takes care of the children, who all attend elite schools through university.

Case 9: Another young Brazilian woman has poorly educated parents. Her mother is a homemaker and her father sells lunches out of a small cart on street corners. She is bright but has no one to guide her or advise her about schooling. When she graduates from high school there is a possibility of college, but she simply doesn't understand the process and what she would need to do to enroll and apply for fellowships or bursaries. At the same time, her parents pressure her to help out with the family business, and she ultimately forgoes college in order to help with a second small cart. At nineteen, the girl marries a young man who also works on the streets and they quickly begin having children. Their economic circumstances are always dire, and their children have to finish their schooling early in order to help their parents. The little family business suffers when two international chains specializing in "fast food" open locations in the area.

Case 10: Finally, consider a young woman with poorly educated parents. Her mother is a homemaker and her father sells lunches out of a small cart on street corners. She is, however, able to attend a private Catholic school without having to pay tuition. There she enjoys small classes with more intensive instruction, including courses in preparation for college. Despite constant financial stressors, the girl remains in school and excels. With the assistance of a school guidance counselor, she applies for and is awarded a scholarship to the local university and eventually she graduates with distinction. She marries a young man in her class. He becomes a lawyer and she becomes an accountant. They have children and are able to lead an upper-middle-class life.

Cases 8 and 9 correspond to the expected pattern and they also illustrate how the problem of poorly educated parents "reproduces" across the generations. That is, poorly educated parents often face financial difficulties which require the shortening of their children's education; those children, in turn, will face financial difficulties and ask the same sacrifices from their children, and so on. Case 8 focuses on a highly educated young couple who capitalize on the opportunities of the global economy by means of their educations. Case 9 represents a terrible bind: although the daughter left school to help, the family business is nevertheless threatened by competition that is likely to put an end to family-owned meal carts. These different patterns of schooling translate into additional, lifelong differences as well. All other things being equal, the couple in Case 8 will live longer, healthier, and happier lives than the parents in Case 9. Case 10, however, is intriguing because it departs from expectations. Here, the proximal environment compensates for the parents' lack of resources and know-how, and it changes the course of the woman's life.

Soviet Russia in a Globalizing Context
If the case of Brazil highlights how people fare in new and foreign contexts, an equally important issue is how people's biographies, their past broadly conceived, "translate" into new environments. What parts of one's biography may be useful or less useful in newly emergent contexts? In fact, systematic inquiry into such questions is in its infancy, as is much of our discussion in this chapter. Consider, however, the collapse of the Soviet Union and its ongoing reconstitution as contemporary Russia and other former Soviet republics and satellites, such as Ukraine and the Czech Republic. Two facts predominate. First, the transition to democracy has greatly transformed the landscape of social power. Although the Communist party was not eliminated (and it continues to be a reasonably successful com-

petitor in open elections), it is no longer the centralized authority that it once was. Whatever the Communist party's political future, it did produce a class of former party members who had earlier commanded considerable social resources and reaped significant economic benefits. Their roles in the new societies have been considerably more ambiguous.

The situation can only be appreciated when placed in the context of the history of the Communist party. The reputations of party members were often clouded in the eyes of non–party members, who typically comprised the vast majority of the citizenry. Party members formed an elite class (called the *nomenklatura*) that enjoyed many privileges unavailable to non–party members. Party members were also often associated with the state's efforts to monitor the activities of citizens. In effect, members (and many nonmembers) were often suspected of being spies for the state. And yet, as members of the elite, the party members also possessed the "know-how" to run the state.

Second, Russia's shift to a capitalist economy has been both quite painful and large in scope. In addition to the growth in the private sector and the expansion of the economy in general, there was a very long recession, the devaluation of the ruble, a collapse of the wage economy which led to a "barter" system and wage arrears (i.e., firms owing wages to workers whom they were unable to pay), widespread unemployment, and considerable regional inequality. With such widespread economic collapse, the tax base was greatly reduced and with this came a decline in most social services. The pain was not evenly distributed and the revitalizing economy of the late 1990s provided opportunities for economic gain. An important question in all this is who are the "winners" and "losers" in the new economy, and more specifically, how have the previous elites fared in the new sociopolitical context?

Theodore Gerber has focused particular attention on the socioeconomic life courses of former Communist party members and their labor-market fortunes in the new capitalist-style economy.[14] Neoclassic economics might expect that an open economy would level the playing field and yield no advantage to former party members, but Gerber hypothesized otherwise. Specifically, he argued that Communist party members would have persistent advantages because they had "acquired superior 'social capital'—personal connections and relations of reciprocity—through the Communist party during Soviet times."[15] Such ties have enduring utility in that they are useful for gaining information on and access to opportunities in the general labor market. Rather than creating leverage for mobility within a given firm, the advantage of former party membership is that it broadens the scope of one's networks and leads to economic advantage in general. In the context of one's economic life course, former Communist party members had lower rates of job loss and lower rates of shifts to low-wage labor. At the same time, mobility between firms (i.e., leaving one company for another) and earnings were higher than among those who were not former party members.

While such findings are a fascinating example of biographical continuity across dramatically different social contexts, the story would not be complete without considering the specifics of political and economic context. Gerber is careful to distinguish between 1991 and the period after. In 1991, the Communist party experienced remarkable political challenge. The party was embattled internally and externally. In July of that year, Boris Yeltsin issued decrees that evicted Communist party members from Russian enterprises and, later in the summer, following a failed coup, he banned the party altogether. The year 1991 was a bad one for Communist party members. After 1991, they had substantially higher job-loss rates and lower rates of mobility. Ordinary members (as opposed to the elite) were likely to shift to lower-wage occupations and had lower earnings.

Yet, despite experiencing eviction from state-run enterprises and then an official ban, former party members were actually more economically successful in the later years of the decade, attesting to the power of social capital to reproduce socioeconomic advantage over the life course. Such work has an interesting parallel with James Coleman's claims that social capital is central in the intergenerational transmission of socioeconomic status by showing how such ties can make a potentially redundant aspect of one's biography remarkably important, given newly emergent conditions.[16]

The story of Communist party membership in transitioning Russia is a useful example of new questions that are emerging in light of a globalizing world. The life course of former party members vividly illustrates a generic problem associated with social change: old biographical patterns (i.e., those of the party members) collide with newly organized social institutions. What is being observed in Russia has likewise played out, albeit to different degrees and with many distinctions, in the other former Warsaw Pact nations (e.g., Poland, Romania, East Germany). Comparisons could also made with politically unstable regions of Africa (e.g., Rwanda after its genocidal civil war), the Middle East (e.g., Iraq after the fall of Saddam Hussein), and Asia (e.g., Iran after the fall of the Shah, or Burma after the military coup of 1962), where the collapse of one political system leads to the formation of classes of people who fit in well with an old system but must then recast themselves in a new environment, which they accomplish with varying degrees of success. With nations around the globe undergoing or expected to undergo similar transitions, this pattern will undoubtedly continue to emerge.

The contingencies surrounding this process are illustrated when we consider the societal, proximal, developmental, and interpretive dimensions of this form of social change. At the societal level, what is the history of the deposed ruling class and how and why did they fall out of power? Party members appear to do better in some places (e.g., Turkmenistan, Russia, Kazakhstan, and, until 2005, Kyrgyzstan) than in others (e.g., Poland, East Germany, the Czech Republic), which likely reflects, in part, the broader societal and historical contexts of the deposed parties. At a more proximal level of analysis, how did old forms of social capital translate into new forms of power, income, and prestige? To what extent does the flourishing of old party members in new systems reflect their competencies versus their social connections?

There is also a critical issue of timing. Among children and adolescents, the possibility of membership was probably rendered moot. Young adult party members could quickly drop their party affiliation if need be, and develop a new social identity, complete with new social networks. Older party members were likely more entrenched in the older social order and thus had to draw upon whatever social resources they had developed as party members. Members in their sixties and upwards at the time of upheaval probably withdrew completely from the economy and public life, hoping to subsist on a pension.

In turn, the issue of timing is closely connected to issues of subjectivity. We would expect to find that the oldest party members simply did not attempt to recast their identity into something other than people who spent their adult lives promoting a Communist vision of society. Children and adolescents likely relegated what was once a possibility of becoming members to something that was never plausible. What of adult members? Perhaps many would recast their sense of identity to de-emphasize their former privileges and their destructive collusions with the state, and instead emphasize their commitment to positive values such as social equality. A considerable number of non–party members, ranging from religious officials to academics to factory workers and farmers, had spied on their fellow citizens, sometimes resulting in deportations, imprisonment, and even death. They, too, had dark autobiographical memories to deal with.

Once again, consider several hypothetical cases that illustrate the diverse patterns of three women. The major point of these cases is that while a basic life course pattern is recognizable, issues of context and timing create manifold biographical contingencies.

Case 11: A twenty-four-year-old Russian woman works as an administrator at a hospital in 1990. Her father and mother are devoted Communist party members, although her husband and his relations are not. The Soviet Union dissolves in 1991 and she retains her job. In fact, owing to connections in both her father's and husband's social networks, she secures a better position at another hospital shortly thereafter.

Case 12: A fifty-three-year old single Czech woman is a professor of psychology in 1989. She is a Communist party member. Czechoslovakians oust the Communists, from power in the "Velvet Revolution" of 1989. As party members are generally viewed with suspicion, there is constant talk of things she may have done or things she may have said that jeopardized the lives of others. The stigma of her previous life ultimately plays out during the restructuring of her university when she is demoted to research assistant, but she retires early to avoid this fate and now lives on a very small pension.

Case 13: Similar to Case 12, but the women is not a Communist party member. Czechoslovakia overthrows its Communist government in 1989. Still, there are similar concerns about what information she may have provided to authorities and how this may have jeopardized lives. Her husband is a famous Protestant pastor who was once imprisoned for protesting against the Communists and his reputation provides a buffer against the challenges to his wife. When the university is restructured, the woman is given the opportunity to retire early with full retirement benefits, which she does.

Case 11 involves a young Communist who probably could have forsaken her Communist identity but for her parents' long-standing and ardent ties to the party. Moreover, being in Russia, she may not have felt great pressure or perceived great incentive to renounce the party. At first she is unaffected by the dissolution of the Soviet Union, but in the ensuing social upheaval she draws upon her father's and husband's diverse social networks to advance her career. The woman in Case 12 is not so lucky on several counts. She is older, with an entrenched Communist identity, and her society is less tolerant of her past involvement. Given the fact that she is too young to retire she is offered a demotion, but because of her past standing in the society she refuses the position and becomes impoverished. Case 13 is almost identical to Case 12 except that the woman in Case 13 has a mitigating factor that evokes sympathy (her husband's imprisonment) and she is able to use his good name to secure benefits for herself. Linked lives are thus critical to distinguishing Case 12 from 13.

Concluding Remarks on Macro-Micro

Wolf Lepennies noted that as sociology emerged in the European context, it had to fight mightily to achieve its status as an independent discipline. Several prominent early novels aspired to social analysis and even to creating a social science (e.g., Honoré de Balzac's *Comédie Humaine* of 1842 originally was to be entitled *Études Sociales*). On the one hand, sociologists sought to distinguish themselves from such efforts by adopting the methodological outlook and tools of the natural sciences. On the other hand, because of its subject matter, sociology could never sit as an equal at the table of the natural sciences. What followed was the emergence of a "third culture" that drew upon both the humanities and the natural sciences. "Internal purification" of this third culture was constantly necessary for the nascent discipline to establish its distinctiveness from the work being done by literary artists.

In the American context, as the historian Dorothy Ross chronicles, the early sociologists expended considerable efforts debating the province and methods of sociology, and its place in the university curriculum. These debates continue to this very day, and are especially understandable when we think about the complexity of macro-micro connections. Phenomena as widely diverse as globalization and molecular DNA are implicated in the study of biography. The perennial questions of identity that the discipline of sociology has always faced are especially salient when thinking about macro-micro linkages: where does one begin in studying such complexities of social phenomena? And what is the province of the sociologist?

We can gain leverage on the first question by considering *entry points,* which refer to the starting points or initial questions that direct or animate one's research. For C. Wright Mills, the entry point appeared to be biographical patterns and forms of daily living. As he wrote in *The Sociological Imagination,* "Within that welter [of daily experience], the framework of modern society is sought, and within that framework the psychologies of a variety of men and women are formulated"[17]— which suggests that behavior and biographical patterns are the entry point, and then the analyst moves to the macro, and then the analyst proceeds to the psychological. Other social scientists take as their entry point macro sociological change. For example, as discussed in Chapter 1, Inkeles and Smith begin with modernization and seek to understand its implications for behavior, including psychological processes. Finally, to our knowledge, the great social scientific studies have rarely, if ever, begun with psychological features of the individual person and "worked their way back to society."

We can gain leverage on the second question by acknowledging that whatever the point of entry, the analyst must appreciate the multilevel nature of the problem, necessarily encompassing both macro phenomena such as historical and spatial variations and also micro phenomena such as proximal processes. A fully developed account of biographical patterns calls for an analysis of the psychological and perhaps even the biological. Realism runs contrary to the "internal purification" that Lepennies observed in earlier sociology. The complexity of people's lives simply does not respect the disciplinary boundaries that academicians have concocted. Although a social perspective is critical to understanding biographical forms, the study of lives is ultimately, inherently interdisciplinary.

. . . And Back to C. Wright Mills

This book was written as a response to C. Wright Mills's *The Sociological Imagination*. All along, our hope has been to formulate an imaginative framework within which people can think about how societies shape biographies. A considerable body of life course research has been covered thus far in this book. But what do all of these studies, all of these concepts, all of these hypotheses, and all of these analytic strategies have to do with an imaginative framework? We turn next, in the final chapter, to this question.

Further Reading

The Macro-Micro Link

Alexander, Jeffrey, Bernhard Giesen, Richard Münch, and Neil Smelser, eds. *The Micro-Macro Link*. Berkeley, CA: University of California Press, 1987.

Huber, Joan, ed. *Macro-Micro Linkages in Sociology.* Thousand Oaks, CA: Sage Publications, 1991.

Gene-Environment Interactions

Moffitt, Terrie E., Avshalom Caspi, and Michael Rutter. "Strategy for Investigating Interactions between Measured Genes and Measured Environments." *Archives of General Psychiatry* 62 (2005): 473–481.

Rutter, Michael, Terrie E. Moffitt, and Avshalom Caspi. "Gene-Environment Interplay and Psychopathology: Multiple Varieties but Real Effects." *Journal of Child Psychology and Psychiatry* 47 (2006): 226–261.

Shanahan, M. J., and S. M. Hofer. "Social Context in Gene-Environment Interactions: Retrospect and Prospect." *Journal of Gerontology: Social* 60B (Special Issue I, 2005): 65–76. (Special Issue on "The Future of Behavioral Genetics and Aging," edited by Jennifer Harris).

Planful Competence

Clausen, John. *American Lives: Looking Back at the Children of the Great Depression.* Berkeley, CA: University of California Press, 1995.

Shanahan, Michael J., and Glen H. Elder Jr. "History, Agency, and the Life Course." In *Nebraska Symposium on Motivation (Life Course Perspectives on Motivation)*, edited by L. J. Crockett, 145–186. Lincoln, NE: University of Nebraska Press, 2002.

Titma, Mik, and Nancy Brandon Tuman. "Human Agency in the Transition from Communism: Perspectives on the Life Course and Aging." 108–143. In *Historical Influences on Lives and Aging*, edited by K. Warner Schaie and Glen H. Elder Jr., New York: Springer, 2005.

> Engaging study of personal agency with the collapse of Soviet Russia, drawing on a truly unique data resource, the authors' "Paths of a Generation" sample.

Changes of Eastern Europe and Russia and the Life Course

Diewald, Martin, Anne Goedicke, and Karl Ulrich Mayer, eds. *After the Fall of the Wall: Life Courses in the Transformation of East Germany.* Palo Alto: Stanford University Press, 2006.

> Rich, multifaceted study of the life course with German Re-Unification by leading life course researchers, with emphasis on occupational careers and social class.

Chapter Six
RETURN TO
THE SOCIOLOGICAL IMAGINATION

Whatever you can do, or dream you can, begin it. Boldness has genius, power, and magic in it.

—William Hutchinson Murray

WE BEGAN THIS BOOK by recounting how C. Wright Mills, in his *Sociological Imagination* of 1959, urged the study of social change and the biography. Since his time, social scientists have developed many conceptual and analytic tools to do just that and, together, they constitute the life course paradigm. Mills's ultimate hope was to reveal how social forces change the contours of the biography. With such an understanding, people could realize the profoundly social nature of their seemingly personal predicaments and move both personally and collectively toward improving their societies. The story of people's lives is a story always in the making because society and people are always changing. Nevertheless, discerning the unfolding plot of this story depends in great measure on increasingly perceptive models of how real people live their lives in the real world.

From its inception, the focus on real people in the real world has been a distinctive element of life course studies. Prior to the emergence of life course studies, much effort in the behavioral sciences was devoted to studying how people behaved in experimental situations in laboratories or how large groups of people answered survey questions, with little sense of their social setting or personal histories. (There are, of course, notable exceptions.) We do not deny the value of these endeavors, but we emphasize that a life course paradigm focuses on tracing societal changes through social institutions and organizations, to communities, neighborhoods, and families, and ultimately to the person. Life course study begins and ends with the actions and experiences of people in the contexts in which they live and in which their lives unfold.

Mills apprehended the significance of social change in the study of biography, and to this awareness a life course perspective adds an appreciation for the developing and aging person, for socially based contigencies, and, as we write this, over forty-five years of conceptual and empirical research. Although we have presented the paradigm as a *fait accompli,* it is in fact constantly being refined and extended as its applicability is explored in diverse fields (e.g., epidemiology and other medical sciences) and as societies change in new and interesting ways.

The examples considered in the previous chapter illustrate how life course concepts and analytic strategies can be used to bridge the macro and micro in the study of biography, and they do indeed suggest a framework for the imagination—"points of inquiry" or "levels of analysis" that students of the life course are constantly probing.

AN IMAGINATIVE FRAMEWORK FOR LIFE COURSE STUDIES

As we noted from the beginning, the life course is not a systematic theory, it probably never will be, and that is probably okay. What is lost in the rigor of theory is gained in the flexibility of a paradigm. The framework offered here captures many of the concerns typically explored in the life course analysis of people's lives. Nevertheless, we offer this imaginative framework with some hesitancy. First, the very word "imagination" denotes something different from a mechanical application of questions. We do not offer a checklist or set of sensitizing concepts but rather a framework that is meant to orient the life course analyst to the way lives unfold within social structures of embeddedness: people's sense of self and their behaviors are embedded within configurations of roles and relationships that are, in turn, embedded within historical contexts and societies, all of which may be continually in flux. Second, given a specific research question, some points of inquiry are more relevant and probative than others. Even when several of the points are relevant, available data may dictate what can and cannot be pursued in empirical terms. Third, the power of this framework derives not from a consideration of each factor in sequence but rather by joining them together in an analysis that integrates the levels of inquiry. For example, the analyst would not pick a societal change at random, but rather focus on a specific societal change that is anticipated to make a difference in the patterning of lives. Caveats in mind, we offer the following levels of inquiry that collectively create an imaginative framework:

1. The Societal Level

The imagination first turns to questions of societal change, ideally viewed historically and across geopolitical units. Instances of social change are especially strategic because they create changes in societies' social institutions and organizations, communities and neighborhoods, and interpersonal relationships. In response to such changes, how do biographies change? As noted, "social changes" may refer to relatively discrete events (like the Great Depression and World War II and, even more so, 9/11), or they may take the form of enduring, though perhaps subtle change (e.g., the demographic transition). Social changes may also be macro, referring to changes spanning large distances and/or swatches of time (e.g., globalization), and they may be micro, referring to changes in a person's life (e.g., a geographic move, marital separation). Oftentimes, macro societal and comparatively micro, household changes will coincide. Concepts discussed in Chapter 3 and appearing in Table 3.4 may be especially relevant. Generations and cohorts may be excellent starting points for thinking about how social changes are affecting different groups in society and how different groups are effecting social change. The "master trend hypotheses"—chronologization, periodization, institutionalization, and individualization—may also guide thinking about how social changes affect the patterning of the life course.

2. The Proximal Level

Again, the "proximal level" refers to how social changes are linked to changes in people's immediate social contexts. Prior research has clearly established the importance of labor markets, workplaces, schools, communities, neighborhoods, and especially families. An appreciation for contigency already colors the analysis, as attention turns to the diverse ways that such proximate settings have been transformed in the wake of social change. Equally important is the degree to which proximal contexts shape the meaning that broader societal-level factors have for the life course. Such contexts can enhance the salience of history and introduce vulnerability to broad macro conditions. Proximal contexts can also insulate an individual from certain social forces and hence limit their meaning and impact. Especially helpful can be a consideration of social location, which we defined earlier as the sum total of our social statuses. Different social locations bring with them different forms of capital—cultural, financial, social, and human—which may profoundly affect how broader change alters a proximal setting. Thus, attention should be paid to variations by socioeconomic status, race/ethnicity, and gender.

3. The Developmental Level

This level directs our attention to two distinct phenomena. First, once social proximal factors have been identified, we turn attention to their dynamic properties and issues of timing. The principles discussed in Chapter 2 and the concepts shown in Table 2.1 are especially helpful at this stage of the analysis, directing our attention to the temporal properties of context and the intersections between aging and social changes. Are old social pathways changing and new ones emerging? Have transitions or turning points been encountered? Can circumstances before, during, and after be characterized? How long has a given situation endured and is it part of a longer-term sequence of events or roles?

Second, what of the dynamic properties of the behaviors being studied? This question links life course studies to developmental psychology, which focuses on change and continuity in behavior over time. The presupposition of this inquiry is that a snapshot view of behavior is often misleading; in other words, long-term behaviors have dynamic properties that may tell us far more about a person than his or her behavior at any one point in time. Questions about the stability of behaviors and patterns and rates of change come to the forefront.

Especially revealing at this point in the analysis may be the study of cases that do not correspond to general patterns. In tracing social changes to proximal settings and developmental patterns, generalizations certainly do begin to emerge—but generalizations in the behavioral sciences never describe the experiences of everyone. So what of these biographical patterns that do not reflect the common pattern? For example, given exposure to traumatic stressors, people may exhibit distress (e.g., depression or antisocial behaviors like substance abuse). Why is it, then, that some people exposed to such stressors never exhibit pronounced distress (i.e., why do they exhibit a pattern of resilience)? And why is that some people who are not exposed to traumatic stressors nevertheless do exhibit pronounced distress (i.e., why do they exhibit a pattern of vulnerability)? Although this example is couched in terms of stress and distress, the detailed analysis of unexpected cases is a strategy advocated broadly.

4. The Interpretive Level
At the distinctly micro level of analysis, we may ask how changes in context and in behaviors are associated with a person's subjective self-understanding. How have aspirations and goals, motives and plans been altered, and how are people making sense of these changes? Concepts and mechanisms dis-

cussed in Chapter 4 (some of which are shown in Table 4.1) may be helpful at this point in the analysis. At the most fundamental level, has a person's basic schemas (or schemata) about their self (e.g., subjective age, autobiographical memory, self-efficacy) and their social location changed? Have they changed in relation to who they were (or thought they were) at an earlier point in their life? Moreover, how do they view the future in terms of plans, motives, and goals, and, broadly, their range of possible selves? In thinking about the person's sense of agency, questions about their sense of the past (the iteration phase), judgments about alternatives in the present (the practical evaluation phase), and their grasp of future courses of action all require consideration.

5. People Changing Society and the Biography

Finally, most of this book has concerned how societies shape biographies. And yet we should also ask how, responding to tensions created by social changes, some people react so as to change social forces and the biography. At the level of the person, who are the "life course innovators" and why? Do life course innovators have a subjective sense of their novel place in the social order and, if so, what does this understanding look like? What do innovators do that both paves the way and fails to the pave the way for new forms of the life course? Of special interest are people who are actively involved in social groups that seek to change the life course. What is their vision and how do they pursue it? And perhaps most challenging, do these groups succeed to some appreciable degree and, if so, under what conditions?

NOTES ON CHANGING THE LIFE COURSE: HOW AND WHAT

This last point of inquiry in the imaginative framework has been almost completely neglected by life course sociology but, given the extraordinarily social and malleable nature of the life course, we must ask how the organization of people's lives could be improved by our purposeful actions. That is, how can the life course be changed through people's efforts? Moreover, in what ways would we wish to change it? These are very large questions that cannot be answered here in any but a cursory fashion.

How to Change the Life Course: First Thoughts

One approach would be through social movements, which refer to groups of people who have organized to effect a specific change in society. For example, the AARP (American Association of Retired Persons) presently has over 35 million members and exerts its influence to enact policies favorable to the elderly. (As we noted in Chapter 3, Samuel Preston would argue that success for the elderly might come at the expense of other age groups.) In so doing, the AARP's efforts might change the life course with respect to, for example, governmental supports for the elderly. Feminism and the wide variety of women's movements have often pressed for equality between the sexes in educational and work settings and for new ways of thinking about women's roles in the family. Historically, the child labor movements of the late nineteenth and early twentieth centuries promoted the removal of children from factories.

Can such social movements actually change the life course, the basic pattern of the biography? This question has not been well researched, but our initial impression is one of skepticism. In the case of the women's and child-labor movements, some historians have argued that their impact was minimal in getting women into the workplace and children into schools, respectively.[1] Rather, it was social and economic changes that encouraged or even necessitated these developments. The issue then becomes whether these social movements were necessary but, by themselves, insufficient conditions. That is, had these movements not occurred, would changes in female and childhood life course patterns have changed anyway? The answer is probably "yes," because strong social and economic realities were calling for such changes. But such a conclusion is highly speculative—more research is needed on this fascinating topic.

Another approach to changing the life course involves people conducting their lives in novel ways, as one finds, for example, in the early birth cohorts of women who postponed their first child until well into their thirties. Such people made "unique" decisions concerning education, work, and family, and, in aggregate, these novel ways of living produced new versions of the life course. But, as we noted with the case of Mozart in Chapter 2, these emerging life course forms often bring with them a wide range of challenges. For example, one can imagine the almost constant barrage of social cues directed at mothers who delayed their first child until their mid-thirties, subtle and otherwise: their mothers saying things like "I had three children before I was your age!" a neighbor weighs in with "Well, I hope the baby will be okay," and the well-meaning clerk observes, "You're not the only one—I've seen a few really old mothers come into the store."

The novelty of life course innovations is well captured in the phrase *"nontraditional* student," which is sometimes used to describe people who have returned to school after an extended hiatus. The very label states that they are breaking a tradition. But, in so doing, the label also suggests a modern person who is not governed by rules premised on "that's the way people have always done things." Life course innovators are thus quintessentially modern people whose biographies may not be widely recognized as "normal" or perhaps even "legitimate," but in fact they are "path-breaking" or "emergent."

The historian John Modell notes that members of age groups do indeed have the capacity to act collectively so as to change the meaning of the life course. His study of American adolescents and their entry into adulthood between 1920 and 1975 finds that "a central theme in their innovation has been the injection of increasing volition into the youthful life course."[2] For example, young people have changed the nature of romantic dating, and the aggregate of their choices has created "demonstration effects" that later cohorts follow. Stability in dating behaviors follows until, for reasons not really understood, innovators reach a critical mass and a new demonstration effect takes hold.

The little research that is pertinent to life course innovators is only suggestive. Research by Richard Settersten (discussed in Chapter 3) and other scholars suggests that violations of age norms (as one find with older mothers, for example) are noticed by society but are not subject to punitive measures. Still, other life course innovators (e.g., the first men and women to be joined in gay unions and to adopt children) have undoubtedly experienced some social disapprobation. Further, as discussed in Chapter 3, John Meyer noted that people want to feel that their lives take on the form of a "legitimate résumé," and perhaps not all life course innovators—particularly innovators who are not supported by a community—interpret their lives as socially legitimate.

Finally, if enough people adopt the same life course innovation (e.g., working mothers with young children), social institutions may change to accommodate them (e.g., by increasing daycare opportunities, funding tax credits for daycare, etc.). But as Matilda Riley has pointed out, "individual aging and social change involve separate dynamisms, and their intrinsic lack of synchronization with one another produces strains for both individuals and society."[3] The first cohorts of women who entered the workplace on a full-time basis had few opportunities for daycare, creating stressors in the home and perhaps also at work. Thus, the first cohorts of innovators pressing for a specific change may well encounter mild disapproval from fellow citizens but major structurally based hindrances and challenges. Nevertheless, the mere fact that the life course can change and indeed is constantly changing suggests a certain excitement and heightened meaning to the struggles of life course innovators.

What to Change About the Life Course

A central aspect of social change is the way in which the interactions of society and biography introduce the need, in some way, shape, or form, to manage risk across the life course, and especially to meet the costs associated with avoiding negative hazards. Angela O'Rand has summarized the problem well: as never before, people are faced with a multitude of choices about schooling, family, work, health and life insurance, and retirement funds.[4] Yet should people be given all these choices nevertheless? If so, who is responsible if bad choices are made?

Through the early twentieth century, there was a trend in the Western industrialized world for the increasing assumption of these risks by the state, vividly illustrated by the case of Sweden (discussed in Chapter 3). As the twentieth century came to a close, a countertrend took hold in countries like the United States whereby people were assuming increasing risks. And now, as the twenty-first century begins, social scientists worry that individuals have assumed too much risk. The dynamics of social change, the complex web of myriad contexts and contingencies, and the multiple layers of biography create a fascinating arena for understanding the human condition, both the good and the bad.

For example, what happens to the elderly widow who has made poor choices with respect to her retirement and is now without sufficient financial resources? What happens to the young adult who becomes seriously ill and is without adequate health insurance? Should the government assume these expenses, in which case taxes might have to be increased? Should the consumer pay a bit more for products and services so that employees can be provided with better forms of insurance? Or should the elderly widow and the underinsured young adult "suffer the consequences because it is his/her own fault?" The obvious solution might appear to be for government to assume more risk. But, as noted in Chapter 3, such efforts may sometimes be associated with lower levels of economic growth, which, in turn, are associated with higher unemployment and lower tax revenues.

An extension of this concept could be applied to circumstances of birth. Everyone born into this world incurs the risk of having inadequate parents: parents with serious psychopathologies, drug and alcohol dependencies, or simply little or no understanding of parenting skills. All of these factors are known to be associated with adjustment problems in adulthood, sometimes of a very serious nature. Arguably, in fact, the most far-reaching risk anyone is exposed to is that of having incompetent parents. Should the government certify adults before they can become parents? States must certify young people before they can drive a car; doesn't poor parenting pose at least as great a cost to society?

In what other ways might the life course be reconsidered? What other broad social tensions have worked their way into the everyday welter of experience? Once again, we must acknowledge that this is a large question. Nevertheless, we can identify a few major points in the life course that are (or should be) part of a national dialogue and we then go on to identify patterns in the life course that conceivably could be changed for the better. We are not, however, policy makers, nor are we sufficiently versed in all of the social, political, economic, and cultural issues raised by these possibilities.

First, socioeconomic deprivation has been a major force in creating distinctly different life course patterns. Black males with only a high-school education or less, and weak attachment to the labor force (e.g., long spells of unemployment), have a high probability of spending time in jail and dying very young.[5] Affluent white females with a college education and steady employment will likely live a much longer, happier, and more-productive life. Does the young black man deserve his life? Can we draw upon scientific knowledge to devise a better life for him—a longer, happier, and more-productive life, which is an improvement for both him and society? The obvious solution might be to increase the incomes of the impoverished and to move people out of their troubled neighborhoods. Research suggests that such changes are enormously challenging and the experiences of relocated people are complex, with both benefits and costs.[6] We simply observe that of all of the social experiences that differentiate people's lives, poverty and educational disadvantage are undoubtedly among the most powerful.

A third area for change—in addition to the reallocation of risk and elimination of deprivation—concerns the age segregation of society. Through the eighteenth century, people spent their days together, the young and old alike. Beginning in the late nineteenth and early twentieth centuries, when children moved from factories into schools, Western societies have become increasingly age-segregated. Children and teenagers spend the day in classrooms with age-mates; young adults congregate in collegiate or vocational settings; entry-level workers tend to spend time with people about their age; retirees associate with retirees.

Matilda and John Riley note that social settings are age-segregated to the extent that age is a criterion (explicit or implicit) for participation *and* to the extent that there is a lack of cross-age interaction.[7] They propose two "Ideal Types," or models, that interrelate aging with social institutions. According to the age-segregated model, children spend their days in schools, adults in workplaces, and older adults in leisure settings. According to the age-integrated model, people of all age groups are engaged in educational, work, and leisure settings from birth to death. A growing body of research suggests that age-integrated settings have many benefits.

Finally, what not to change. Many phases of the life course are seemingly under constant assault by "crisis coalitions" who urge their social reconstitution. Adolescence has always been a magnet for "crisis theorists," but virtually every phase of life has been the target of hyperventilating public discourse. Nevertheless, great care must be exercised in evaluating the claims of pressure groups, who typically argue that a phase of life has become pathological. The basic structure of the "crisis argument" is that a specific group of people is suffering from a syndrome-like malady (usually psychological and social) because of the social and cultural circumstances of their age group.

Christina Hoff Sommers, for example, examined the "girl crisis" of the 1980s and 1990s in her provocative book *The War Against Boys*.[8] According to her analysis, the girl crisis started in the early 1980s with Carol Gilligan's book *In a Different Voice,* which claimed that males and females have fundamentally different styles of moral reasoning and, as girls realize this during early adolescence, they withdraw, becoming silenced, and ultimately depressed. "Proof" of this crisis was that girls were doing worse in school than boys.

The book garnered widespread mass-media attention and prompted various women's rights groups and the federal government to form a coalition committed to gender equity in schools by way of curricular changes. But Sommers argues that as early as 1984, Gilligan's research had been challenged by papers appearing in excellent scientific journals and, indeed, substantial evidence showed that girls were actually outperforming boys in the classroom. By the late 1990s, the "girl crisis" was supplanted in the popular media and the public's imagination by a "boy crisis," fomented by William Pollack's book *Real Boys: Rescuing Our Sons from the Myths of Boyhood* and then widespread outrage at the Columbine High School shootings. The book had little basis in scientific research and there was much evidence to rebut its central ideas, but once again a coalition of educators, the mass media, and government officials rendered the "boy crisis" a matter of vital and urgent public concern.

While the particulars of these cases cannot be explored here, the overarching point of these examples is that caution should be observed when encountering enthusiastic claims that a particular group is in crisis and in need of social re-engineering. Some claims require a great deal of empirical research and scientific exchange before being validated. The danger of prematurely accepting such claims is that the putative solution to the crisis can often be worse than the actual nature of the crisis itself. For example, if girls are actually doing better than boys in school (contrary to the claims of proponents of the "girl crisis"), then programs to bolster girls' educational aspirations and study habits only heighten the real inequalities. Purported crises in the life course can easily direct the public's attention to problems that may not actually exist, at the expense of addressing real injustices and inequities.

A Final Word

A final word about the imaginative framework laid out in this chapter: it is incomplete. You may well ask, "Why offer an incomplete framework?" And the answer is: because we must extend beyond Mills's call for an imaginative framework to study lives and we must actually attempt to formulate it. Given that society is constantly changing, given that people are constantly changing, given that our scientific understanding is constantly changing, the framework will *always* be incomplete. Yet, as the eminent social historian Charles Tilly once commented, the point is not to provide all the answers, but rather to "join the conversation and change it." In this spirit, we have offered one view of the progress that has been made in the study of lives since the time of C. Wright Mills. And the conversation will undoubtedly continue, animated by anticipation of the many life courses to come.

FURTHER READING

Age Integration

Uhlenberg, Peter. "Introduction: Why Study Age Integration?" *The Gerontologist* 40 (2000): 261–308.

> This is an excellent introduction to a series of essays on age integration.

Risk in the Modern Life Course

O'Rand, Angela M. "Risk, Rationality, and Modernity: Social Policy and the Aging Self." In *The Evolution of the Aging Self: Societal Impact on the Aging Self*, edited by K. W. Schaie and J. Hendricks, 225–249. New York: Springer, 2000.

Learning More about the Life Course—Syllabi

Fettes, Danielle, Fang Gong, Sigrun Olafsdottir, and Eliza K. Pavalko, eds. *The Life Course: A Handbook of Syllabi and Instructional Materials*. Washington, DC: ASA Publications, 2002.

Harris, Diana K., ed. *Teaching Sociology of Aging and the Life Course*. Washington, DC: ASA Publications, 2000.

Wright, Sue Marie, ed. *Sociology of Children and Childhood*. Washington, DC: ASA Publications, 2003.

> The American Sociological Association (*www.asanet.org*) publishes "Syllabi Sets," which are collections of syllabi from professors teaching in specific areas. For students

with a basic knowledge of the life course, these are fascinating and rich resources to help you further your studies. These collections are often updated.

The Future of the Life Course

Dannefer, Dale, and Peter Uhlenberg. "Paths of the Life Course: A Typology." In *Handbook of Theories of Aging,* edited by V.L. Bengtson and K.W. Schaie, 306–326. New York: Springer, 1999.

The following essays appear in the *Handbook of the Life Course,* edited by Jeylan T. Mortimer and Michael J. Shanahan (New York: Kluwer/Plenum, 2003). These essays were written by leading scholars of the life course and represent creative reflections on the future of life course studies.

Dannefer, Dale. "Toward a Global Geography of the Life Course: Challenges of Late Modernity for Life Course Theory." 647–659.

Furstenberg, Frank F. "Reflections on the Future of the Life Course." 661–670.

George, Linda K. "Life Course Research: Achievement and Potential." 671–680.

Hogan, Dennis P. and Frances K. Goldscheider. "Successes and Challenges in Demographic Studies of the Life Course." 681–691.

O'Rand, Angela M. "The Future of the Life Course: Late Modernity and Life Course Risks." 693–701.

Weymann, Ansgar. "Future of the Life Course." 703–714.

NOTES

INTRODUCTION

1. Salman Rushdie, *Midnight's Children* (New York: Alfred A. Knopf, 1995), 8.

2. C. Wright Mills, *The Sociological Imagination* (London: Oxford University Press, 1959).

3. Ibid., 25.

4. Ibid., 7.

5. D. J. Frank, J. W. Meyer, and D. Miyahara, "The Individualist Polity and the Prevalence of Professionalized Psychology—A Cross-National Study," *American Sociological Review* 60.3 (1995): 360–377. See also D. J. Frank and J. W. Meyer. "The Profusion of Individual Roles and Identities in the Postwar Period," *Sociological Theory* 20.1 (2002): 86–105.

CHAPTER ONE   WHAT IS THE LIFE COURSE?

1. William Shakespeare, *As You Like It* (New York: Washington Square Press, 2004).

2. W. H. Auden, *Collected Poems* (New York: Vintage Press, 1991).

3. A. Georg Simmel, *The Sociology of Georg Simmel,* trans. Kurt H. Wolf (New York: Free Press, 1964).

4. Norbert Elias, Michale Schroter, and Edmund Jephcott, *Mozart: Portrait of a Genius* (Boston: Blackwell Publishing, 1994).

5. Quoted in Bruce Mazlish, *A New Science: The Breakdown of Connections and the Birth of Sociology* (Oxford: Oxford University Press, 1989).

6. Ferdinand Tönnies, *Community and Society* (Mineola, NY: Dover, 2002).

7. Emile Durkheim, *The Division of Labor in Society* (New York: Free Press, 1984).

8. David Riesman, *The Lonely Crowd: A Study of the Changing American Society* (New Haven, CT: Yale University Press, 1965).

9. Herbert Marcuse, *One-Dimensional Man: Studies in the Ideology of Advanced Industrial Society* (Boston: Beacon Press, 1991).

10. Irving Louis Horowitz, *C. Wright Mills: American Utopian* (New York: Free Press, 2002).

11. Dennis H. Wrong, "The Oversocialized Conception of Man in Modern Sociology," *American Sociological Review* 26 (1961): 183–193.

12. Karl Mannheim, "The Problem of Generations," in P. Kecskemet (Ed.), *Essays in the Sociology of Knowledge* (Boston: Routledge and Kegan Paul, 1952), 276–322.

13. Kenneth Keniston, *Young Radicals: Notes on Committed Youth* (New York: Harcourt, Brace, and World, 1968).

14. Kenneth Keniston, "The Sources of Student Dissent," *Journal of Social Issues* 22 (1967): 108–137.

15. James S. House, "Social Structure and Personality," in Morris Rosenberg and Ralph Turner (Eds.), *Social Psychology: Sociological Perspectives* (New York: Basic Books, 1981), 525–561.

16. Alex Inkeles and David Horton Smith, *Becoming Modern: Individual Change in Six Developing Countries* (Cambridge: Harvard University Press, 1976).

17. Ibid., 143.

18. Melvin Kohn, *Class and Conformity: A Study in Values* (Chicago: Chicago University Press, 1989).

19. Ibid., 192.

20. Glen H. Elder Jr., *Children of the Great Depression*, 25th Anniversary Edition (Boulder, CO: Westview Press, Perseus Books, 1999; originally published 1974, University of Chicago Press).

21. The girls did not suffer these adverse effects, perhaps because they were exposed to a strong maternal role model.

CHAPTER TWO   THE LIFE COURSE AS A PARADIGM

1. Adrian Desmond and James Moore, *Darwin: The Life of a Tormented Evolutionist* (New York: Norton, 1994).

2. E. Janet Browne, *Charles Darwin: Voyaging* (Princeton, NJ: Princeton University Press, 1996).

3. John Bowlby, *Charles Darwin: A New Life* (New York: Norton, 1992).

4. Glen H. Elder Jr., *Children of the Great Depression*, 25th Anniversary Edition (Boulder, CO: Westview Press, Perseus Books, 1999; originally published 1974, University of Chicago Press).

5. Erik Erikson, *Identity: Youth and Crisis* (New York: Norton, 1968), 92.

6. Ibid.

7. Erik Erikson, *Young Man Luther* (New York: Norton, 1993; originally published 1953), 209.

8. Ibid., 206.

9. Dale Dannefer, "Adult Development and Social Theory: A Paradigmatic Reappraisal," *American Sociological Review* 49 (1984): 100–116; and Dale Dannefer, "The Role of the Social in Life-Span Developmental Psychology, Past and Future: Rejoinder to Baltes and Nesselroade," *American Sociological Review* 49 (1984): 847–850.

10. Robert Havinghurst, *Development Tasks and Education* (London: Longman Group United Kingdom, 1972), 2.

11. A. M. Pallas, "Educational Transitions, Trajectories, and Pathways," in *Handbook of the Life Course*, ed. J. T. Mortimer and M. J. Shanahan (New York: Plenum, 2003), 165–184.

12. M. J. Shanahan, J. T. Mortimer, and H. Kruger, "Adolescence and Adult Work in the Twenty-First Century," *Journal of Research in Adolescence* 12 (2002): 99–120.

13. D. R. Entwisle, K. L. Alexander, and L. S. Olson, "The First-Grade Transition in Life Course Perspective," in *Handbook of the Life Course*, ed. J. T. Mortimer and M. J. Shanahan (New York: Plenum, 2003), 239.

14. Ibid.

15. A. C. Kerckhoff, *Diverging Pathways: Social Structure and Career Deflections* (New York: Cambridge University Press, 1993).

16. H. S. Becker, "Notes on the Concept of Commitment," *American Journal of Sociology* 66. 1 (1961): 32–40.

17. I. Schoon, J. Bynner, H. Joshi, S. Parsons, R. W. Wiggins, and A. Sacker, "The Influence of Context, Timing, and Duration of Risk Experiences for the Passage from Childhood to Mid-Adulthood," *Child Development* 73.5 (2002): 1486–1504.

18. M. J. Bane and D. T. Elwood, "Slipping Into and Out of Poverty: The Dynamics of Spells," *Journal of Human Resources* 21.1 (1986): 1–23.

19. P. McDonough, G. J. Duncan, D. Williams, and J. House, "Income Dynamics and Adult Mortality in the United States, 1972 through 1989," *American Journal of Public Health* 87.9 (1997): 1476–1483.

20. M. E. J. Wadsworth, S. M. Montgomery, and M. J. Bartley, "The Persisting Effect of Unemployment on Health and Social Well-Being in Men Early in Working Life," *Social Science and Medicine* 48 (1999): 1491–1499.

21. A. Caspi, D. J. Bem, and G. H. Elder Jr., "Continuities and Consequences of International Styles across the Life Course," *Journal of Personality* 57.2 (1989): 375–406.

22. F. F. Furstenberg Jr., T. D. Cook, J. Eccles, G. H. Elder Jr., and A. Sameroff, *Managing to Make It: Urban Families and Adolescent Success, Studies on Successful Adolescent Development: The John D. and Catherine T. MacArthur Foundation Series on Mental Health and Development* (Chicago: University of Chicago Press, 1999).

23. Matthew E. Dupre, "Educational Differences in Age-Related Patterns of Disease: Reconsidering Cumulative Disadvantage and Age-as-Leveler," *Journal of Health and Social Behavior* (forthcoming).

24. Michael Rutter, *Developing Minds: Challenge and Continuity across the Lifespan* (London: Basic Books, 1993).

25. A. M. Pallas, "Educational Transitions, Trajectories, and Pathways," in *Handbook of the Life Course*, ed. J. T. Mortimer and M. J. Shanahan (New York: Plenum, 2003), 165–184.

26. Reuben Hill, *Family Development in Three Generations* (Cambridge, MA: Schenkman Books, 1970).

27. X. Ge, F. O. Lorenz, R. D. Conger, G. H. Elder Jr., and R. L. Simons, "Trajectories of Stressful Life Events and Depressive Symptoms During Adolescence," *Developmental Psychology* 30.4 (1994): 467–483.

28. T. E. Moffit, "Adolescence-Limited and Life-Course Persistent Antisocial Behavior: A Developmental Taxonomy," *Psychological Review* 100.4 (1993): 674–701; and T. E. Moffitt, A. Caspi, N. Dickson, P. Silva, and W. Stanton, "Childhood-Onset Versus Adolescent-Onset Antisocial Conduct Problems in Males: Natural History from Age 3 to 18," *Development and Psychopathology* 8 (1996): 399–424; T. E. Moffitt, A. Caspi, H. Harrington, and B. J. Milne, "Males on the Life Course Persistent and Adolescence-Limited Antisocial Pathways: Follow-Up at Age 26 Years," *Development and Psychopathology* 14.1 (2002): 179–207.

29. F. F. Furstenberg Jr., J. Brooks-Gunn, and S. P. Morgan, *Adolescent Mothers in Later Life* (New York: Cambridge University Press, 1987).

30. R. J. Sampson and J. H. Laub, *Crime in the Making: Pathways and Turning Points Through Life* (Cambridge, MA: Harvard University Press, 1993).

31. John H. Laub, and R. J. Sampson, *Shared Beginnings, Divergent Lives: Delinquent Boys to Age 70* (Cambridge: Harvard University Press, 2003).

32. K. S. Schiller, "Effects of Feeder Patterns on Students' Transition to High School," *Sociology of Education* 72 (October 1999): 216–233.

33. S. Maruna, *Making Good: How Ex-Convicts Reform and Rebuild Their Lives* (Washington, DC: American Psychological Association, 2001).

34. John A. Clausen, "Gender, Contexts, and Turning Points in Adults' Lives," in *Examining Lives in Context: Perspective on the Ecology of Human Development*, ed. P. Moen, G. H. Elder Jr., and K. Lushcer (Washington, DC: APA Press, 1995), 365–389.

35. Duane F. Alwin, Robert M. Hauser, and William H. Sewell, "Colleges and Achievement," in *Education, Occupation and Earnings: Achievement in the Early Career*, ed. W. H. Sewell and R. M. Hauser (New York: Academic Press, 1975), 114–142

36. R. B. Cairns and B. Cairns, *Lifelines and Risks: Pathways of Youth in Our Time* (Cambridge: Cambridge University Press, 1994).

37. See L. F. Katz, J. Kling, and J. Liebman, "Moving to Opportunity in Boston: Early Impacts of a Housing Mobility Program," *Quarterly Journal of Economics* 116.2 (2001): 607–654; and J. Ludwig, G. J. Duncan, and P. Hirschfield, "Urban Poverty and Juvenile Crime: Evidence from a Randomized Housing-Mobility Experiment," *Quarterly Journal of Economics* 116.2 (2001): 655–680.

38. Jeffrey R. Kling, Jeffrey B. Liebman, and Lawrence F. Katz, "Bullets Don't Get No Name: Consequences of Fear in the Ghetto" (National Bureau of Economic Research, 2001).

39. This discussion draws on Adrian Desmond and James Moore, *Darwin: The Life of a Tormented Evolutionist* (New York: Norton, 1994); E. Janet Browne, *Charles Darwin: The Power of Place* (Princeton, NJ: Princeton University Press, 2003); and Frank F. Sulloway, "Darwin and His Finches: The Evolution of a Legend," *Journal of the History of Biology* 15 (1982): 1–53; "Darwin's Conversion: The *Beagle* Voyage and Its Aftermath," *Journal of the History of Biology* 15 (1982): 325–396; "The Legend of Darwin's Finches," *Nature* 303 (1983): 372; and "Darwin and the Galapagos: Three Myths," *Oceanus* 302: 79–85.

40. Joseph Ellis, *Founding Brothers: The Revolutionary Generation* (New York: Vintage, 2002).

41. Doug McAdam, *Freedom Summer* (New York: Oxford University Press, 1990).

CHAPTER THREE   MACRO VIEWS OF THE LIFE COURSE

1. Peter Uhlenberg, "Historical Forces Shaping Grandparent-Grandchild Relationships: Demography and Beyond." *Annual Review of Gerontology and Geriatrics* 24 (2004): 77–97.

2. D. Snow and L. Anderson, "Identity Work among the Homeless: The Verbal Construction and Avowal of Personal Identities," *American Journal of Sociology* 92.6 (1987): 1336–1371.

3. Norman B. Ryder, "The Cohort as a Concept in the Study of Social Change," *American Sociological Review* 30 (1965): 856.

4. Phillipe Ariès, *Centuries of Childhood: A Social History of Family Life* (New York: Vintage, 1965).

5. Ibid., 128.

6. John Gillis, *Youth and History: Tradition and Change in European Age Relations, 1770–Present* (New York: Academic Press, 1974).

7. Joseph Kett, *Rites of Passage: Adolescence in America, 1790 to Present* (New York: Basic Books, 1977).

8. D. F. Alwin and R. J. McCammon, "Generations, Cohorts, and Social Change," in *Handbook of the Life Course,* ed. Jeylan T. Mortimer and Michael Shanahan (New York: Plenum Publishing, 2003), 2–49.

9. José Ortega y Gasset, *History as a System* (New York: Norton, 1962).

10. As quoted in Alwin and McCammon.

11. Allen Ginsberg, *Howl and Other Poems* (San Francisco: City Light Publishers, 1956).

12. As quoted in Michael Davidson, "Beat Generation," 62–64, in *Companion to American Thought,* ed. Richard Fox and James Kloppenberg (Boston: Blackwell Publishers, 1998).

13. Matilda White Riley, "Aging and Cohort Succession: Interpretations and Misinterpretations," *Public Opinion Quarterly* 37 (1973): 35–49; and Matilda White Riley "On the Significance of Age in Sociology," *American Sociological Review* 52 (1987): 1–14.

14. Alice Rossi, *Feminists in Politics: A Panel Analysis of the First National Women's Conference* (New York: Academic Press, 1982).

15. David L. Featherman and Robert M. Hauser, *Opportunity and Change* (New York: Academic Press, 1978).

16. Ibid., 13.

17. This is not a strictly correct procedure in that it ignores the standard errors of the estimates, but it will suffice for our purpose of illustrating the use of cohorts in macro studies of the life course.

18. Glen H. Elder Jr., "War Mobilization and the Life Course: A Cohort of World War II Veterans," *Sociological Forum,* no. 2 (1987): 449–472.

19. Richard Easterlin, *Birth and Fortune* (New York: Basic Books, 1980).

20. Gordon, 4.

21. Fred C. Pampel and H. Elizabeth Peters, "The Easterlin Effect," *Annual Review of Sociology* 21 (1995): 163–194.

22. Samuel Preston, "Children and the Elderly in the U.S.," *Scientific American* 251 (1984): 44–49.

23. Fred Pampel, "Population Aging, Class Context, and Age Inequality in Public Spending," *American Journal of Sociology* 100 (1994): 153–195.

24. Michael Mitterauer, *A History of Youth (Family, Sexuality, and Social Relations of Past Times)* (Boston: Blackwell Publishing, 1992).

25. Lutz Leisering, "Government and the Life Course," in *Handbook of the Life Course,* ed. Jeylan Mortimer and Michael J. Shanahan (New York: Kluwer Publishing, 2003).

26. See Martin Kohli, "The World We Forgot: A Historical Review of the Life Course," in *Later Life: The Social Psychology of Aging,* ed. V. W. Marshall (Beverly Hills, CA: Sage, 1986), 271–303.

27. Karl U. Mayer, "Structural Constraints on the Life Course," *Human Development* 29 (1986): 163–170.

28. James Rosenbaum, *Beyond College for All* (New York: Russell Sage Foundation, 2001).

29. Harvey Graff, *Conflicting Paths: Growing Up in America* (Cambridge: Harvard University Press, 1995), 47.

30. Ibid.

31. Phyllis Moen and Patricia Roehling, *The Career Mystique: Cracks in the American Dream* (Lanham, MD: Rowman & Littlefield Publishers, 2004); and Phyllis Moen, "Midcourse: Navigating Retirement and a New Life Stage," in *Handbook of the Life Course,* ed. Jeylan Mortimer and Michael J. Shanahan (New York: Kluwer Publishers, 2003).

32. Phyllis Moen, *It's About Time: Couples and Careers* (Ithaca, NY: Cornell University Press, 2003), 274.

33. Elizabeth Fussell and Frank F. Furstenberg Jr., "The Transition to Adulthood during the Twentieth Century: Race, Nativity, and Gender," in *On the Frontier of Adulthood: Theory, Research, and Public Policy,* ed. Richard Settersten, Frank Furstenberg, and Rubén Rumbaut (Chicago: University of Chicago Press, 2005).

34. Jeffery Jensen Arnett, *Emerging Adulthood: The Winding Road from the Late Teens through the Twenties* (Cambridge: Cambridge University Press, 2004).

35. Becky Pettit, and Bruce Western, "Mass Imprisonment and the Life Course: Race and Class Inequality in U.S. Incarceration," *American Sociological Review* 69 (2004): 151–69.

36. Edgar Friedenberg, *The Vanishing Adolescent* (Boston: Beacon Publishing, 1967).

37. Alice Schlegel, "The Social Criteria of Adulthood," *Human Development* 41 (1998): 323–325.

38. Peter R. Uhlenberg, "A Study of Cohort Life-Cycles: Cohorts of Native-Born Massachusetts Women, 1830–1920," *Population Studies* 23 (1969): 407–420.

39. John Modell, Frank F. Furstenberg, and Theodore Hershberg, "Social Change and Transitions to Adulthood in Historical Perspective," *Journal of Family History* 1 (1976): 7–32.

40. Ronald Rindfuss, Karin L. Brewster, and Andrew L. Kavee, "Women, Work, and Children: Behavioral and Attitudinal Change in the United States," in *Population and Development Review* 22 (1996): 457–482.

41. Martina Morris, Mark Stephen Handcock, Marc A. Scott, and Annette D. Bernhardt, *Divergent Paths: Economic Mobility in the New American Labor Market* (New York: Russell Sage Foundation, 2001).

42. Martin Kohli, "The World We Forgot: A Historical Review of the Life Course," in *Later Life: The Social Psychology of Aging*, ed. V. W. Marshall (Beverly Hills, CA: Sage Publications, 1986), 271–303.

43. John Modell, *Into One's Own: From Youth to Adulthood in the United States, 1920–1975* (Berkeley: University of California Press, 1991).

44. Dennis P. Hogan, *Transitions and Social Change: The Early Lives of American Man* (New York: Academic Press, 1981).

45. Marlis Buchmann, *The Script of Life in Modern Society: Entry into Adulthood in a Changing World* (Chicago: University of Chicago Press, 1989).

46. John Meyer, "Self and the Life Course," in *Institutional Structure: Constituting State, Society, and the Individual,* ed. G. M. Thomas, J. W. Meyer, F. O. Ramirez, and J. Boli (Beverly Hills, CA: Sage Publications, 1987), 242–260.

47. Ibid., 208.

48. Harvey Graff, *Conflicting Paths: Growing Up in America* (Boston: Harvard University Press, 1995).

49. Ibid.

50. Anthony Giddens, *Modernity and Self-Identity: Self and Society in the Late Modern Age* (Palo Alto, CA: Stanford University Press, 1991).

Chapter Four   Micro Views of the Life Course

1. The actual name has been changed, as have various details, to prevent deductive disclosure of this person's identity.

2. John Reynolds, Michael Stewart, Ryan MacDonald, and Lacey Sischo, "Have Adolescents Become Too Ambitious? High School Seniors' Educational and Occupational Plans, 1976–2000," *Social Problems* 53 (2006): 186–206.

3. John W. Meyer and Ronald L. Jepperson, "The 'Actors' of Modern Society: The Cultural Construction of Social Agency," *Sociological Theory* 18 (2000): 100–120.

4. William H. Sewell, Archibald O. Haller, and Alejandro Portes, "The Educational and Early Occupational Attainment Process," *American Sociological Review* 34 (1969): 82–92; and William H. Sewell, Archibald O. Haller, and George W. Ohlendorf, "The Educational and Early Occupational Status Attainment Process: Replication and Revision," *American Sociological Review* 35 (1970): 1014–27.

5. Mustafa Emirbayer and Ann Mische, "What Is Agency?" *American Journal of Sociology* 103 (1998): 962–1023.

6. Samuel R. Lucas, *Tracking Inequality: Stratification and Mobility in American High Schools* (New York: Teachers College Press, 1999).

7. Cathy Spatz Widom, "The Cycle of Violence," *Science* 244 (1989): 160–166.

8. Ibid., 164.

9. See Martin Brookes, *Extreme Measures: The Dark Visions and Bright Ideas of Francis Galton* (New York: Bloomsbury, 2004).

10. Bill Henry, Terrie E. Moffitt, Avshalom Caspi, John Langley, and Phil Silva, "On the 'Remembrance of Things Past': A Longitudinal Evaluation of the Retrospective Method," *Psychological Assessment* 6 (1994): 92–101.

11. See Howard Schuman, Barry Schwartz, and Hannah D'Arcy, "Elite Revisionists and Popular Beliefs: Christopher Columbus, Hero or Villain?" *Public Opinion Quarterly* 69

(2005): 2–29; also Howard Schuman and Amy D. Corning, "Collective Knowledge of Public Events: The Soviet Era from the Great Purge to Glasnost," *American Journal of Sociology* 105 (2000): 913–956; also Howard Schuman, Hiroko Akiyama, and Barbel Knauper, "Collective Memories of Germans and Japanese about the Past Half Century," *Memory* 6 (1998): 427–454.

12. Howard Schuman, Cheryl Rieger, and Vladas Gaidys, "Collective Memories in the United States and Lithuania," in *Autobiographical Memory and the Validity of Retrospective Reports,* ed. N. Schwarz and S. Sudman (New York: Springer-Verlag, 1994), 313–333.

13. Mustafa Emirbayer and Ann Mische, "What Is Agency?" *American Journal of Sociology* 103 (1998): 994.

14. Ibid.

15. George H. Mead, *Mind, Self, and Society* (Chicago: University of Chicago Press, 1934).

16. S. Stryker and R. Serpe, "Commitment, Identity Salience, and Role Behavior: Theory and Research Example," in *Personality, Roles, and Social Behavior,* ed. William Ickes and Eric S. Knowles (New York: Springer-Verlag, 1982), 199–218; and Sheldon Stryker, "Identity Theory: Its Development, Research Base, and Prospects," *Studies in Symbolic Interaction* 16 (1994): 9–20.

17. Bernice Neugarten, Joan Moore, and John Lowe, "Age Norms, Age Constraints and Adult Socialization," *American Journal of Sociology* 70 (1965): 710–717.

18. Richard A. Settersten Jr., "The Salience of Age in the Life Course," *Human Development* 40 (1998): 257–281 and accompanying commentary. See also Richard A. Settersten, "A Time to Leave Home and a Time Never to Return? Age Constraints on Living Arrangements of Young Adults," *Social Forces* 76 (1998): 1373–1400.

19. Margaret M. Marini, "Age and Sequencing Norms in the Transition to Adulthood," *Social Forces* 63 (1984): 229–241.

20. Michael J. Shanahan, Erik J. Porfeli, Jeylan T. Mortimer, and Lance D. Erickson, "Subjective Age Identity and the Transition to Adulthood: When Do Adolescents Become Adults?," in *On the Frontier of Adulthood: Theory, Research, and Public Policy,* ed. Richard A. Settersten Jr., Frank F. Furstenberg Jr., and R. G. Rumbaut (Chicago: University of Chicago Press, 2005), 225–255; and Jeylan T. Mortimer, Sabrina Oesterle, and Helga Kruger, "Age Norms, Institutional Structures, and the Timing of Markers of Transition to Adulthood," *Advances in Life Course Research* 9 (2005): 175–203.

21. John R. Logan, Russell Ward, and Glenna Spitze, "As Old as You Feel: Age Identity in Middle and Later Life," *Social Forces* 71 (1992): 451–467.

22. Victor Gecas, "The Social Psychology of Self-Efficacy," *Annual Review of Sociology* 15 (1989): 291–316.

23. See Albert Bandura, *Self-Efficacy: The Exercise of Control* (New York: Freeman, 1997).

24. Gecas, 300.

25. Leonard I. Pearlin, and Marilyn McKean Skaff, "Stress and the Life Course: A Paradigmatic Alliance," *Gerontologist* 36.2 (1996): 239–247.

26. Lorie Schabo Grabowski, and Kathleen Thiede Call, "Global and Economic Self-Efficacy in the Attainment Process," *American Sociological Association (ASA);* and Lorie Schabo Grabowski, Kathleen Thiede Call, and Jeylan T. Mortimer, "Global and Economic Self-Efficacy in the Educational Attainment Process," *Social Psychology Quarterly* 64.2 (June 2001): 164–79; and Kathleen Thiede Call, Lorie Schabo Grabowski, Jeylan T. Mortimer, Katherine Nash, and Chaimun Lee, "Impoverished Youth and the Attainment Process," American Sociological Association, Toronto, Canada, 1997.

27. Hazel Markus and Paula Nurius, "Possible Selves," *American Psychologist* 41 (1986): 954–969.

28. Barbara Schneider and David Stevenson, *The Ambitious Generation: America's Teenagers, Motivated but Directionless* (New Haven, CT: Yale University Press, 2000).

29. Bradley R. Entner Wright, "Behavioral Intentions and Opportunities among Homeless Individuals: A Reinterpretation of the Theory of Reasoned Action," *Social Psychology Quarterly* 61 (1998): 271–286.

30. James Rosenbaum, *Beyond College for All* (New York: Russell Sage Foundation, 2001).

31. W. Sewell and V. Shah, "Social Class, Parental Encouragement, and Educational Aspirations," *American Journal of Sociology* 73 (1968): 559–572.

32. William H. Sewell, Archibald O. Haller, and Alejandro Portes, "The Educational and Early Occupational Attainment Process," *American Sociological Review* 34 (1969): 82–92; and William H. Sewell, Archibald O. Haller, and George W. Ohlendorf, "The Educational and Early Occupational Status Attainment Process: Replication and Revision," *American Sociological Review* 35 (1970): 1014–27.

33. Sandra L. Hanson, "Lost Talent: Unrealized Educational Aspirations and Expectations among U.S. Youths," *Sociology of Education* 67 (1994): 159–183; and Sandra L. Hanson, *Lost Talent: Women in Science* (Philadelphia, PA: Temple University Press, 1996).

34. Jerry Jacobs, "The Dynamics of Young Men's Career Aspirations," *Sociological Forum* 6 (1991): 609–639.

35. Jay MacLeod, *Ain't No Makin' It: Aspirations and Attainment in a Low-Income Neighborhood* (Boulder, CO: Westview Press, 1995).

CHAPTER FIVE FROM MACRO TO MICRO

1. See Shanahan and Hofer, ibid.

2. It is unlikely that there is a gene for "age of first sexual intercourse." Rather, we are interested in genetic variation that, because of a wide array of biological and psychological processes, leads some people to intercourse before others.

3. M. P. Dunne, N. G. Martin, D. J. Statham, W. S. Slutske, S. H. Dinwiddie, K. K. Bucholz, P. A. F. Madden, and A. C. Heath, "Genetic and Environmental Contributions to Variance in Age at First Sexual Intercourse," *Psychological Science* 8 (1997): 211–216.

4. R. J. Rose, D. M. Dick, R. J. Viken, and J. Kaprio, "Gene-Environment Interaction in Patterns of Adolescent Drinking: Regional Residency Moderates Longitudinal Influences on Alcohol Use," *Alcoholism: Clinical & Experimental Research* 25 (2001): 637–643.

5. D. M. Dick, R. J. Rose, R. J. Viken, J. Kaprio, and M. Koskenvuo, "Exploring Gene-Environment Interactions: Socio-Regional Moderation of Alcohol Use," *Journal of Abnormal Psychology* 110 (2001): 625–632.

6. This statistic is called "h^2" and represents the proportion of total variance in drinking attributable to genetic variance, and thus it ranges from 0 (drinking has no genetic component) to 1.0 (drinking is fully predictable in terms of genetic variation).

7. Caspi et al.

8. M. J. Shanahan, G. H. Elder, and R. A. Miech, "History and Agency in Men's Lives: Pathways to Achievement in Cohort Perspective," *Sociology of Education* 70 (1997): 54–67.

9. John Clausen, "Adolescent Competence and the Shaping of the Life Course," *American Journal of Sociology* 96 (1991): 805–842.

10. John W. Meyer, John Boli, George M. Thomas, and Francisco O. Ramirez, "World Society and the Nation-State," *American Journal of Sociology* 103 (1997): 144–181.

11. Evan Schofer and John W. Meyer, "The Worldwide Expansion of Higher Education in the Twentieth Century," *American Sociological Review* 70 (2005): 898–920.

12. William I. Thomas and Florian Znaniecki, *The Polish Peasant in Europe and America* (Chicago: Badger, 1918–20).

13. David Lam and Letícia Marteleto, "Small Families and Large Cohorts: The Impact of the Demographic Transition on Schooling in Brazil," in *Changing Transitions to Adulthood in*

Developing Countries: Selected Studies, ed. Cynthia B. Lloyd, Jere R. Behrman, Nelly P. Stromquist, and Barney Cohen (Washington, DC: National Research Council, 2005), 56–83.

14. Theodore P. Gerber, "Structural Change and Post-Socialist Stratification: Labor Market Transitions in Contemporary Russia," *American Sociological Review* 67.5 (2000): 629–659; see also Theodore P. Gerber, "Membership Benefits or Selection Effects? Why Former Communist Party Members Do Better in Post-Soviet Russia," *Social Science Research* 29.1 (2000): 25–50.

15. Gerber, *American Sociological Review,* 636.

16. James C. Coleman, "Social Capital in the Creation of Human Capital," *American Journal of Sociology* 94 (1998): 95–120.

17. C. Wright Mills, *The Sociological Imagination,* 5.

CHAPTER SIX   RETURN TO *THE SOCIOLOGICAL IMAGINATION*

1. See Robert Max Jackson, *Destined for Equality* (Cambridge: Harvard University Press, 1998), on women's rights. See Paul Osterman, "Education and Labor Markets at the Turn of the Century," *Politics and Society* (Fall 1979), on child labor.

2. Modell, *Into One's Own,* 331.

3. Matilda White Riley, Anne Foner, and Joan Waring, "Sociology of Age," in *Handbook of Sociology,* ed. Neil Smelser (Newbury Park, CA: Sage Publications, 1988), 243–290.

4. Angela M. O'Rand, "The Future of the Life Course: Late Modernity and Life Course Risks," in *Handbook of the Life Course,* ed. Jeylan T. Mortimer and Michael J. Shanahan (New York: Kluwer/Plenum, 2003), 693–701.

5. See discussion of Petit and Western, Chapter Three.

6. L. Rubinowitz and J. Rosenbaum, *Crossing the Class and Color Lines: From Public Housing to White Suburbia* (Chicago: University of Chicago Press, 2000).

7. M. W. Riley and J. W. Riley Jr., "Age Integration: Historical and Conceptual Background," *The Gerontologist* 40 (2000): 266–272.

8. Christina Hoff Sommers, *The War Against Boys: How Misguided Feminism Is Harming Our Young Men* (New York: Simon & Schuster, 2000).

INDEX

AARP (American Association of Retired Persons), 285

accentuation as life course principle, 54–55, 58–59

adolescence:
alcohol consumption during, 246
Ariès on, 109–10
in Brazil, 261–67
emergence of, 153
generational analysis of, 122
Gillis on, 111–12, 144
global efficacy and, 213
Great Depression and, 250
identity theory on, 207
Kett on, 115–19
lost talent, 227
modernization and, 113–14
occupational aspirations, 217–19, 222, 229–30
planful competence and, 251
social change and, 120
transitions to adulthood, 258–74

adolescence-limited offenders, 80

adulthood:
age effects and, 138
emerging, 155, 157–58
globalization and, 258–74
Great Depression and, 250
identity theory on, 207
lost talent, 227
occupational aspirations, 229–30

as phase of life, 111
subjective age identity, 207–8
transition to, 154–55, 160, 163–64, 207–8, 258–74

Afghanistan, 200

Africa, 270–71

age:
cohort effects and, 137
further reading, 294
occupational aspirations and, 229–30
segregation in society, 291
social, 52
subjective age identity and, 209

age effects, 138

age-graded roles:
defined, 40–41
expectations of, 169–70
grandparenthood, 106
identity theory on, 206–7
institutionalization and, 159
in premodern society, 161
social age and, 52–53
social pathways, 67

agency:
alcohol abuse and, 248
causal, 211
in childhood, 187
contextual contingencies and, 250–58
defined, 182, 232
future-oriented, 219
as life course principle, 51, 55, 58

agency (cont.)
    measuring, 251
    in micro view, 182–87
    planful competence and, 256
    social context and, 255
    timing and, 255
age norms, 232
Ain't No Making It (McLeod), 230
alcohol abuse, 239, 245–49
alienated student, 28–29
Almond, Paul, 168
Alwin, Duane, 87, 120–21
The Ambitious Generation (Schneider and
    Stevenson), 218–19
American Association of Retired Persons
    (AARP), 285
Anabaptist Church, 170–71
analytic dimension, 30
Anderson, Leon, 108
anticipatory identification, 215–20
antisocial behavior, 80, 239, 247
Apted, Michael, 168
Ariès, Philippe, 109–11, 153, 157
Arnett, Jeffrey, 155
ascriptive process, 130–35
Asia, 271
Auden, W. H., 6
Australia, 241–42
autobiographical memory, 197–201,
    232

Baby Boom generation, 123
Balzac, Honoré de, 274
Bandura, Albert, 211
Beat Generation, 124–25
Becker, Howard, 71
Becoming Modern (Inkeles and Smith), 30,
    32
Beethoven, Ludwig van, 94
Beginning School Study (Baltimore), 69

behavior:
    antisocial, 80, 239, 247
    behavioral sciences on, 7–8
    cohort effects of, 138
    defined, 7
    Easterlin hypothesis on, 140
    influence of genetics on, 238
    modernization and, 114
    sexual, 114, 116, 240–44
    social control and, 239
    society and, 26–29
behavioral change, 12, 21
behavioral sciences:
    on "behavior," 7–8
    on influences of genetic factors, 237
    modernization and, 19
    sociology and, 5–13
Bem, Daryl, 74
Beyond College for All (Rosenbaum), 147,
    222–23, 228
binding, 112
biographical availability, 98
biography:
    life course and, 40
    memory and, 197–201
    John Meyer on, 174
    presuppositions of, 8
    as social construct, 63
    societal change and, 284
    sociology and, 13–34
    studying links between society and, xviii–xix
Birth and Fortune (Easterlin), 137
birthrates, 113, 137–39
bourgeoisie, 15
Bowlby, John, 46
Brazil, 261–67
Brontë, Charlotte, 18
Browne, Janet, 46
Buber, Martin, 235
Buchmann, Marlis, 165

Burma, 271
Burroughs, William, 124

Cairns, Beverly, 87
Cairns, Robert, 87
Canada, 145
careers, 78
    See also occupations
Caspi, Avshalom, 74–75
causal agency, 211
Centuries of Childhood (Ariès), 109–11
Chaga's Disease, 45
The Changing Transition to Adulthood in Developing Countries (Lam and Merteleto), 261–62
character, society and, 22–26, 35
Charles II, 95
child abuse, 194–96, 247
childhood:
    agency in, 187
    experiences as predictors, 76
    identity theory on, 207
    in premodern society, 110–11
    religious identity in, 170–71
    theory of symbolic interactionism, 204
Children of the Great Depression (Elder), 35–42, 47, 49–50, 55
Christianity, 61–62, 170–71
A Christmas Carol (Dickens), 18
chronologized life course, 146, 175
Class and Conformity (Kohn), 32
Clausen, John, 84, 251
cohort effects, 138
cohort flow, 128–37, 175
cohorts:
    age strata and, 137
    birth, 38–39, 127
    cohort analysis and, 127–28
    comparing modes of analysis, 142–44
    defined, 127

further reading, 177–78
Great Depression and, 250, 252
macro view of, 175
planful competence and, 256
relationships among, 137–42
sexual behavior by, 240–41
social change and, 128–37
World War II and, 253
Coleman, James, 270
Coleridge, Samuel Taylor, 91
collective memory, 199–201
Columbine High School shootings, 293
Comédie Humaine (Balzac), 274
Communism, xii, 267–74
conduct-of-life books, 115, 117
control, 99
control cycles, 52
coordination, strategies of, 80
counterfactuals, 99
Covington, Syms, 45
criminality:
    age and cohort effects, 138
    child abuse and, 195–96
    life phases and, 156
    schemata/scripts, 193–96
    social control and, 239
crisis, life phases in
crisis, stage model of, 60–64
cross-fertilization of modes of analysis, 142
cross-national comparisons of life course, 144–52, 178–79
cultural practices, 111–14, 118
cumulative continuity, 77, 86
cumulative disadvantage, 75
cumulative processes in life course, 71–77, 86
Czech Republic, 267, 271

Dannefer, Dale, 63–64
Darwin, Charles, 44–46, 90–100

Darwin, Emma, 95
Darwin, Erasmus, 96
decision-making in life course, 202–14
defined contributions to pensions, 154
demographic patterns:
  cohort analyses and, 129
  cultural practices and, 111–14
  phases of life and, 118
demographic transitions, 259–67
desistance process, 83–84
Desmond, Adrian, 46
developmental level (life course studies),
  282–83
developmental task, 65–66
developmental trajectory, 79
Dick, D. M., 245
Dickens, Charles, 17–19
Dictionary of Occupational Titles, 228
diseases, cumulative processes and, 75–76
drug abuse, social control and, 239
Dunne, M. P., 240–41
Dupre, Matthew, 76, 80
Durkheim, Émile, 20–21, 24

Easterlin, Richard, 128–40, 175
economic recessions, 48, 255
education:
  in Brazil, 261–67
  cohort analysis, 132–34
  cohort effects and, 138
  cross-national comparisons, 150–51
  cumulative processes and, 75–76
  expansion of, 260
  feeder patterns in, 83–84
  institutionalization in, 159
  life courses and, 48
  life phases and, 155
  lost talent, 227
  market economy and, 148
  migration for, 246

occupations and, 191, 254
  planful competence and, 253–54,
    256
  in premodern society, 109–10
  schemata/scripts and, 190–93
  social pathways and, 68–71
  Sewell-Haller-Portes model, 186
  timing of transitions and, 81
  vocational training, 116–17
educational aspirations:
  increase in, 222–23
  parental encouragement and, 225
  Sewell's study on, 226
  social mobility and, 185–87
educational careers, 78
educational efficacy, 213
ego development, 27, 29, 59–60
Einstein, Albert, 6
Elder, Glen H., Jr.:
  on childhood personalities, 75
  on cohort analysis, 127
  life course principles, 47, 49–50, 55
  life course sociology and, 35–42
  Mannheim and, 38
elderly, cohort analysis of, 141–42
Elias, Norbert, 14–16
Eliot, George, 18
Ellis, Joseph, 92–93
emerging adulthood, 155–58
Emirbayer, Mustapha:
  on elements of agency, 187
  on narrative construction, 221
  on practical evaluation, 202
  on projection, 214–15, 224
empiricism, 5, 119
employment, *See* occupations
England, *See* Great Britain
entry points, 275
Entwisle, Doris, 69–70
epigenetic sequence of crises, 60, 63

Erikson, Erik:
  on adolescence, 122
  on ego development, 27, 29, 60
  on identity, 60–61
  ontogenetic fallacy and, 63–64, 102
  on self, 60
  stage model of crises, 60–64
  Young Man Luther, 61
evolution, theory of, 44, 90
exogenous processes, 88, 104
expected self, 216
experimental enactment, 223–25

Falaris, Elizabeth, 140
Falchikov, Nancy, 117
feared self, 217
Featherman, David, 129–35, 185
fertility rates, 259, 261–62
FitzRoy, Robert, 95–96
France, 112, 145
Frankenstein (Shelley), 18
Franklin, Benjamin, 171
Friedenberg, Edgar, 157
friendships, self-concept and, 77
Furstenberg, Frank:
  on cumulative disadvantages, 75
  on implications of transitions, 81
  on life course patterns, 160
  on life phase changes, 155
future states:
  acting on images of, 221–26
  defined, 232
  possible selves in, 215–20

Galton, Francis, 197–98
Gaskell, Elizabeth, 18
Ge, Xiaojia, 79
Gecas, Victor, 210–11
Gemeinschaft, 19–20, 22, 131; see also,
  Gesellschaft

gender:
  adolescence based on, 115
  life course paradigms and, 49–50
  status and, 11
  subjective age identity and, 209
gene-environment interaction, 238–39, 277
generations:
  comparing modes of analysis, 142–44
  defined, 38, 120–21
  differing experiences by, 39
  further reading, 177–78
  generational analysis, 120–27
  macro view of, 175
  sociology on, 26–27
Generation X, 120, 123, 125–26
genetics, life course and, 238–49
genocide, 270–71
Geoffrey St. Hilaire, Etienne, 91
geographic region, 48, 115, 245
Gerber, Theodore, 269
Germany:
  cross-national comparisons and, 145,
    150–52
  modernization in, 17
  premodern society in, 112
  social change and, 271
  social pathways in, 68
  Warsaw Pact and, 270
Gesellschaft, 20, 131
G.I. Bill, 36
Giddens, Anthony, 172
Gilligan, Carol, 292
Gillis, John, 111–12, 114, 144
Ginsberg, Allen, 124
Girl's Club, 181–84
global efficacy, 213
globalization, 237, 258–74
Golden Rule, 11
goodness of fit, 53
Gorbachev, Mikhail, 200

Gordon, Robert, 139
Grabowski, Lorie Schabo, 213
Graff, Harvey, 147, 157, 171
grandparenthood, 105–6
Grant, Robert Edmond, 96
Great Britain:
    cross-national comparisons and, 145
    life course predictability in, 160
    mapping life course in, 168
    modernization in, 17–18
    premodern society in, 112
    social pathways in, 68, 70
Great Depression:
    differences in cohorts for, 250, 252
    Elder on, 35–39, 41, 47
    Greatest Generation and, 122–23
    life course principles and, 47–53
    planful competence and, 255
Greatest Generation, 122–23

h² statistic, 308n6
Haller, Archibald O., 186
Hanson, Sandra, 227–28
Hauser, Robert, 129–35, 185
Havinghurst, Robert, 65
health, marriage and, 81
Henslow, John Stevens, 95
Hershberg, Theodore, 160
Hill, Reuben, 78
historical time/place:
    Darwin's life course, 91–94
    as life course principles, 48, 55, 57
    listed, xiv
    modernization and, 162
    planful competence and, 253–54
Hogan, Dennis, 164
homelessness, 219–20
home ownership, 208
homogenization of society, 259
Horowitz, Irving, 24

House, James, 29–30
Howl (Ginsberg), 124
human development, xv, 122
human relationships as social structures,
    9–10
Hussein, Saddam, 271
Huxley, Thomas, 97
hypothesis, 7
hypothetical resolution, 222–23, 225,
    230

identity:
    Giddens on, 172–74
    identity confusion vs., 61
    possible selves, 216
    role-related, 210, 212
    Stryker on, 205
    subjective age, 207–10
identity salience, 205
identity theory, 204–7, 211
identity work, 108
immigration, 56–57
impressionable years hypothesis, 122
In a Different Voice (Gilligan), 292
income:
    cumulative processes of, 73
    distribution of, 144
    loss of, 47, 51
    mortality and, 73
individualization, 165, 172, 175
industrialization:
    anxieties about, 18
    ascription and, 132
    birthrates and, 113
    meritocracy and, 131
    modernization and, 17
inheritance, 112–13
Inkeles, Alex, 30–34
inner-directed person, 22–23
institutional isomorphism, 259

institutionalization:
  defined, 147
  macro view of, 175
  modernization and, 161, 163–64
  social structures and, 159
  transitions and, 160
institutions:
  cumulative processes and, 77
  institutionalization of, 147, 159
  social pathways and, 67–68
intergenerational transmission of violence
  thesis, 194
interpretive level (life course studies),
  283–84
IQ, 81–82, 185–86
Iran, 271
Iraq, 271
ISI Web of Science, 125
iteration in life course:
  autobiographical memory, 197–201
  defined, 187, 232
  schemata and scripts, 188–96

Jacobs, Jerry, 228–29
Japan, 68
Jepperson, Ronald, 184
juvenile delinquents, 114, 195, 239

Kazakhstan, 271
Keniston, Kenneth, 27–29, 143
Kerckhoff, Alan, 70–71, 74
Kerouac, Jack, 124, 144
Kett, Joseph, 115–19
Kidder, Tracy, 105
Kling, Jeffrey, 90
knifing-off experience, 83
Kohli, Martin, 164
Kohn, Melvin, 32–34
Krushchev, Nikita, 201
Kyrgyzstan, 271

Lam, David, 262–63
Lamarck, Jean-Baptiste, 91
Laub, John, 82
Leisering, Lutz, 146
Lepennies, Wolf, 274, 276
LexisNexis database, 125
Liebman, Jeffrey, 90
life course:
  agency in, 184–87
  behavioral sciences and sociology,
    5–13
  chronologized, 146, 175
  cohort analysis of, 127–42
  comparing modes of analysis, 142–44
  contextual contingencies in, 250–58
  cross-national comparisons of, 144–52,
    178–79
  cumulative processes in, 71–77, 86
  decision making in, 202–14
  developmental tasks in, 65–66
  difference in, 235–36
  emergence of life course sociology,
    34–42
  framework for studies, 279–84
  further reading on, xxv–xxvi, 103–4,
    277, 294–95
  generational analysis of, 120–27
  genetic expression and, 238–49
  on genetic factors, 237
  globalization and, 237
  grandparenthood, 106
  how to change, 285–88
  iteration in, 187–202
  mapping, 168
  master trends in, 153–74, 179–80
  overview, 3–5
  as paradigm, 46
  periodization of, 146, 175
  perspective on Darwin's life, 90–100
  practical evaluation in, 187, 202–14

life course (*cont.*)
  predictability of, 159–66
  principles of, 47–59, 101–2
  projectivity in, 187, 214–31
  sameness in, 235–36
  self-efficacy in, 210–13
  social history and, 108–19, 177
  social pathways in, 66–71, 86
  sociology and biography, 13–34
  stage model of crises, 60–64
  standardization of, 147, 161, 164
  as subjective project, 167–74
  trajectories and transitions, 78–82,
    86
  trend toward individualization, 165
  turning points in, 82–86
  variability in, 144–52
  vocational training and, 150–51
  what to change, 288–93
life-course persistent offenders, 80
life course sociology:
  on biography as social construct, 63
  emergence of, 34–42
  further reading, 43
  on transitions to adulthood, 258–59
Life magazine, 125
life phases:
  adolescence as, 109–12
  adulthood as, 111
  changes in, 109–11
  childhood as, 110–11
  cohort analyses and, 129
  demographic patterns and, 118
  emergence of, 153–58
  emerging adulthood as, 155
  macro view of, 175
  midcourse as, 153–56
  predictability of timing, 146
life-stage principle, 52–55, 58, 97–98
Lincoln, Abraham, 148

linked lives:
  Darwin's life course, 95–97
  as life course principle, 50–51, 55,
    57–58
linking mechanisms, 47
Lithuania, 200–201
Logan, John, 209
The Lonely Crowd (Riesman), 22–25
Lord of the Rings trilogy (Tolkien), 18–19
lost decade, 262
lost talent, 227
Lucas, Samuel, 191
Luther, Martin, 61–63, 94
Lyell, Charles, 92, 95

macro view:
  cohort analysis and, 127–42
  comparing modes of analysis, 142–44
  cross-national comparisons of life course,
    144–52
  defined, xvi
  further reading, 177–80, 276
  generational analysis and, 120–27
  master trends in social change, 153–74
  questions asked in, xvii
  social history and, 108–19
  social structures and, 29–30, 106
Malthus, Thomas, 91–92
Mannheim, Karl:
  Elder and, 38
  on generational units, 26–27, 120–21,
    125
MAOA gene, 247
Marcuse, Herbert, 24
Markus, Hazel, 216–17, 220
marriage:
  adulthood and, 158
  age effects and, 138
  careers and, 78
  cumulative processes and, 71

identity theory on, 206
institutionalized children and, 77
modernization and, 113
physical health and, 81
planful competence and, 253
in premodern society, 112–13
subjective age identity and, 208
timing of transitions, 81
Maruna, Shadd, 84
Marx, Karl, 19, 21, 24
mastery, concept of, 212
Mayer, Karl Ulrich, 146, 148, 159
McAdam, Doug, 98
McCammon, Ryan, 120–21
McDonough, Peggy, 73–74
McLeod, Jay, 230
Mead, George Herbert, 204–5
Meadows, Sarah, 80
mechanization, modernization and, 17
memory, autobiographical, 197–201
men, See gender
meritocracy, 70, 131
Merteleto, Letítica, 262–63
Merton, Robert K., 225
Meyer, John:
    on age-grading, 170
    on agency, 184
    on biographies, 174
    on expansion of education, 260
    institutional isomorphism, 259
    on life course innovators, 287–88
    on self, 167–69
micro view:
    agency in life course, 182–87
    defined, xvi
    example, 181–84
    further reading, 233–34, 276
    iteration in life course, 187–202
    practical evaluation in life course, 187,
        202–14

projectivity in life course, 187, 214–31
questions asked in, xvii
subjectivity in life course, 183–87
midcourse phase of life, 153–56
Middle East, 271
Midnight's Children (Rushdie), ix–x
migration, substance abuse and, 245–49
military service, cohort analysis of, 136–37
Millennial Generation, 123
Mills, C. Wright:
    entry points for, 275
    Horowitz on, 24
    on social change, 278–79, 293
    on social study, 3
    on sociological imagination, x–xiii,
        23–24, 100
Mind, Self, and Society (Mead), 204
Mische, Ann:
    on elements of agency, 187
    on narrative construction, 221
    on practical evaluation, 202
    on projection, 214–15, 224
Mitterauer, Michael, 144
mobility aspirations, 225
Modell, John, 160, 162, 164, 287
Modernity and Self-Identity (Giddens), 172
modernization:
    anxieties about, 18
    behavioral sciences and, 19
    birthrates and, 113
    chronologized life course and, 146
    demographic transitions and, 259
    further reading, 42
    historical changes and, 162
    Inkeles and Smith on, 30
    institutionalization and, 161, 163–64
    meritocracy and, 131
    predictable life course and, 166
    sexual behavior and, 114, 116
    social structures and, 20

modernization (*cont.*)
  of society, 17–18, 30
  urbanization and, 17, 161
modern personality, 30–31
Moen, Phyllis, 153–54
Moffitt, Terri, 80
Moore, James, 46
Morris, Martina, 163
mortality, 74–76, 259
Moving to Opportunity (MTO), 88
Mozart: Portrait of a Genius (Elias), 14–16
Mozart, Wolfgang Amadeus, 13–16, 94,
  148, 286
Murray, William Hutchinson, 278

Naked Lunch (Burroughs), 124
narrative construction, 221
National Longitudinal Survey of Youth,
  215
National Research Council, 261–62
National Women's Conference, 128
natural selection, evolution by, 44, 90
Neugarten, Bernice, 205
nomenklatura, 268
Nurius, Paul, 216–17, 220

observations, 5–7
occupational aspirations:
  of adolescents, 217–19, 222, 229–30
  in adulthood, 229–30
  aging and, 229–30
  social mobility and, 185–87
  stability of, 228
occupations:
  cross-national comparisons, 151
  education and, 191, 254
  identity theory on, 206
  life course paradigms and, 48–50
  migration for, 246
  progression of work roles, 40

social pathways and, 68–69
subjective age identity and, 208
transitions in, 81, 163
vocational training and, 150
On the Road (Kerouac), 124, 144
ontogenetic fallacy, 63–64, 102
Opportunity and Change (Featherman and
  Hauser), 129
O'Rand, Angela, 288
organizations, 67–68, 147
Ortega y Gasset, José, 121
other-directed person, 23–24
"The Oversocialized Conception of Man"
  (Wrong), 25–26

Pallas, Aaron, 78
Pampel, Fred, 140–42
Panel Study of Income Dynamics, 73
paradigms, 7, 46
parental encouragement, 225
parenthood:
  age effects and, 138
  careers and, 78
  certification for, 290
  differences by social class, 32–33
  grandparenthood, 106
  identity theory on, 206
  planful competence and, 253
  subjective age identity and, 209
  timing of transitions and, 81
Parsons, Talcott, x–xi
pathways in life course, 66–71
Pearlin, Leonard, 212–13
perestroika, 201
periodization of life course, 146, 175
personality, social structure and, 29–34
personal responsibility, xxi
Pettit, Becky, 156
phases of life, *See* life phases
planful competence, 251–56, 277

Plinian Society, 96
Poland, 270–71
The Polish Peasant in Europe and America
(Thomas and Znanieck), 260–61
political-economic systems, 118, 144–52,
270–71
Pollack, William, 293
Portes, Alejandro, 186
possible selves in future states, 215–20,
230, 232
poverty, 72–73, 88–89, 141
practical evaluation in life course:
defined, 187, 202–3, 232
identity theory, 204–7
self-efficacy, 210–13
subjective age identity, 207–10
premodern society:
adolescence in, 112
age-graded roles in, 161
childhood in, 110–11
Durkheim on, 21
Inkeles and Smith on, 30
life phases and, 109–10
moral support in, 113
nature of social change and, 19–20
Preston, Samuel, 141, 175, 285
presuppositions:
of biography, 8
defined, 8
of psychology, 8
of sociology, 8, 17
"The Problem of Generations"
(Mannheim), 26–27
projectivity in life course:
acting on images of the future,
221–26
complications and contingencies,
227–30
defined, 187, 214–15, 230, 232
future and possible selves, 215–20

Protestant Church, 61, 171
proxies, 135
proximal level (life course studies),
281–82
proximal settings, 242, 256
psychology, presuppositions of, 8
psychometrics, 197
punishment, social class and, 33

race/ethnicity:
child abuse and, 195
criminality and, 156
cumulative processes and, 72
MTO study, 88–89
status and, 11
turning points and, 82
Real Boys (Pollack), 293
reciprocal continuity, 78, 86
relationships:
among cohorts, 137–42
structure in, 9–10
religious identity, 170–71
replication, empiricism and, 119
representations of youth, 115–19
retirement, 154, 289
Ribbentrop-Molotov pact, 201
Riesman, David, 22–25, 39
Riley, John, 291
Riley, Matilda, 128, 288, 291
Rindfuss, Ronald, 163
Rites of Passage (Kett), 115
Roman Catholic Church, 61, 170
Romania, 270
Rose, Arnold, 209
Rose, R. J., 245
Rosenbaum, James, 147, 223, 228
Ross, Dorothy, 275
Rossi, Alice, 128–29
Rushdie, Salman, ix–x
Rushing, William, 225

Russia:
  further reading, 277
  globalization and, 267–74
  Lithuania and, 200–201
  modernization in, 17
Rutter, Michael, 77, 83
Rwanda, 270–71
Ryder, Norman, 108, 122

Salzburg, Archbishop of, 15–16
Sampson, Robert, 82
Savonarola, Girolamo, 94
schemata, 188–96, 232
Schiller, Katherine, 84
Schlegel, Alice, 158
Schneider, Barbara, 218–19
Schofer, Evan, 260
Schoon, Ingrid, 72
Schuman, Howard, 199
Schwartz, Morrie, 181
science:
  anxieties about, 18
  defined, 7
  modernization and, 17
  nature of, 5–8
scientific theory, 7
script:
  defined, 189, 232
  iteration in life course, 189–96
The Script of Modern Life (Buchmann), 165
secularization, modernization and, 17
self:
  concern with, xix–xx
  Erikson on, 60
  expected, 216
  feared, 216
  identity theory on, 204
  society and, 27–28, 43
  theory of symbolic interactionism, 204
self-actualization, xix

self-authenticity, xix
self-awareness, xix
self-concept, xix, 77
self-determination, xxi
self-direction, 32–35
self-efficacy:
  concern with, xix
  defined, 232
  homelessness and, 220
  in life course, 210–13
self-esteem, xix
self-help, xix–xx
self-improvement, xix–xx
SES, See socioeconomic status (SES)
Settersten, Richard, 206, 287
Seven Up! (documentary series), 168
Sewell, William, 186, 224–26
sexual behavior, 114, 116, 240–44
Shah, Vimal, 224–26
Shakespeare, 3–4
Shanahan, Michael, 210, 251–52, 258
Shelley, Mary, 18
Simmel, George, 9–10
simple functionalism, x
situational imperatives as life course principle, 49–50, 52, 55, 57
Sixties Generation, 128, 143
Smith, Adam, 91
Smith, David, 30–34
Snow, David, 108
social age, 52
social change:
  behavioral change and, 12, 21
  cohort flow and, 128–37
  economic collapses and, 255
  generational linkages and, 27
  globalization and, 260, 264, 271
  life course principles on, 56
  master trends in, 153–74
  Mills on, 278–79, 293

role of society and, xiv
sexual behavior and, 240–44
social life and, 16–21
social classes:
  adolescence based on, 115
  binding and, 112
  birthrates and, 113
  cumulative processes and, 72–73
  distribution of income across, 144
  education and, 116–17
  Kohn on, 32
  Marx on, 19
  modernization and, 113–14
  parental encouragement and, 225
  parenting differences by, 32–33
  punishment and, 33
  status and, 11
  turning points and, 82
social context:
  agency and, 255
  gene-environment interaction and,
    238–39
  life course sociology on, 63
  pathways in, 66–71
  timing and, 255
social control, 239–49
social history:
  of adolescence, 144
  changes in life phases, 109–11
  comparing modes of analysis, 142–44
  cultural practices and, 111–14
  demographic patterns and, 111–14
  epochal studies of, 143
  further reading, 177
  overview, 108–9
  representations and, 115–19
social mobility, 185–87
social pathways in life course, 66–71, 86,
  118–19
social scientific theory, 42

social structures:
  adolescence based on, 115, 118
  codes and rules, 11
  cultural practices and, 111
  human relationships as, 9–10
  institutionalization and, 159
  macro view and, 29–30, 106
  meaning of, 8–9
  modernization and, 20
  personality and, 29–34
  possible selves and, 217
  social location and, 11–12
  sociology and, 9
  status as, 10
social timing, 52–53
societal level (life course studies), 280–81
society:
  age segregation, 291
  behavior and, 26–29
  character and, 22–26, 35
  homogenization of, 259
  modernization of, 17–18, 30
  Riesman on, 22
  self and, 27–28, 43
  social change and, xiv
  status within, 11
  studying links between biography and,
    xviii–xix
  Tönnies on, 20
socioeconomic status (SES):
  adolescence based on, 115
  aspirations based on, 224–25
  duration effects of stressors, 74
  education and, 254
  modernization and, 21
  social mobility and, 185–86
  social pathways and, 69
  as social structure, 10–11
  Wisconsin model of attainment, 185,
    187, 190, 224

The Sociological Imagination (Mills), x–xiii,
  23–24, 275
sociology:
  behavioral sciences and, 5–13
  biography and, 13–34
  distrust of, xxi
  further reading, 42
  on generations, 26–27
  presuppositions of, 8
  on social change and social life,
    16–21
  on social structures, 9–12
  See also life course sociology
Sommers, Christina Hoff, 292
"Sources of Dissent" (Keniston), 28
Spitze, Glenna, 209
Stalin, Joseph, 19
standardization:
  of life course, 147, 161, 164
  of transitions, 160–61
Stevenson, David, 218–19
Stryker, Sheldon, 205
subjective age identity, 207–10, 232
subjectivity:
  alcohol abuse and, 248
  defined, 183, 232
  in micro view, 183–87
  planful competence and, 256
substance abuse, 239, 245–49
Sweden, 151, 289
symbolic interactionism, 204, 211
synchronization, strategies of, 80, 86

temporality in people's lives, xv–xvi
"The Self and the Life Course" (Meyer),
  167–68
Thomas, William I., 260–61
Tilly, Charles, 294
timing:
  agency and, 255

of migrations, 247–49
social context and, 255
of transitions, 80–82, 146–47
Tolkien, J. R. R., 18–19
Tönnies, Ferdinand, 19–22
topical dimension, 30
Tracking Inequality (Lucas), 191
tradition-directed person, 22
trajectories, 78–79, 86
transitions:
  to adulthood, 154–55, 160, 163–64,
    207–8, 258–74
  cross-national comparisons, 152
  defined, 78, 86
  demographic, 259–67
  institutionalization and, 160
  MTO study, 88–89
  sequencing markers of, 164–65
  standardization of, 160–61
  timing of, 80–82, 146–47
  in workplace, 81, 163
trust vs. mistrust, 60
Turkmenistan, 271
turning points, 82–86

Uhlenberg, Peter, 105, 160–61
Ukraine, 267
unemployment, cumulative processes and,
  74
United States:
  cross-national comparisons and,
    145
  life course predictability in, 160
  social pathways in, 68–69
  vocational training in, 148
University of Chicago, 204
urbanization:
  birthrates and, 113
  modernization and, 17, 161
  sexual behavior and, 240

The Vanishing Adolescent (Friedenberg), 157
verbal ability, 238–39
vocational training:
  life course and, 150–51
  modernization and, 116–17
  social pathways and, 69
  in United States, 148

Wadsworth, M. E. J., 74
Wallace, Alfred Russell, 44
The War Against Boys (Sommers), 292
Ward, Russell, 209
Warsaw Pact, 270
Washington, George, 93
Western, Bruce, 156
Widom, Cathy Spatz, 193–96
Wisconsin model of status attainment, 185, 187, 190, 224
women:
  life course paradigms and, 49–50
  life course patterns of, 159–60
  subjective age identity and, 209
Wordsworth, William, 18

workplace, *See* occupations
World War II:
  cohort analysis of military service, 136–37
  differences for cohorts, 252
  Great Depression and, 36–38, 53
  Greatest Generation and, 122
  life courses and, 48
  Lithuania and, 200–201
Wright, Brad, 220
Wrong, Dennis, 25–26

Yeltsin, Boris, 270
Young Man Luther (Erikson), 61
Youth and History (Gillis), 111–12
Youth Development Study, 208, 213
youth groups:
  generational analysis of, 120
  modernization and, 113–14
  phases of life and, 118
  in premodern society, 113
  representations of, 115–19

Znaniecki, Florian, 260–61